# MAJOLICA

British, Continental and American Wares
1851–1915

*St. George's Fountain, London International Exhibition, 1862.*
*Designed by John Thomas for Minton.*

# MAJOLICA

British, Continental and American Wares
1851–1915

VICTORIA BERGESEN

BARRIE & JENKINS
LONDON

First published in Great Britain by
Barrie & Jenkins Ltd
289 Westbourne Grove, London W11 2QA

British Library Cataloguing in Publication Data
Bergesen, Victoria
    Majolica: British, Continental and American wares
    1851–1915
    1. Majolica, 1851–1915
    I. Title
    738.3'7

    ISBN 0–7126–2077–X

Designed by Nigel Partridge
Typeset by DP Photosetting, Aylesbury, Bucks
Printed by Printer Portuguesa, Portugal

This book is dedicated to
my husband Lewis Pierotti
& our children Nicholas & Jessica
without whose encouragement and support
it could not have been written

# CONTENTS

## ACKNOWLEDGEMENTS

Tessa Aldridge, Sotheby's, London. Mrs. Armitage, Librarian, American Museum, Bath. Alf Barnes for photography of author's collection. Gaye Blake-Roberts and her staff, Wedgwood Museum, for access to the Wedgwood Museum and Archives. L. A. Compton. Robert Copeland, Spode Museum, Royal Worcester Spode for his aid in assembling the list of Copeland majolica patterns. Carl DeMilia, Reference Librarian, New Milford Public Library. Christine Fife, Special Collections, Keele University Library. Susan Finkel, Assistant Curator, New Jersey State Museum, Trenton. Harry E. Frost, Curator, Dyson Perrins Museum, Worcester. Nigel Gaspar, Curator, Clive House Museum, Shrewsbury. Geoffrey Godden for the use of many valuable records and documents pertaining to the British majolica manufacturers. R. K. Henrywood. Tony Herbert. Joan Jones and her staff, Minton Museum, Royal Doulton Tableware Ltd. for access to the Minton Museum and Archives, and many useful suggestions. Don Kelly and Warren Fitzsimmons. Captain Jefferds Inn, Kennebunkport, Maine. Katherine Krile, Assistant Curator and Wes Sollenberger, Assistant Librarian, Chester County Historical Society, West Chester, Pennsylvania. Barry Lamb, Reference Works. My mother, Beverley Lockwood, for all her help in researching the American firms, and my stepfather, Richard Lockwood, for his help with the photography. John Mallett, Keeper of Ceramics, Victoria & Albert Museum. Ruth Neuendorffer, Librarian, Historical Society of the Tarrytowns. Phillips, New York and London. Martin & Rosalind Pulver. John Powell, Librarian, Ironbridge Gorge Museum Trust. Alan Rumrill, Cheshire Co. Historical Society, Keene, New Hampshire. Henry Sandon. Rita & Ian Smythe, Britannia, Grays Market, London. Kenneth R. Trapp, Oakland Museum, Oakland, California. John Twitchett.

To my friends in the Spode Society and Friends of Blue for their encouragement and many helpful suggestions.

The librarians and staff of the British Library, the National Art Library, the Public Record Office, the Hanley Reference Library, and the New York Public Library.

Special thanks to Allison May, Karan Carlsen and, most specially, Joan Locke for all their help at home, freeing me to write this book.

CHAPTER ONE

# INTRODUCTION

The trade name 'Imitation Majolica' was coined by Minton to describe a wide range of brilliantly glazed earthenwares introduced at the Great Exhibition of 1851 in London. While some pieces were indeed imitations of Italian maiolica, most were not. Maiolica is a biscuit-fired earthenware dipped in a stanniferous glaze. After drying it is decorated with high-temperature colours, or sometimes with lustre. Although different in style, French faience and the English and Dutch delft wares were made in the same way.

Majolica, of course, is an Anglicization of *maiolica*. It has been frequently said that the name derives from wares made on the island of Majorca, and the *Oxford English Dictionary* quotes J. C. Scaliger's *Exoteric, Exercit* of 1557 to this effect.

With regard to the pronunciation of the word, some people refer to majolica as 'maiolica', possibly because they think that it actually is maiolica, or that majolica is an Italian word. However, majolica is not maiolica, no Italian firm manufactured majolica and majolica originated in England, overwhelming reasons for this author to approve the 'j' pronunciation of the *Oxford English Dictionary*.

The question of just what constituted Victorian majolica wares is a complicated one. Whichever definition one uses, it seems that some wares are left out. For that reason it is wise to consider majolica as a loosely defined genre. The body is usually earthenware, but sometimes stoneware or even Parian. It was painted with or dipped into lead glazes, although some majolica was gilded or painted with enamels in addition to this. The majority of majolica was relief-moulded. However, not all the relief-moulded earthenwares decorated with lead glazes were necessarily majolica, and it is here that the genre classification becomes useful.

The most important distinction is that which must be made between majolica and the art pottery wares. These two genres are differentiated by style. The characteristics of majolica style are discussed at length below, but briefly the art pottery wares were simpler in design, more subdued in colour and wholly lacking in the odd combination of humour and fascination with the macabre, which characterizes so many of the most notable pieces of majolica.

Two other classes of wares which have sometimes been confused with majolica are green glazed wares and rockingham glazed wares. These two groups should not

*1. A selection of green glazed wares, which were also made with majolica glazes.* Author's collection

be considered to fall into the majolica genre for two reasons. The first is that both had been made for many years before majolica was introduced. The second is that, even after the introduction of majolica, the manufacturers themselves did not consider these wares to fall within the majolica classification. There is abundant evidence for this in the advertisements, catalogues and shape books of the period, all of which consistently differentiated between the three types of wares. Although some shapes were made in all three glazes, when regarded as three separate classes of wares, the differences in style become quite evident.

## THE INTERNATIONAL EXHIBITIONS

The international exhibitions of the second half of the nineteenth century played an enormous role in the development of British ceramics, both technically and stylistically. Firstly, the enormous range of goods exhibited by manufacturers from all over the globe served to disseminate traditional styles as well as new developments more widely and more rapidly than ever before. Secondly, the competition encouraged manufacturers to invest in the development of new techniques, and to employ the best designers, modellers and decorators to execute them. The major international exhibitions of this period (including the number of visitors to the first five) were:

Great Exhibition of the Industry of All Nations, London, 1851 (6,039,135)
Universal Exhibition, Paris, 1855 (5,162,330)
International Exhibition, London, 1862 (6,211,103)
Universal Exhibition, Paris, 1867 (8,805,969)
International Exhibition, London, 1871 (6,740,500)
Universal Exhibition, Vienna, 1873
International Exhibition, London, 1874
Philadelphia Centennial Exhibition, Philadelphia, 1876
Universal Exhibition, Paris, 1878
International Exhibition, Sydney, 1880
Universal Exhibition, Paris, 1889

One can begin to understand the enormous impact of these exhibitions when one learns that the total number of visitors to the first five exhibitions was 32,959,037 – more than the population of the United Kingdom in 1871. The number of exhibitors at these exhibitions can be gauged from the number of awards given at Paris in 1878: 100 grand prizes, 2,000 gold medals, 4,000 silver medals, 8,000 bronze medals and 8,000 honourable mentions. This exhibition was the scene of much fierce competition among majolica manufacturers. *Pottery and Glass Trades' Review*, September 1878, decided:

> In Majolica Mintons exhibit the largest pieces, but Wedgwood's colours are the most brilliant and pure. There are many French exhibitors in this class and the competition with Mintons and Wedgwood is very keen. T. C. Brown-Westhead, Moore & Co. are, in my opinion, quite equal to Mintons in this department, but on the whole Wedgwood's is superior to anything in the Majolica class, and although the pieces are not so large, the colours are unapproachable and the execution of their works unsurpassed.

The majolica manufacturers were appreciated by the judges, according to the official list of awards: Minton won the Grand Prix for their tiles and pottery ware, Brown-Westhead Moore won a gold medal for their earthenwares and majolica wares, and Wedgwood won a gold medal for their pottery.

## THE RISE AND FALL OF MAJOLICA

As early as 1868, Charles Eastlake in *Hints on Household Taste* complained:

> Indeed, there is no branch of art-manufacture exposed to greater dangers, in point of taste, than that of ceramic design. … The tendency of the uneducated eye is, in most cases, to admire the smart and showy but effeminate hues of the day rather than the subtle and refined combinations of colour which distinguish ancient pottery and porcelain. Extravagance of form is preferred to a sober grace of contour, and neatness of execution to the spirit of artistic design.

An economic depression in both Britain and America in 1873–8 hit the ceramics industry particularly hard. The industry had been expanding not only by providing useful wares, but, as will be seen, by providing a vast array of speciality tablewares which were luxury items and among the first things the public could do without during a depression.

As will be seen in Chapter Five, the demand for majolica in America did not really develop until after the Philadelphia Exhibition in 1876, and it was not until 1878, when the economy recovered, that Americans could afford to indulge themselves. Indulge they did, and the 'majolica craze' was born, with a consequent boom in sales in Staffordshire. *Pottery and Glass Trades' Review*, February 1878, reported, '… majolica is just now in great demand in America and seems to suit the Yankee's ideal of beauty. Several extensive orders, and that for the more expensive class of goods – large specimens being most enquired after, and meeting with a ready sale.' In June of the same year, they announced:

> Judging from our experience, we should say that majolica ware is now the most popular class of decorated pottery. The taste for this class of wares appears to be rapidly on the increase, and is spreading itself throughout every branch. Designs to suit majolica decoration are in demand, and anything in the way of novelty stands the best chance on the market and ultimate success.
>
> Of course, a demand of this sort is not without its evil side, which seems to be in sacrificing in many particulars good form to merely 'catchy'. However, we hope that the exuberance will sober down and that we shall have elegance as well as colour, and that the chaste in design will be studied as well as the novel and surprising.

This boom was, ironically, largely responsible for the ultimate decline of majolica in the estimations of Victorians and succeeding generations. Under pressure of large orders, the quality of the goods of even the best manufacturers deteriorated. This period also saw the entrance of many small firms into the trade, and most of their productions were of very poor quality indeed. *Pottery Gazette*, September 1881, reported of Tunstall, Burslem and District:

> The demand for majolica has induced several manufacturers of other wares to add this to their list of industries, but from want of proper management in the mixing of the colours and glazes, or the unsuitable firing have decided to let the few majolica makers in the district have that particular branch to themselves.

This they may have done, but only temporarily. No one wanted to miss out on the majolica bonanza. There were over 130 British majolica manufacturers all told, and many of these operated only briefly during the 1880s.

None the less, the pressures for simpler, more 'tasteful' designs were increasing. Dr. Christopher Dresser in *Principles of Decorative Design* (1880) complained:

> If potters would be content themselves, in order to the production of such articles as we require in common life, with the 'potter's wheel', we should be almost sure of a certain amount of beauty in domestic earthenware, but such is not the case. They make fancy moulds of plaster of Paris, and of wire gauze, and roll out clay as the pastrycook does dough, and manipulate it as so much pie crust, instead of applying it with simple skill.

Such criticisms were heard by the public, and the industry was forced to respond. *Pottery Gazette*, January 1883, explained:

> A change has also crept over the productions of the district. America refuses to have crazy majolica, and the consequence has been that the hitherto bright colours of that

class have become sobered down. The merchants want hard fused ware, ware that will stand rough usage, as well as smooth; this is particularly the case with majolica teapots. A crazy teapot is an abomination not to be tolerated in any well-organized household. Amongst the more noticeable features of decorators this year is the 'sunflower' placed upon every conceivable style of ornament – as centres of plates, on the sides of teapots, jugs, mugs, boxes, creams, cuspadores, spills.

The sunflower was, of course, with the peacock one of the motifs of the Aesthetic Movement, which in and of itself was quite opposed to flamboyant majolica. An article in the *London Daily Mail* in 1881 spoke of 'the lean and melancholy virgins who decorate themselves with peacock feathers and carry sunflowers'.

*2. Majolica argenta basket with typical japonesque design. Unmarked. Height 22 cm. c.1880.* Collection of Don Kelly and Warren Fitzsimmons

During this period argenta wares with cream grounds became more popular than pieces with coloured grounds (Plate 2).

None the less, *Crockery and Glass Journal*, 24 January 1883, reported of Staffordshire, 'Majolica continues, in some instances, to be as brisk as ever.' However, another depression in the mid 1880s once again sent crockery sales plummeting. Majolica was never to regain the popularity it had enjoyed earlier in the decade.

*Pottery Gazette*, January 1889, reported:

The Parian, majolica, jet, furnishing and speciality manufacturers have been constant in their efforts to produce new designs and bodies of a most pleasing and artistic character. ... the influence of Japanese art has been widely felt and the demand for such designs continues. Efforts are, however, being made to obtain designs of a more English type, which may command the home markets. It is possible that too much attention has been paid to the art of other countries and in endeavors to adapt it to English pottery, whilst that of this country has been sorely neglected.

Perhaps the majolica flowerpots in the forms of Derbyshire hash pots sold as fire-screen decorations, described by the *Pottery Gazette* in June of the same year, were efforts in that direction.

*Pottery and Glass Record*, June 1914, explained:

That the taste of the public in pottery designs is improving is certain. There is a lessening demand for flamboyant and riotous patterns and colouring; a simpler, quieter and altogether more artistic article is being asked for. It was in America that the demand for greater simplicity was first noticed, but the same requirement is now extending to other countries.

The *Pottery and Glass Record,* June 1915, summed it up this way:

> Between ten and fifteen years ago the much criticised and not a little despised 'New Art' became the rage. In its epidemic form it became a terrible disease. ... it reduced patterns to a series of dots and dashes, or splashes and blobs, or, still worse, weird wriggly forms like things of torture. Some of those who had rebelled against the monstrosities of Early Victorian days may have enjoyed the revolutionary change, but some of us there were who wondered if the remedy were not worse than the disease. It was not quite. ... But the *Art Nouveau* has had a kindly, beneficent effect. When the virulent form of the epidemic had given way to a milder form of the disease, it became possible to see that good would result. The New Art, at any rate, has simplified design and has largely resulted in the well-considered and restrained decoration which we more often find nowadays.

## FORM AND STYLE - ORIGINS AND INFLUENCES

One of majolica's chief characteristics is its historicism, using many styles from the past both singly and simultaneously. Nearly every piece displays characteristics derived from earlier periods, and yet the bold execution of old forms in a new medium gives majolica an originality and vigour which is unique. The plethora of styles found in majolica was aided, if not entirely due, to the English potters' new exposure to the ceramics of other nations at the international exhibitions, and of other periods at the new museums. The Minton Archives contain a number of

*3. A pair of foliage and Greek key border plates, a typical design showing a combination of influences.* Right: *impressed '4' and 'C'. Diameter 21.5 cm.* Left: *impressed '*' and '7'. Diameter 21 cm.* Author's collection

sketches made at the Louvre and the South Kensington Museum. Also during this period there were increasing efforts to classify ornament, and such books as Owen Jones's *Grammar of Ornament* (1856) offered a wealth of material to designers.

As the century progressed there were increasing cries against the flamboyance and inappropriateness of majolica designs. The idea that ceramics should be fun or even funny became heresy. However, to appreciate majolica today, we must remember the spirit in which it was made. To judge these wares with 'high seriousness' is to judge them unfairly.

*Trompe-l'oeil* plays a large part in majolica design. Surfaces were glazed to represent malachite, tortoiseshell and other materials. Garden seats were made to look like tree stumps entwined with vines. Tureens were shaped like fruits and vegetables, or in one case a boar's head. These latter designs were copied from eighteenth-century designs, made in porcelain or French faience. *Trompe-l'oeil* was also copied from Italian maiolica, where it can be seen in such items as bowls of fruit. Della Robbia's wreaths of fruit, flowers and vines were also much admired and copied. As decribed below, the works of Bernard Palissy were rife with lifelike molluscs, insects and reptiles.

The Arts and Crafts movement, however, objected to *trompe -l'oeil* on principle. As early as 1849, in *Seven Lamps of Architecture*, John Ruskin had criticized the painting of surfaces to represent different materials as 'deceits'. In *Principles of Decorative Design* (1880), Dr. Christopher Dresser challenged the idea of *trompe-l'oeil.* 'We have all seen earthen jugs made in imitation of wicker-work, although to

*4. Meissen porcelain leaf dish. Painted crossed swords and dot in underglaze blue, impressed 'K'. Length 19.4 cm. c.1765-70. Sotheby's*

*5. Spode cabbage tureen. Impressed mark. Height 14.5 cm.* c.1820. Sotheby's

*6. Begonia leaf bread tray. Unmarked. Length 34 cm.* Author's collection

I. *Left to right:* Staffordshire pineapple teapot, probably Whieldon.
Height 12.5 cm. *c.*1760; Leeds creamware punch pot. Height 21.5 cm. *c.*1765;
Staffordshire teapot, Astbury-Whieldon type. Height 12.5 cm. *c.*1745–50. *Sotheby's*

II. George Jones Punch Bowl. Diamond registration mark for 13 September
1875. Height 25.5 cm. Diameter 34 cm. *Phillips, New York*

III.  Minton Negro Male and Female, modelled by Carrier de Belleuse. Shape
numbers 1157 and 1158. Height 179.5 cm. *c.*1870. *Sotheby's*

do so is obviously foolish, as no wicker vessel could hold water, and the thing imitated is much less beautiful than a thousand forms which clay is capable of representing.'

The historicism of majolica is also reflected in the large number of designs called 'Gothic', 'Elizabethan' or 'Tudor'. Design elements from these periods, most notably the Gothic arch were freely incorporated into shapes and patterns. These are not usually very successful, a notable exception being the bread plate designed by A. W. N. Pugin for Minton. One of Wedgwood's most popular early designs was the Cambridge Ale Jug, which copied a medieval leather vessel.

The Victorian passion for natural history is reflected in the large number of designs depicting plants. *The Artist,* July 1882, announced that a number of new

*7. Villeroy & Boch Bamboo Fan dessert plate. Impressed '977/7'. Diameter 20.5 cm.* Author's collection

plants had been certified by the Royal Horticultural Society and thus, 'some decorative resources have been added to our gardens and homes'. Designers went to the botanical gardens, or, in the case of Brown-Westhead, Moore's famous majolica tigers, to the London Zoo, to sketch from the originals.

*Japonaiserie* pervaded the ceramics industry after exhibitions of Japanese wares at South Kensington in 1862 and at Paris in 1867. In majolica this took the form of decorating typically Western shapes with storks, fans, prunus blossom and pine branches. Most often these motifs are found on argenta wares which had cream-coloured grounds.

These were some of the most popular majolica wares ever made, but in retrospect they are rather feeble. Most of these were made during the majolica boom in the early 1880s, and under pressure of large orders, even the better class of manufacturers turned out some poorly executed work.

*Crockery and Glass Journal,* 16 June 1881, said of these designs:

> … they have the form, the peculiarities, the eccentricities of the Japanese, but not the spirit. There seems to be a general idea that if a sprig of apple or hawthorn blossom is thrown across a piece of ware in a slovenly manner, and a few stamps and panels are stuck in front, without form or order, that a Japanese design is secured.

## ITALIAN MAIOLICA

The maiolica copied by the Victorian potters was fifteenth-century faenza. An earthenware body, slightly fired, was dipped in a white tin enamel. Once dried, the wares were painted with enamels, usually in white, green, yellow, cobalt blue or

*8. Savona maiolica jar and cover. Height 56 cm. c.1722.*
Sotheby's

brownish purple. The ware was then glazed with a clear glaze, which gave depth to
and protected the design. Maiolica, and the related tin-glazed earthenwares, faience
and delft, were very fragile, the glazes chipping away quite easily. These wares were
superseded by other more durable wares, most notably English creamwares,
during the eighteenth century. It was not the maiolica technique that was copied

in England then, but the shapes and decoration. The principal subjects of maiolica decoration were:

Trofei: weapons, armour and musical instruments
Rabeschi: interlaced lines and foliage
Cerquate: oak leaves
Groteschi: ornaments ending in human figures or heads
Foglie: leaves
Fiori: flowers
Paesi: landscapes

All of these motifs may be found on those majolica items imitating maiolica. Also copied were the so-called marriage plates, with portraits in the centre. Most of the maiolica-inspired majolica was made during the 1850s. After that the genre increasingly evolved away from its original inspiration.

## PALISSY WARES

Palissy wares were just as important as Renaissance maiolica in the formation of majolica wares. Bernard Palissy was born at La Chapelle-Biron near Agen in 1510. He trained as a glass painter and a surveyor, before travelling through Germany and the Low Countries. In 1542, he married and settled at Saintes. While working as a painter, glass painter and surveyor, he learned to make peasant pottery. His attempts to perfect a stanniferous glaze such as that used in maiolica brought him to destitution. In his biography he told of how he burnt the furniture, and even floorboards, of his home in order to keep his kilns burning. During this time, Palissy became a Protestant.

Palissy was eventually successful, and his white glaze became the basis for all the richly coloured glazes to follow. In 1548, Palissy gained the patronage of the Constable of France, Anne de Montmorency, which brought him great repute, as well as protection against a 1562 ordinance seizing all Protestant property. He obtained an appointment of '*inventeur des rustiques figulines du Roy*', and settled in Paris. In Paris he fulfilled commissions for Catherine de Medici, and lectured on natural history. However, in 1588 he was finally thrown into the Bastille for his religious beliefs, and died there four years later.

Palissy's work can be divided into three periods. In the first period, his works were covered with brilliant enamels. During the second period he made his rustic pieces of enamelled earthenware, statuettes, dishes, plates, ewers and vases with moulded ornaments. He applied to them realistic figures of fishes, reptiles, shells, plants and fossil shells, all meticulously modelled and painted realistically. It is these pieces which are most often associated with Palissy today. During the third period his pieces had geometrical patterns in relief with pierced borders, as well as pieces moulded after the work of goldsmith François Briot. Work in the Palissy style continued in the region until the middle of the seventeenth century. According to Chaffers there were also works of this sort being made in Manerbe, Normandy, during the second half of the sixteenth century.

During the 1830s several different French potters revived Palissy wares. Some of these imitations are so well done that even museum curators and Palissy experts cannot be certain of their authenticity. The majority of the copies were, however, identifiably different from or inferior to the real Palissy works. They were called Palissy wares not only because they were in fact imitations of Palissy's wares, but because Palissy enjoyed considerable celebrity during the nineteenth century. The Portuguese also began to imitate Palissy later in the nineteenth century. These works have merit of their own, but are not exact copies.

The Palissy revival in France would have been familiar to Léon Arnoux at Minton. However, the general popularity of Palissy wares in England, both the originals, which commanded hitherto unheard-of prices, and the copies, was largely due to a biography of Palissy by Henry Morley, first published in 1852. Palissy was greatly admired by the Victorians for his perseverance and industry, as well as for his Protestant martyrdom.

## TYPES OF WARES

The manufacturers divided their wares into two categories, the ornamental and the useful. Within the category of ornamental wares fall the exhibition pieces. These were individually produced by the manufacturer's best designers, modellers and decorators, usually at enormous cost. *Pottery and Glass Trades' Review*, November 1878, explained:

> There seems to be just now almost a rivalry among some manufacturers for the production of big pieces of pottery. ... To such wealthy houses ... it matters little that these large pieces never pay the potter, however amazing and interesting they may be to beholders who seldom buy.

9. A trompe-l'oeil *effect leaves-on-basketweave bread tray. Unmarked. Diameter 26 cm.* Author's collection

These pieces were, however, very effective advertising. They were described in detail again and again in contemporary journals, books and magazines. If the exhibition pieces themselves were not purchased, they often induced the spectator to purchase the smaller items which were displayed at the firms' stalls.

Large *animalier* figures, sometimes life size (as was the famous Minton peacock), figured prominently at the international exhibitions. These were made in limited quantities and are very rare today. They were generally intended for use in conservatories. On a smaller scale, vases, flower holders, spill vases, flower baskets and brackets were made in abundance.

The largest class of ornamental majolica wares were those relating to the garden

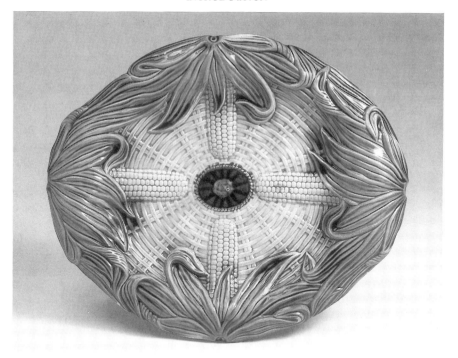

*10. Corn bread tray. Unmarked. Length 34 cm.* Author's collection

and conservatory. Jardinières, flowerpots and garden pots were not only the most popular majolica items during its heyday, but continued to be made up until the First World War. These were frequently accompanied by stands or pedestals.

Majolica furniture should also be regarded as largely ornamental, due to the fragility of the ware. Garden seats and umbrella stands are the items most commonly found, but flower tables were also made. In the Minton Archives there is a drawing of a majolica chair with cabriole legs, but it is not certain that the item was actually produced, as there are no recorded examples.

The useful wares are most importantly tablewares. *Crockery and Glass Journal*, 7 June 1883, declared:

> It was in former years, the fashion to purchase an entire outfit of one ware, shape and color; but, ... art and good taste have decreed that this monotonous habit shall be broken, and we now rarely sit at a well appointed table that has not upon its cloth a succession of dishes changing with the courses and varying in style – a sure index of the taste and culture of the owner.

The author then goes on to say that the service for the soup course must 'of necessity' be of French porcelain, but recommends English majolica, preferably argenta, for the fish course. 'The decoration must consist of fish, shells or marine plants, or, still better all three.' For the game course one must again resort to French porcelain, and for the main course blue and white wares, preferably Chinese.

Majolica salad sets are recommended for the next course: 'a pretty salad dish is tall in shape, with panels at the side, in which are raised representations of lobsters, vegetables, etc.' He further warns that the raised surfaces on the accompanying plates may be 'awkward for use'. He specifies next the ice cream and berry sets, preferably of glass. However, as so many of these were made in majolica, they must have been a popular choice. These are followed by the fruit or dessert plates, 'after dinner coffees' and finger bowls.

Having procured all of the above, the hostess is far from finished. 'The little things upon the table – outside of and belonging to no course – are like conjunctions and prepositions in language, connecting or adding to the various services; and in these seemingly insignificant details lies the beauty or ugliness of the entire collection.' The items here mentioned are individual butter plates (porcelain or majolica), individual or table salts (cut glass), sugar bowl, cream pitcher and syrup pitcher (all of Wedgwood jasperware, preferably of more than one colour).

This cacophony of tablewares explains a great deal about the logic behind the range of majolica table wares generally offered by the manufacturers. The relative fragility of majolica made it impractical for dinner services, but less so for the fish, salad, fruit and dessert courses. The 'little things', which had even less need to be durable, were made in abundance, as were the large items not mentioned by the author, namely centrepieces and even table fountains, which frequently were as large as eighteen inches high.

There is also the matter of lighting the dinner table. A 'fashion writer' in *Crockery and Glass Journal*, 2 November 1882, recommends that the dinner table be lighted by candelabra on either side of the centrepiece. 'Usually the foundation is a mirror, and the support the figure of a child or mythological subject.'

This writer then goes on to explain that 12 o'clock breakfast and 4 o'clock tea

must be served in the boudoir upon a revolving table. This of course required a special set of dishes which was comprised of a muffin dish and toast rack (for breakfast use only), cups, a teapot, a tea kettle, cream jug, milk pitcher and sugar bowl. To compensate for the expense of all this, it is pointed out that 'By their use the attendance of a servant is dispensed with.'

Among the most popular majolica items were covered butter dishes, covered cheese dishes and the magnificent covered Stilton cheese stands. The

*11. George Jones cheese stand. Impressed mark and registration mark. Base diameter 27 cm.* Sotheby's

sardine boxes require explanation today.
Sardines enjoyed a new popularity during
the height of the majolica craze. They
keep poorly, and so were prime candi-
dates for the new canning industry of the
period. Mrs. Beeton specified a box of
sardines as one of the ingredients of a
Family Tea. Sardines were something of a
novelty and had not fallen into their
current ill repute. Thus, a showy sardine
box served to call attention to the fact that
this new delicacy was being served. Oyster plates are another majolica speciality
which is greatly sought after.

*12. Minton oyster stand. Shape number
636. Height 26 cm. c.1862.* Sotheby's

Game pie dishes were first introduced
in the beginning of the nineteenth century when, due to the Napoleonic Wars,
flour was scarce. These early game pie
dishes in caneware were made to look like a pie crust, and the pie filling was baked
in them. Majolica game pie dishes, which were not ovenproof, could be bought
with ovenproof liners in which the pies were actually baked. The liners were then
placed inside the elaborate dish, before serving.

*13. George Jones hare game pie dish. Diamond registration mark. Pattern no.
3371. Length 38 cm. c.1875.* Sotheby's

It is not surprising that almost none of the majolica toilet wares have survived. The ware was wholly unsuited to the hard usage given to toilet wares. These sets were generally confined to ewer and basin. No majolica chamber pots have been recorded. Thus, although majolica toilet wares were made by quite a few manufacturers, they are extremely rare today. Dressing table wares and trinket trays were a far more suitable use for majolica. A dressing table set might include a powder box, match box, candlestick, ring stand or tray, pin tray, match stand, comb tray and pomade box. They were not, however, made in any great quantities, and are also rare today.

There are a large number of majolica wares which were related to smoking. Complete smoking sets comprised of a spill case, cigar box, ashtray, match box and tobacco box were made by a number of firms, but complete sets are today almost unknown. A great many ashtrays were made, and can be easily found today. In many cases these have been mistaken for pickle dishes, as they do not have the impressions today associated with ashtrays. Similarly, the Wedgwood Net Cigar Tray has frequently been called a trinket tray, presumably because it seems far too attractive for its original purpose. The number of match holders and match boxes is not surprising considering that in 1885 some 8,000 million boxes of matches were sold in Britain.

Spittoons and cuspadores were produced copiously and are very common today. They are probably the most affordable majolica items to be found today, as their original purpose was rather unpleasant (Plate 14).

## TECHNICAL ASPECTS

Majolica's translucent glazes are responsible for its unique brilliance. In most cases, the wares were covered with an opaque white glaze before being dipped in or painted with coloured glazes. Sometimes, however, the body used was of sufficient whiteness to omit this step. This coloured glaze was usually quite thick, as can be

seen occasionally on the undersides of wares where it has pooled. In many cases, the glazes have a delicate iridescence. The pieces were fired at a higher than normal temperature which resulted in the subtle blending of colours typical of majolica.

Léon Arnoux, of Minton, the greatest ceramic chemist of the nineteenth century, was a master of glaze preparation, yet he wrote, 'To prepare a glaze is one of the most delicate operations possible, and failures attended with most serious

*14. Pineapple spittoon. Painted mark '14'. Base diameter 19.5 cm.* Author's collection

*15. Oak leaf dish, showing typical running glazes. Painted mark 'X'. Length 27.5 cm.* Author's collection

consequences.' As the perfection of the glazes was essential to majolica production, it is not surprising that many majolica producers bought their colours and the glazes they mixed them into from specialists in that field. Perhaps the largest majolica glaze manufacturer was A. Wenger. Other large producers were James Hancock & Son of Worcester, Harrison & Son of Hanley and S. Fielding & Co. (Wenger and Fielding were also majolica manufacturers and are discussed in Appendix A and Chapter Four, respectively.) As late as the 1880s the Americans were still importing *all* of their colours, mostly from England and Germany.

Yet these lovely glazes were death to those who worked with them in the potteries. The widespread use of rockingham, raw majolica glazes and the cheaper sanitary glazes was credited with the large increase in lead poisoning during the late nineteenth century. In Furnival's *Researches on Leadless Glazes* (1898), he cites the cases of two boys aged fourteen and fifteen, who had worked in the dipping house only six and twelve months respectively before their deaths from lead poisoning. Of 156 cases, 'twelve resulted in total blindness, two of these being paralysed and insane, three of them died since being reported; of nine cases liable to go blind, three have lost the sight of one eye; two other victims are paralysed and in bed and nineteen paralysed and rendered unfit for work.'

Yet, ceramic manufacturers insisted that leadless glazes were impossibly inferior. Even the compromise of fritting the lead before use resulted in hardness, tendency to craze, and the loss of brilliancy and purity of colour. None the less, public pressure increased and leadless glazes were introduced during the first forty years of the twentieth century. Majolica glazes made after that time, and up to this day, lack the glossiness, brightness and iridescence found in the Victorian examples.

In general the body of majolica is a simple earthenware body. Some Parian majolica was made, and Wedgwood used a close-grained pearlware on some of their majolica. Both Copeland and Dudson made majolica with a stoneware body. Some of the coarser grades of majolica have a terracotta body.

Most majolica was relief-moulded. However good the colours, glazes and decoration, a poorly moulded piece makes for a poor end product. The importance of the modeller in this process cannot be overemphasized. Presented with a design, it is the job of the modeller to decide how to divide the item into pieces which will be moulded individually and then assembled. A jug would only have two pieces – the body and the handle; a teapot, three – the body, spout and handle. Figures or pieces with figures attached were far more complicated, as heads and limbs were all moulded separately. The more intricate the design, the more difficult it becomes to extract from the mould. The making of the plaster of Paris mould is itself a very highly skilled job, and if poorly done, no amount of decoration can hide it.

Once the mould is made, the item is cast. First, the clay slip is poured into a hole at the top of the mould. After standing and settling, excess clay is poured away. The mould is left standing until the clay stiffens and contracts, enabling it to be removed from the mould. The piece is then assembled and sponged to remove seams from the mould and to smooth over joins. This last step seems simple enough, but it is one which was most often skimped upon by manufacturers. It is not unusual to find ugly seams under the handle and running from base to spout on poor-quality jugs.

The major advantage of the relief-moulding process was that the item could be merely dipped in glazes or dabbed with glaze to highlight the moulded design –

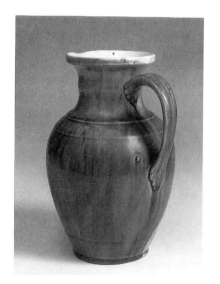

a process much cheaper than painting a design. The chief disadvantage was that the moulds wore out, and with repeated use the impressions become less crisp. Some factories sold their worn moulds to lesser manufacturers, explaining the poor-quality pieces one may find which seem identical to better-quality pieces known to have been made by the higher class of manufacturers.

*16. An atypically simple jug with mottled majolica glazes. Height 20 cm.* Author's collection

# CHAPTER TWO

# MINTON MAJOLICA

T he firm that first introduced majolica was established as Minton & Poulson in 1793 by Thomas Minton, Joseph Poulson and William Pownall, a Liverpool businessman. Initially they produced transfer-printed earthenware, introducing porcelains in 1798. In 1817, Minton took his two sons into partnership. Although this partnership was dissolved in 1828, Herbert Minton continued to work with his father. Upon the death of Thomas Minton in 1836, Herbert formed a partnership with John Boyle. The firm operated under the style Minton & Boyle until 1841, when the partnership was dissolved. They then traded as Herbert Minton & Co. until 1873 when the name changed to 'Mintons'.

In 1842, Minton took into partnership his nephew, Michael Daintry Hollins, and in 1849 another nephew, Colin Minton Campbell. Campbell took over the factory upon his uncle's death in 1858. Hollins stayed on with the firm until 1868, when he left to run Minton, Hollins & Co., a new firm formed to carry on Minton's tile manufacture. A full account of the factory from 1793 to 1850 may be found in Geoffrey Godden's *Minton Pottery and Porcelain of the First Period.*

## LÉON ARNOUX

Léon Francis Arnoux was born in Valentine near Toulouse in 1816. His father, Antoine Arnoux *fils*, was a successful potter, who became mayor of Toulouse in 1830. Antoine Arnoux the elder and his brother-in-law, Joseph-Jacques Fouque, had established the Fouque-Arnoux pottery at Toulouse in 1800. They made urns, vases and useful wares in faience and other glazed earthenwares. They also experimented with hard-paste porcelain. By 1832 the firm was run by Fouque's sons, François and Henri, and Arnoux's son, also Antoine. They had moved to Valentine, and traded as Fouque, Arnoux et Cie. The firm began to produce transfer-printed wares and lavishly gilded and decorated hard-paste porcelains.

Arnoux studied engineering at l'Ecole des Arts et Manufactures in Paris. He went on to gain practical experience at the Paris depot of Sèvres. He then managed the family firm in Valentine. He came to England in 1848, escaping the political upheaval in France and difficulties at Fouque-Arnoux. Herbert Minton employed him to reproduce a formula for French hard-paste porcelain. His responsibilities increased until he was appointed Art Director in 1849, and, eventually, Director of the works until his retirement in 1892. He continued to work as a consultant to the firm until his death in 1902.

Generally considered the greatest ceramicist of the nineteenth century, Arnoux excelled not only in the technical side of ceramic production, creating bodies and glazes and inventing the Minton Patent Oven, but the artistic side. Under his leadership, Minton became the best pottery in the world. Their porcelains vied with

*17. Minton pedestal. Impressed marks, date code and numbers 871 and 2217. Height 53 cm. c.1872. Sotheby's*

those of Sèvres and Worcester, and at the same time their earthenwares surpassed those of Wedgwood. Majolica was only one of the innovative new styles in pottery and porcelain introduced by Arnoux. He received the Legion of Honour and the Order of Francis Joseph in 1878, among many other international honours.

## THE INTRODUCTION OF MAJOLICA

One story goes that Herbert Minton obtained some specimens of Italian maiolica formerly in the possession of the Duke of Buckingham. These inspired him to attempt reproduction maiolica. Another story says that Minton was inspired by some lead-glazed flower pots he saw while travelling in France. Both stories may well be true, as what would become majolica was inspired by both sources. In 1849, two prizes were offered at the School of Design in the Potteries, by Smith Child, for the best and second-best designs for a wine cooler in the old maiolica style. One of these prizes was awarded to Simon Birks, who had recently completed his apprenticeship with Minton. The vase for which he received the prize was exhibited by Minton at the Exhibition of 1862 (although the colouring had been somewhat modified by other artists).

Arnoux began majolica manufacture in 1849 or 1850. His knowledge of the continental methods of producing lead-glazed wares was invaluable, but the English clays, which were harder and less calcareous than continental clays, at first presented difficulties. He also perfected, through endless experimentation, the majolica colours. As will be seen, the Minton palette was a major factor in the superiority of the ware, which was maintained throughout the majolica period.

Initially, the wares were meant to be reproductions of Italian maiolica, and Minton called them 'Imitation Majolica'. Arnoux sent artists to public and private collections throughout England and in France, to make detailed drawings of various Renaissance wares, including maiolica, Della Robbia's work and Palissy wares. These drawings, many of which survive in the Minton Archives, were then closely copied. In 1851, Minton began to manufacture Della Robbia and Palissy wares, which fall within the majolica genre. However, over the next decade, Arnoux's majolica glazes were applied to an ever-increasing range of wares.

Arnoux was instrumental in attracting many of the leading continental ceramic artists and artisans to join the Minton team. Some of these men also taught at

*18. Minton jardinière and stand. Height 97 cm. c.1880.* Sotheby's

the local art school, thus training local artists and craftsmen, many of whom are discussed in Appendix C.

When majolica was officially introduced at the Great Exhibition, it produced a great sensation. The jury commended '... the garden pots and vases exhibited by Messrs. Minton, modelled in imitation of the old majolica ware and not only remarkable for the success with which the effect of that ware is attained, but for the novelty and beauty of design.'

*The Industry of All Nations* illustrated a swagged jardinière with goat's head handles, 'coloured after the style of the old Majolica. The quiet tone of colour he has adopted for their fanciful surfaces evinces the very best taste.'

The first clearly majolica designs registered by Minton were the bamboo and bow Jardinière and Stand (No. 480) and Garden Seat (No. 481), registered on 4 December 1851. (For more information on design registration see Chapter Eight.) From this we may assume that by the end of 1851, Minton had produced some five hundred majolica designs. Of these, many would have been earlier shapes now made in majolica. For example, the Harvest Wreath Jug (No. 268) was illustrated in the *Art Journal*, October 1849, originally produced in stoneware.

The Hop Pickers Jug, designed by Henry Townsend, was illustrated in the *Art-Union*, September 1847. This jug was awarded the Gold Medal of the Society of Arts, 1848 for 'the Union of Superior Art & Manufacture'. Originally made in brown earthenware, a majolica example of this jug may be seen at the Victoria and Albert Museum. Bell's Bread Tray (No. 367), presumably designed by John Bell, was registered in 1848, but it was later made in majolica. It must have proved a good steady seller, because pieces have been recorded with date marks as early as 1861, and the shape appeared in the *Minton Shape Book* of 1884. 'Pugin's Bread Plate' (No. 368) was originally made in encaustic style with coloured clays, but later made in majolica.

Some shapes were combinations of earlier pieces. For example, the Cherub Tazza (No. 836) is a combination of a 'Support and Pedestal' (No. 539) and a 'Basket' (No. 734).

It was at the Paris Exhibition in 1855 that Minton really displayed a full line of majolica wares for the first time. Perhaps the most remarkable exhibition piece displayed was a seven-foot flower stand, painted with bands of grotesques in the style of the Duke of Urbino service decorated by Orazio Fontana, c.1565. It may have been designed by Emile Jeannest. Also of importance were the pair of maiolica-style plaques with portraits of Queen Victoria and the Empress Eugénie, painted by Thomas Kirkby.

In 1856, the Jacques Soulages Collection was displayed at Marlborough House. It was subsequently purchased for the nation by a public subscription to which Herbert Minton contributed £1000. This collection, which included 115 examples of maiolica, was to be a rich resource for Minton designers and decorators. The Soulage Ewer and Stand (No. 732) was modelled by Hamlet Bourne from a Palissy ewer in the Soulages collection.

On 5 October 1858, Minton registered the Pineapple Jug (No. 538), which was made in Parian as well as in majolica. This design proved very popular and was still

*19. Minton oyster plate. Diameter 25 cm.* Sotheby's

shown in the *Minton Shape Book* of 1884. In 1859, the Crystal Palace Art Union commissioned a Minton majolica Christmas dish, one of the earliest products commissioned by that union. The dish was decorated with various Christmas motifs, and incorporated a shield reading, 'Crystal Palace Art Union'.

Majolica was again featured at the London International Exhibition of 1862. The most important Minton piece was the majolica and stone fountain, known as St. George's Fountain, erected under the eastern dome of the Crystal Palace (see frontispiece). Designed by John Thomas (see Appendix C), it was the greatest attraction of the exhibition. The *Vide Times*, 17 May 1862, proclaimed, 'If there were no other object in the Building but this grand work alone, it would be well worth a shilling entrance to see it.'

*Cassell's Illustrated*, from which the frontispiece illustration was taken, reported that the fountain had several times been successfully perfumed by Rimmel of Paris.

> Here every afternoon may be heard the strains of beautiful music from the Grand Pianofortes . . . and here beauty and fashion meet and mingle with the representatives of labour – the working men and working women of our world. On crowded days – and almost every day is crowded – the eastern dome is a sight to behold.

*20. Pair of Minton flower brackets. Impressed 'M' and date code for 1859 on one. Height 34 cm.* Sotheby's

The fountain was 36 feet high by 39 feet in diameter. It was comprised of 369 separate pieces which took two months to assemble. The group of St. George and the Dragon at the summit of the fountain (now on display at the City Museum and Art Gallery, Hanley) was supported by four winged victories, holding crowns of laurel surrounding a central pavilion inscribed with the motto, 'For England and for Victory'. Beneath this were tiers of smaller fountains which received the water and further distributed it. One of these, supported by a heron, was a copy of a fountain designed for the Queen's dairy under the personal supervision of Prince Albert. The outer circumference of the fountain was ornamented with oak leaves and acorns, alternating with roses of England and divided by eight flower vases. The fountain as a whole was not, of course, meant as a marketable item, but several of the smaller fountains comprising the whole, especially the crane and the griffin, were sold as conservatory fountains.

The list of majolica displayed by Minton at the Exhibition is reproduced in full below as it gives an accurate idea of the range then produced by Minton. It will be noticed, firstly, that these pieces fall into one of several groups: Italian, Alhambra, Oriental, Louis XV, Elizabethan, Palissy and, predominantly, those with motifs from classical myth. The naturalistic motifs which are most familiar to majolica collectors today are poorly represented. This is because they were reserved for the 'useful classes of Pottery, in Dinner, Dessert, Toilet, and Tea and Breakfast services' which were, indeed, displayed at the Exhibition, but were not listed in the Catalogue, which confined itself to the 'Works of an Ornamental character'.

IV. French asparagus dish. Length 38.5 cm. *Author's collection*

V. Wedgwood Vine Bread Tray. Length 30 cm. *Author's collection*

VI. Minton Monkey Garden Seat, c.1873. Impressed mark and date code.
Height 44 cm. *Sotheby's*

D 1.   Pair of Vases. No. 804, orange ground, decorated with the figures representing Justice, Theology, Philosophy, and Poetry, painted by Raphael in the Stanza Della Signatura, in the Vatican.

D 2.   Pair of Vases and Pedestals, No. 788, white enamel in imitation of Porphyry, finished in gold.

D 3.   Pair of Alhambra Bottles, No. 624, in imitation of Malachite.

D 4.   Pair of Vases, No. 804, in imitation of Porphyry, finished with white enamel and gold.

D 5.   Cornucopia, No. 808, Cupid riding on a Dolphin.

D 6.   Pair of Vases and Pedestals, No. 788, painted grotesque subjects in the Italian style.

D 7.   Pair of Groups and Stands, (Children and Goat), No. 257 and 258, on pedestals.

D 8.   Pair of large Oriental Flower Pots and Pedestals, No. 720, orange and green.

D 9.   Pair of Tall Bottles, No. 625, blue and green mottled.

D 10   Tripod Jardinière, No. 718, in Louis 15th style,

D 11.   Oval Dish, painted in green Camaïeu, representing the competition of Apollo and Marsyas.

D 12.   Pair of large Baskets, No. 949, supported by three Cupids.

D 13.   Pair of large Oriental Flower Pots and Pedestals, No. 720, chocolate ground and blue ornaments.

D 14.   Daisy Basket, No. 860, Cupid support.

D 15.   Wine Cooler, No. 762, blue ground, Elizabethan style.

D 16.   Wine Cooler, No. 762, chocolate ground, Elizabethan style.

D 18.   Round Dish, painted subject, representing the 'Judgment of Paris.'

D 19.   Round Tray, painted subject, representing the 'Metamorphosis of Jupiter, by Julio Romano.'

D 20.   Fish Dish, No. 982, bulrush embossed.

D 21.   Comport Palissy, No. 773.

D 22.   Tazza, No. 465, painted female bust.

D 23.   Italian Cistern. No. 842, blue ground.

D 24.   Pair of Garden Pots and Stands, No. 713, blackberry, Turquoise ground.

D 25.   Pair of Vases. No. 768, blue ground, coloured wreaths of flowers.

D 26.   Amorini Fountain, No. 911.

D 27.   Shell Centre Piece, supported by three Tritons.

D 28.   Inkstand, No. 837.

D 29.   Shell Comport, No. 852, merman support.

D 30.   Shell Comport, No. 853, mermaid support.

D 31.   Jug, No. 900, barrel shape, with four Cupids.

D 32.   Garden Pot and Stand, fern and foxglove, blue ground.

D 33.   Tazza, No. 782, painted Cupids on blue ground.

D 34.   Round Dish, No. 771, embossed figures of Henry 4th, and Mary of Medici, in blue ground.

D 40   Vintagers supporting Basket, No. 728.

D 41.   Palissy Tray, No. 537, painted subject in centre.

D 42.   Flower Stand, No. 922, Turquoise ground, green ivy snake handles.

D 44.   Cream Bowl and Stand, No. 709, Palissy.

D 45.   Triangular Basket, No. 981.

D 46.   Tall Candelabra, 10 lights, No. 871, supported by a group of figures, representing Love, Peace, & Abundance.

D 47.   Wine Cooler, Victoria, No. 631, surrounded by four hunting groups, with a group of boys and basket of grapes on the top.

D 48.   Custard Stand, No. 605.

D 49. Oval Victoria Basket, No. 942, perforated, with two Oriental figures reclining at foot.

D 50. Oval perforated Basket, No. 937, supported by two mermaids.

D 51. Large centre Basket, No. 948, supported by figures, representing the Seasons.

D 52. Pair of Vases, No. 766, Turquoise ground.

D 53. Pair of large Cupid Brackets, No. 767.

D 54. Flower Holder, No 778, triple horn with steel chains.

D 55. Wine Cooler, No. 806, painted Landscapes.

D 56. Pierced Basket, No. 734, supported by a Bacchante.

D 57. Pierced Basket, No. 735, supported by a Satyr.

D 58. Jug, No. 654, blue ground, painted Cupids and garlands.

D 59. Jug, No. 596, Verulam, in imitation of Malachite.

D 60. Low Comport, pierced, No. 742, painted Cupids.

D 61. Mussel Dish and Stand, No. 736.

D 62. Candlestick, No. 765, in Palissy ware.

D 63. Table, No. 847, Cupid supports, painted subject from Van Loo.

D 64. Pompeian Cup, No. 346, Eagle.

D 65. Set of five round Dishes, representing the triumph of Julius Cæsar.

D 77. Pair of Vases, No. 895, painted allegorical figures and Cupids.

D 78. Pair of Vases, Snake handle, No. 630, painted subjects after Raphael.

D 79. Oval Dish, painted subject under the glaze, representing Venus and Vulcan.

D 80. Oval Tray with handles, painted subject under glaze, representing Samson and Delilah, after Titian.

D 81. Pair of Jardinières, with wreath in high relief, round the basin.

D 82. Oval Cistern, No. 614, blue ground supported by two Cupids.

D 84. Garden seat, No. 940, white ground.

D 85. Garden seat, No. 940, Turquoise ground.

D 86. ditto No. 772, orange ground.

D 87. ditto No. 772, crimson ground.

D 88. ditto No. 838, blue ground.

D 89. ditto No. 786, Chinese brown ground.

D 90. Bamboo Garden Seat, No. 481, coloured naturally.

D 91. Large Shell supported by Red Coral, No. 966, coloured naturally.

D 92. Oak Garden Pot and Stand, No. 650, crimson ground.

D 84½. Pair of Large Vases, No. 980, Maskhead, in imitation of Porphyry.

D 95. Soulage Ewer and Stand, Palissy, No. 732.

D 96. Vase, No. 714, orange ground, green key border.

D 97. Stilton Cheese Stand, No. 969, beehive and blackberry, coloured naturally.

D 98. Fountain, No, 705, from a design by Lady Marian Alford.

D 100. Oval Comport, No. 930, imitation of Porphyry, supported by two Cupids, ornamented in gold and white enamel.

D 101. Suspension Basket, No. 578.

D 116. Suspension Basket Bark, No. 423, coloured naturally.

D 117. Inkstand, (Lizard) in imitation of Malachite, finished in gold.

D 118. Jug and Stand, No. 654, in imitation of Malachite, finished in gold.

D 120. Ewer and Stand, No. 787, white embossed, marine subjects.

D 121. Pair of Large Vases, No. 990, Ramshead handles, deep violet ground, festoons of fruit, supported by a group of four Cupids.

D 122. Flower Holder, No. 991, Chinese leaf in Palissy, richly coloured, on a black stand.

D 125. Vase, No. 600, painted in Raphael style, chiaro oscuro, on deep blue ground.

D 126. Pair of Vases, No. 901, painted under glaze, with Cupids, after Boucher, subjects framed with oak and laurel wreath, blue ground.

D 127. Pair of Large Vases, No. 980, in imitation of Malachite, with Maskhead, ropes and fruit.

D 128. Round Dish, painted battle subject from Julio Romano.

D 130. Nautilus Shell, No. 992, in imitation of Malachite, marine Venus on the top, embossed Cupids on the Shell, supported by two mermen.

D 131. Large Round Tazza, 'Time rescuing truth from Envy and Jealousy', in white enamel and gold, in the Limoges style.

D 132. Pair of Garden Seats, Malachite and gold.

D 133. Pair of Bottles, No. 624, gilt marbling, in imitation of Lapis Lazuli.

D 136. Large Ewer and Stand, No. 616, painted under glaze, figures of the Gods after Polidoro Carvagio, on the ewer, and the labors of Hercules on the stand.

D 137. Ewer and Stand, No. 787, painted under glaze, with Cupids.

D 139. Salt, imitation of Henry 2nd ware, brown & buff inlaid.

D 140. Antique Jug, Lion handle and spout, brown and buff inlaid.

D 141. Round Tray, painted under glaze, female head in centre surrounded with a garland of fruit.

D 142. Vase, No. 658, snake handles, painted subjects.

D 143. Pair of Vases, No. 944, in imitation of Malachite, solid gilt ropes.

Minton again exhibited majolica at the Paris Exhibition of 1867. *The Art Journal* in 1868 remarked of their successful display there:

> There is, however, one description of decorative porcelain in which Messrs. Minton leave all rivals, whatever their nation, in the rear; it may indeed be called, without the least disparagement of their other works, that in which they pre-eminently excel; certain it is that no firm in England, and but few on the Continent, have paid so much unremitting attention to it. We refer to the class of Faience usually designated Majolica; that massive ware, of bold design, and bolder ornaments and positive colours, principally blues, yellows and greens.... The variety of objects of this kind exhibited by them was great and they were not seen alone in the space allotted to them in the building, but dispersed about the gardens in the form of garden-seats, flower pots, and flower-vases.

Minton once again enjoyed great success with their majolica at the Vienna Exhibition of 1873. A sales log from the Exhibition stall in the Minton Archives, reveals that majolica was certainly fashionable among the Viennese aristocracy. Among others, it notes majolica jardinières purchased by Princess Stefani de Croy and Prince von Lichnowsky; a majolica fountain (at £35.10.0, an enormous sum for the times) and a majolica chestnut dish to Count Heneker Donnersmarck.

The Minton Peacock, probably their most famous piece of majolica, was modelled by Paul Comolera (see Appendix C) around 1873. Comolera also modelled the heron umbrella stand, a stork and a faun, all nearly lifesize.

At the Centennial Exhibition in Philadelphia in 1876, they received a mixed reception. The judges' report said of their majolica wares:

*21. Minton 'Lazy Susan'. Diameter 46 cm. c.1873.* Sotheby's

The majority of these are commendable, but occasionally overglazed, and somewhat hard in effect. A pair of full-sized storks are remarkable as successful specimens of modelling and potting. The glaze of the majolica ware sometimes shows a tendency to craze.

Nevertheless, Minton carried on a large and profitable majolica trade with America during the late 1870s and early 1880s.

On 21 December 1877, they registered the design for their Boar's Head Tureen, which was copied from a model made at Chelsea about 1755. Similar tureens were made in faience at Strasbourg *c.*1748–54. This particular piece is often cited as one of Minton's ugliest efforts, but it is certainly no less attractive than its predecessors.

By 1878, Minton's pre-eminence among majolica manufacturers could no longer be taken for granted. High-quality wares were being produced by their great rivals Wedgwood and Copeland, as well as by many newer concerns, such as George Jones, Brownfields, and Brown-Westhead & Moore. These firms hired designers and modellers used by Minton, so the actual quality of potting and decoration became ever more important. The creation of new colours, at which Léon Arnoux excelled, was a relatively cheap way to keep abreast of the market. Old shapes could be used, with novel effect. *Pottery and Glass Trades' Review*, October 1877, described new combinations of celadon and white, and Venetian green with Turkish dark blue.

None the less, *Pottery and Glass Trades' Review*, September 1878, said of Minton's exhibit at Paris, 'There is nothing from the English side of the Channel to beat or even vie with Messrs. Minton's costly crowd of majolica and Palissy wares.' Among the majolica wares at Paris was a large fountain modelled by Paul Comolera.

In 1879, they had the honour to produce from the design of and at the special request of Queen Victoria, a magnificent majolica dish intended by the Queen for a present to the Emperor and Empress of Germany on the occasion of their golden wedding. The design was a floral one surrounded by the arms of the Emperor and the monogram of the Queen.

By the 1890s majolica was long past its prime. A catalogue of pottery exhibited at the Imperial Institute in 1894 lists only four pieces of Minton majolica – two jardinières, a faun and a pair of peacocks. By this time, majolica was generally regarded as too garish for display anywhere but in the garden or conservatory. None the less, Minton did continue to produce some pieces, most notably game pie dishes, as late as 1910.

*22.* Left: *Minton garden seat. Impressed mark, shape number and date code for 1872. Height 46.5 cm.* Sotheby's

*23.* Right: *Minton pedestal of Chinese inspiration. Shape number 2081. Height 72.4 cm.* c.*1878.* Sotheby's

*24. Pair of Minton posy vases. Impressed marks and date codes for 1865 and 1867. Height 23.5 cm. Sotheby's*

*25. Pair of Minton putti riding goats. Height 26.5 cm. c.1875. Sotheby's*

In 1902, Minton introduced Secessionist Wares. The name derives from the Viennese Secession movement. A group of Viennese artists and architects seceded from the Viennese Akademie der bildenden Kunste in 1897, in protest against the Akademie's conservatism. They formed the Wiener Sezession which was highly influential in Austrian decorative arts until the 1920s. As evidenced by Minton's wares, their influence extended throughout Europe.

These designs, employing majolica glazes, were slip-trailed, relief-moulded or block-printed. The colours were mustard, pink, olive green, purple, red, inky blue, pale lime and copper brown – more subdued than the shades used on the earlier majolica wares. They were quite similar to the art wares of James Macintyre & Co., designed by William Moorcroft, but mass-produced and, hence, much cheaper. The range was produced until 1914.

## TYPES OF WARES

The Minton majolica should properly be divided into three groups in order to fully appreciate and understand them: the exhibition or commissioned pieces, the ornamental pieces and the useful wares. (Minton's tiles are discussed in Chapter Seven.) Within these categories, Minton made nearly every type of ware imaginable. The only major group avoided was dinner ware. This was not made by Minton or most other manufacturers, because it was felt that majolica's fragile nature made it impractical.

*26. Minton game pie dish. Impressed mark, pattern number 964, date code for 1864. Length 36 cm. Sotheby's*

There were two major stylistic groups: the Renaissance wares, which include the imitations of maiolica, Palissy and Della Robbia, and the more truly Victorian wares, which were a polyglot of styles freely interpreted and boldly executed. Most of the exhibition pieces fall into the first group and most of the useful wares into the latter group, but the ornamental wares include many pieces from both groups. This division is, however, of very limited usefulness, as so many pieces fall outside or between the two categories. All of the major stylistic influences discussed in Chapter One are well represented among the Minton majolica wares.

The *Minton Shape Book* of 1884 gives a good idea of the wide range of items available, although it only includes 147 of the many hundreds of shapes they had made in the previous thirty-five years. It is quite surprising how many of these shapes were old ones. Of the 143 shapes with numbers, 55 are below 1000, 44 between 1000 and 1999 and 44 are between 2000 and 3100. The highest number listed is 3076. One would normally expect a preponderance of recent, higher-numbered shapes to be featured.

The class of exhibition pieces includes pieces such as the St. George's Fountain, which were never meant for manufacture because of their prohibitive size and cost. They also include various costly pieces which were made in extremely limited numbers because they required the personal attentions of Minton's best artists and craftsmen. Although these exhibition pieces are now usually only seen in museums, they are of interest to the collector because they illustrated the utmost

*27.* Left: *Minton match pot. Impressed Minton, shape number 1692 and date code for 1872. Height 19 cm.* Sotheby's

*28.* Right: *Minton 'Queen's Vase'. Impressed mark, shape number 649 and date code for 1866. Height 69.5 cm.* Sotheby's

29. *Minton baptismal font. Shape number 614. c.1870. Length 90 cm.* Sotheby's

skill of the manufacturers. Similarly the ornamental pieces such as the great peacocks are beyond the reach of most collectors, but they display characteristics which can explain why so many of the useful wares are successful. These pieces were made in limited numbers, and, like the exhibition pieces, they required the skills of the factory's best craftsmen.

It cannot be said that all of the Minton majolica was of such high standard. Overall, the quality of the mass-produced useful wares was probably the best in the world, but some pieces were poorly designed, or the designs poorly conceived. For example, the Cat Milk Jug (No. 1924) is relatively attractive, but the Cat Cream Jug (No. 2012) is a disaster. To create a cream jug, the cat's head was flattened and the face squashed to accommodate a differently shaped spout.

As a rule, the pieces are finely potted, but moulds grew old at Minton, just as at any other factory, and some pieces are more crisply moulded than others. In general the colours and glazes are truly beautiful, but some are unattractive. When a piece was first designed the colours were very carefully worked out, usually to brilliant effect. However, as new colour combinations were conceived they were often applied indiscriminately to all previous shapes, sometimes disastrously. As will be seen, these were the practices of all potters, and these criticisms are not confined to Minton wares.

It must also be pointed out that some of the pieces which find their way into collections were, in fact, factory seconds. These were supplied to jobbers by the crate, many of which found their way to America.

*30. Minton jardinière and stand, painted by J. Thorley. Impressed mark, date code and shape number 1256. Height 25.3 cm.* Sotheby's

## CHARACTERISTICS

As stated above, there was more than one class of Minton majolica. A recipe book by George Smith in the Minton Archives recommends, 'The best glaze for [the] best class of majolica is 2 of the above [recipe] and one of [illegible] but the above will suit almost all kinds of majolica.' Léon Arnoux's recipe book includes a section for 'Transparent Glazes in C.C. [cream-colour] body fired in majolica kiln'. These handwritten recipes are somewhat difficult to read as Arnoux employed his personal version of 'franglais' in the instructions. The recipe for majolica glaze was as follows:

| Pounds | Ounces | Drachms | |
|--------|--------|---------|------------------|
| 47 | 7 | 3 | red lead |
| 8 | 7 | 4 | Borax |
| 3 | 6 | 2 | carbonate of lime |
| 1 | 11 | 1 | nitre |
| 22 | 0 | 4 | sand |
| 16 | 15 | 2 | cornish stone |

Fritted and ground without any addition at the mill.

From this it can be seen why the majolica glazes are called lead glazes. The recipe for majolica buff body is as follows:

257 Flint
118 stone
 50 cornish clay
352 buff marl
478 Ball clay
Blunged together [a blunger is a wet mixing tank].

The enormous pains that were taken with the colours can be seen from the following list of twenty-one different '*Emaux opaque blancs de majolique*' found in the book:

Blanc ordinaire
Pinky white ou blanc rose de majolique
Email de plomb (opaque)
Blanc ordinairement employé pour les moorish tiles
Blanc grissâtre à majolique
Blanc rossâtre qui feut servie pour peindre déssins
Blanc rosé pour l'interieur des coquilles
Blanc verdâtre de majolique
Blanc verdâtre que j'ai fait pour assorter des carreaux [illegible] un celadon très
  affaibli
Blanc de Majolica, tirant au verdâtre
Blanc rosé de majolica par la chromate ou fer
Blanc pour marbrures
Email Blanc pour passer mince sur biscuit buff qui duit être peint en plus émaille
  par déssin over l'émail transparent
Blancs opaques très durs pour suprebiancho [three recipes]
Pour peindre [two recipes]
Email blanc très dur de majolique
EB principalement employé pour cloisonné sur le Turquoise
EB, [illegible]

Arnoux also listed fourteen reds, ten yellows and oranges, thirty-one greens, thirteen blues, fourteen turquoises, twelve chocolats violété, nine browns, and two blacks. Some of these are given specific names and uses; some are merely indicated by number. The original art work for the majolica designs was painted in water-colours, and the colours chosen usually indicated by these numbers.

## DESIGNERS, MODELLERS AND DECORATORS

Lady Marian Alford
Thomas Allen
John Bell
Simon Birks
Hamlet Bourne
Albert Carrier de Belleuse
Paul Comolera
Theodore Deck
Christopher Dresser
John Henk

Louis M. Jahn
Pierre Emile Jeannest
Thomas Kirkby
Emile Lessore
Sir Coutts Lindsay
Francis Wollaston Moody
M. W. Mussill
Eugene Phoenix
Hughues Protât
A. W. N. Pugin

Edouard Rischgitz
Alfred Stevens
John Thomas

J. Thorley
Henry Townsend
William Wise

## MARKS AND DATE CODES

Most Minton majolica is impressed 'Minton' or after 1873, 'Mintons'. It also usually bears a date cipher, a system instituted in 1842. These impressed marks are usually clear enough to be interpreted using a standard chart (see e.g. Godden or Cushion). The ornament (shape) number may also be found on the piece. The Minton shapes known to have been made in majolica are listed in Appendix D. Minton marked their wares 'England' from 1891, and 'Made in England' from 1910.

*31. Minton Vulture and Python Teapot. Impressed mark, shape number and date code. Height 22.2 cm. Sotheby's*

# CHAPTER THREE

# WEDGWOOD MAJOLICA

A lthough they came comparatively late on the majolica scene, Wedgwood may well have produced more majolica than any other manufacturer. In general, the pieces are well designed, modelled and potted, but the quality is extremely variable. The glazes range from superb glossy, clear colours to watery or nearly opaque ones. Some of their mottled glazes are wonderfully fused, and others hardly at all. Similarly the choice of colours is frequently unsuccessful. More than any other firm, Wedgwood would concoct a new colour combination and revive all of the popular shapes of previous years, subjecting them to the new colours. The quality of the decoration itself is also inconsistent: some pieces are beautifully done and others quite simply sloppy.

The history of the first hundred years of the Wedgwood firm has been well documented in many places. For a thorough survey of the firm from 1850, one should consult Maureen Batkin's *Wedgwood Ceramics 1846-1959*. A number of the other books about Wedgwood which will be useful for the majolica collector are listed in Appendix E.

Josiah Wedgwood I established the Wedgwood pottery in 1759 in Burslem. The firm moved to Etruria between 1769 and 1773. Josiah Wedgwood II succeeded his father in 1795, and was in turn succeeded in 1841 by his sons Josiah III and Francis. It was Francis who controlled the firm during the period 1842-70, when majolica was introduced at Wedgwood.

Francis Wedgwood was faced with a daunting task. According to Batkin, 'The company was in a parlous state following several decades of inadequate management and family indifference, and for many years it had been trading largely on the strength of its 18th-century reputation.' Francis took as his partner John Boyle, Herbert Minton's former partner. Boyle helped raise the capital needed to modernize the factory before his death in 1845. Francis's new partner was Robert Brown, who injected considerable capital into the firm, accelerated the modernization programme and encouraged the introduction of new lines until his death in 1859.

In 1859, Francis took into partnership his eldest son Godfrey, who was to be Art Director for many years, during which he attracted many fine artists such as Emile Lessore to the factory. Clement Francis Wedgwood joined the firm in 1863 and became the firm's ceramic chemist. Francis's youngest son, Lawrence, joined in

*32. Wedgwood Shell Jug. Phillips, New York*

1865. It was Godfrey and Clement Francis, then, who were largely responsible for the development of majolica, the former for the design and decoration, and the latter for the development of the all-important majolica glazes.

The three men's sons took over during the 1880s, when the expansion of the previous years lost its impetus and the firm suffered severely from reverses in the economy.

## GREEN GLAZED WARES

Josiah Wedgwood I perfected his recipe for green glaze during his partnership with Thomas Whieldon. Josiah Wedgwood later annotated this recipe No. 7, dated 23 March 1759 in his Experiment Book:

> This No. is the result of many Expts. which I made in order to introduce a new species of ware ... to be of an even colour, and laid upon the ware in the form of a coloured glaze. This No. has been used for several years very successfully, in a great variety of articles for both home and foreign consumption.

The glaze was used on finely modelled creamware cauliflower, melon and pineapple shapes, as well as on plates with leaf, vine and strawberry patterns. Green glazed wares have been made at Wedgwood continuously to the present day, usually in traditional shapes. As discussed in Chapter One, green glazed wares are not majolica. However, Wedgwood produced many of their green glazed shapes in majolica (Plate 1).

## EARLY WEDGWOOD MAJOLICA

As mentioned above, the Wedgwood factory was experiencing considerable difficulties during the period when majolica was first introduced. Struggling to regain its former prestige, the firm would have hesitated before investing in the production of a new ware, whose popularity might prove ephemeral. By 1861, however, Wedgwood decided that they had stood by and watched their

*33.* Left: *Wedgwood Peacock Pickle Dish. Impressed 'WEDGWOOD', date code for August 1883. Length 22 cm.* Author's collection

*34.* Right: *Wedgwood Shell Dessert Plate in mottled glazes. Impressed 'WEDGWOOD', date code for 1866. Length 22 cm.* Author's collection

competitors garner all the glory and profits associated with majolica for long enough.

None the less, they started production in a very modest way. The vast majority of the early pieces in the Wedgwood Majolica Pattern Books are old shapes with the new glazes applied. The first pattern (No. 30) in the Pattern Books is for the Cambridge Ale Jug. Registered on 4 November 1850, this jug was a copy of a

*35. Wedgwood 'Caterer Jug'. Impressed 'WEDGWOOD', diamond registration mark for 1867, date code for 1870. Painted pattern number 674. Lid marked 'EPBM James Dixon & Sons Sheffield'. Height 16.5 cm.*
Author's collection

VII. Pair of Minton umbrella stands, 1875 and 1876. Impressed marks, date code and pattern number 1916 and 1917. Height 101.5 cm. *Sotheby's*

VIII. Pair of Minton agate-ground jardinières, 1871. Impressed marks, date codes, shape numbers 1023. Height 44.5 cm. *Sotheby's*

IX. *Left to right:* Manerbe or Pred'Auge oval dish, 17th Century, School of
Palissy. Length 48 cm.; Saintonge oval dish, 17th Century. Length 33 cm.
*Sotheby's*

X. Minton Group of Three Putti and a Ram, 1862. Impressed mark and date
code. Height 38.1 cm. *Sotheby's*

medieval leather jug. Already quite successful, the jug was produced in twenty-eight different majolica versions during the next fifteen years. The Doric Jug (No. 155), registered 29 November 1861, was equally popular, with twenty-eight versions produced in seventeen years. These sometimes bear the impressed mark 'DORIC' on the base. The Howard Teapot (No. 129), also introduced in majolica in 1861, was offered in eighteen different patterns during a ten-year period. The Dolphin Salt (No. 498), modelled by John Bell for Summerly's Art Manufactures c.1848, had been previously made in a number of different bodies and glazes. It can thus be seen that the expense of developing the new product was minimized by using existing shapes.

The late 1860s brought the introduction of several more very successful designs. The Sickle Bread Tray (No. 594), registered in 1867, had been made in nine different versions by 1879. These seem to have been made in considerable quantities, as they are among the most commonly found pieces of Wedgwood majolica today. The Caterer Jug (No. 674), also registered in 1867, was made in twenty-one different versions during the next twelve years (Plate 35). A Caterer Tankard (No. 638) was also made, but only in the one coloration, and can be considered quite rare. The Caterer pieces and the Flowering Rush Jug (No. 750) were both designed by Frederick Bret Russel, whose initials may be found on the bases of some pieces.

The Trentham pattern pieces, modelled by Rowland Morris, were also introduced in the late 1860s. These were some of the relatively few maiolica type wares made by Wedgwood. The Trentham Vase (No. 678) has two beautifully modelled cherubs supporting it. It was made in eight different versions over a ten-year period. Wedgwood also produced a Trentham Centre (Nos. 915, 1425, 1585) and a Trentham Flower Basket (Nos. 1774, 2282).

## TREMBLAY WARES

The *émail ombrant* technique consists of flooding majolica glazes over intaglio designs stamped in the body of the ware. The cavities of the stamped design appear as shadows of various depths, the parts of the design in high relief being highlighted. The most vital part of this process was the mould making. Those who tried to imitate Tremblay's techniques were frustrated by the difficulties associated with gauging the relative depths of various parts of the designs. For this reason, when Tremblay's concern went bankrupt the demand for the moulds was considerable.

The Baron Paul-Charles Amable was the owner of a patent for this technique taken out in 1827. His early experiments were carried out at a creamware pottery owned by the firm of Darte & Billele in rue de la Roquette, Paris. Upon this factory's closure in 1836, he moved to a pottery at Montreuil-sous-Bois, and later in the same year he went into partnership with his friend Baron Hocédé Alexis du Tremblay. They built a factory at Rubelles, where Tremblay owned a château. The partners renewed the patent for fifteen years in 1842, at which time they expanded their works. Du Tremblay was succeeded by his son-in-law, J. Hocédé, in 1850.

*36. A selection of unmarked* émail ombrant *comports.* Author's collection

Initially, the technique had met with great success. The *Jury's Report of the Exhibition of 1851* stated:

Le Baron A. de Tremblay [sic], Rubelles near Melun, exhibits a series of articles equally remarkable for cheapness, for novel and agreeable effect, and for the ingenuity of the process by which that effect is attained ... Much taste is evinced in the selection of designs to which the process has been applied, and perhaps there is no other in the ceramic art by which at so cheap a rate designs of high artistic merit can be reproduced in the most harmonious tinting for dessert or table services and for other useful domestic purposes. The jury have awarded the Baron de Tremblay a prize medal.

Despite this success, in 1852 the firm was forced to cut costs, and the new glazes introduced were dry, brittle and easily scratched. Apparently, J. Hocédé was not a very efficient manager. In 1857 the factory closed and the moulds were sold to Wedgwood and three French firms, Hautin Boulenger, Vallauris and Golfe-Juan. Of these latter, only Hautin Boulenger is known to have made use of the moulds (see Chapter Six). A good selection of the early Tremblay wares is on display at the Musée des Beaux Arts in Paris.

Batkin quotes a letter from Wedgwood to Thomas Goode & Co., dated 18 September 1863, indicating that trials to produce Tremblay wares were already under way. A small number of these wares were made from 1864, and marketed exclusively by Thomas Goode & Co., but they do not appear in the Majolica Pattern Books. In 1872, Wedgwood sent Henry Brownsword to France to ascertain the condition of the Tremblay moulds, which were being offered for sale. With the assistance of solicitor Alfred Lessore (a son of Emile), he bought over 2,500 moulds and designs, recipes for shading enamels and the original patent.

During the 1870s Wedgwood introduced some 173 Tremblay majolica patterns, ranging from No. 1385 to No. 2726. Although there were other English majolica manufacturers who made use of this technique, it was not used by Wedgwood's major rivals, Minton and George Jones. The 'Tremblay' centres were usually in green glaze, but occasionally in blue or grey. Although most of Wedgwood's Tremblay wares were dessert wares, they made a great many tiles, plaques and trays. The technique was really only effective on flatwares, but other shapes were attempted, even a knife handle.

## PRIME-PERIOD WEDGWOOD MAJOLICA

The period 1875–80 was Wedgwood's peak majolica period, when approximately 1,300 designs were introduced. The great novelty of this period was argenta ware, apparently first made by Wedgwood, but soon made by Simon Fielding and others. Most of the new argenta patterns were new japonesque designs, but many of the firm's old favourites were revived with the new cream-coloured ground and pastel decoration. In 1879, Wedgwood's Ocean argenta pattern was introduced. It was very successful, and was still being produced in 1888. More than twenty shapes were produced in this pattern. It was particularly successful in America. *Crockery and Glass Journal*, 28 April 1881, recommended, 'For summer use, Wedgwood's "Ocean" majolica will be found very acceptable to the cultivated taste, the colors having a rich, quiet effect, and being free from gross liberties with nature.'

The most popular majolica pattern ever created by Wedgwood was the Fan pattern, sometimes erroneously called 'Bird & Fan'. The first item produced was the flower pot (No. 2746). The Fan Jug (No. 2761), registered in 1879, is the most common of the Fan wares and was made in twelve different colorations. Although Fan wares were usually decorated in argenta colours, they were made in many different pastels. The pattern was still being made in 1888, when the Pattern Books end. The pieces made were: tea ware, jugs, toilet wares, garden seats, cremes or mustards, biscuit boxes, flower pots, strawberry sets, cheese bells, punch bowls, dessert ware, salads, cruet sets, comports, teapots, umbrella stands, bread trays and beer sets.

In 1882, Wedgwood brought out the fantastically successful St. Louis argenta pattern. The jug (No. 3211) was the most popular shape, but they also made flower pots, bread trays, salads, strawberry trays, dessert wares, oyster trays, molasses jugs, ice trays, fish dishes, pickle dishes, punch bowls, sardine boxes, butters, tea wares, sandwich trays and milk sets. This japonesque pattern was still made in 1888.

In 1884, the Grosvenor Tobacco Jar (No. 3390) was registered, but it seems that other pieces in this pattern had been issued the previous year. Among the many wares created in this pattern was a line of dinner ware, which is most unusual for majolica. It had always been thought that majolica was too fragile for dinner ware, but this must have been fairly successful, for it was made in six different colorations. Wedgwood did not, however, introduce dinner wares in any other majolica patterns.

One of the last new items introduced in the Pattern Books was the Italian Flower Pot. This must have been an enormous success: it was made in fifty-eight different colorations in a very short time, the first being No. 3837, and the last No. 4153.

Another type of ware usually regarded as majolica is the Vigornian ware. The wares were made in simple shapes, glazed in monochrome or mottled majolica glazes, and then acid-etched with simple, usually floral, patterns. These pieces are not, however, included in the Majolica Pattern Books, probably because they were sent out to John Northwood to be decorated.

## LATE WEDGWOOD MAJOLICA

Unfortunatately, the Pattern Books end with 1888, so although we know that Wedgwood majolica continued until 1910, we know relatively little about the wares. A great number of salads were made, and they continued their emphasis on garden and conservatory-related items, as did most manufacturers of the period. The story did not end there, however, for as late as 1947 a Wedgwood Catalogue offered 'Coloured Vine and Strawberry' plates.

## WEDGWOOD MAJOLICA PATTERNS

The Wedgwood Majolica Pattern Books (see Appendix D) are the most complete records of majolica patterns extant for any factory. The M series entries begin with

*37. Wedgwood Fly Match Box. Length 14 cm. c.1875.* Sotheby's

No. 30 in 1861 and continue to No. 41. The next pattern is No. 104, followed by No. 124, the numbers then continuing to No. 1909. The next entry is No. 2000. There is no space left in the book to indicate that the missing numbers were ever used, and unless someone comes forward with pieces bearing these lost pattern numbers, it can be assumed that, for some unknown reason, they were never used. The numbers then continue to No. 3349, c.1880.

The K series then begins with No. 3350 and continues to No. 4189, c.1888. There is no evidence in the Pattern Books that the M series ever continued beyond No. 3349, nor any evidence that there were any K patterns before No. 3350. It is not known why the prefix was changed at this time. However, the Vine Bread Tray in Plate V is clearly marked K1515; and M1515 is a Basket Salt. The author would be very interested to hear of any other pieces bearing such mysterious K series marks.

Majolica tiles are included in the M series, but not in the K series. The Pattern Book includes a Q series for tiles; entries have only been made for Nos. 421–44. There is also a blank page headed 'V SERIES – TILES'. It seems that after the K series was begun, the tiles were placed in either the Q or V series of patterns. (Tiles are discussed in detail in Chapter Seven.)

There are several ways to fix dates to these patterns, none entirely reliable. The first is by using the dates on which designs were registered. The difficulties with this method are: (1) comparatively few designs were registered; (2) some shapes were registered and made in other bodies and/or glazes for some time before being introduced as majolica patterns; (3) apparently some designs were in use for some time before being registered. The second method of assigning dates to patterns is by the occasional notations in the pattern books themselves, such as that for No. 803, the Bamboo Kettle, 'Sent to Messrs. Goode Nov. 15, 1869'. These notations can be taken as reliable if they were obviously written at the time of the original entry. Unfortunately, there are only a handful of such references. The last and least reliable method is by noting the date codes on recorded pieces. This can tell us that a particular piece was made in a certain year, but not when the pattern or shape was actually introduced.

The following chart will aid the collector in ascertaining the approximate date of introduction of a given pattern. Unfortunately, the design registrations after 1883 are not descriptive enough to determine the pattern to which they refer.

WEDGWOOD REGISTERED DESIGNS IN MAJOLICA
(1850–83)

| Pattern No. | Name or Description | Date of Registration |
|---|---|---|
| 30 | Cambridge Ale Jug | 4 November 1850 |
| 155 | Doric Jug | 29 November 1861 |
| 317 | Griffin Flower Stand | 2 February 1864 |
| 354 | Limoges Dessert | 22 September 1864 |
| 369 | Sprite Flower Stand | 22 September 1864 |
| 594 | Sickle Bread Tray | 4 April 1867 |
| 606 | Disraeli Flower Pot | 15 July 1867 |
| 644 | Stanley Butter & Stand | 29 October 1867 |

| Pattern No. | Name or Description | Date of Registration |
|---|---|---|
| 674 | Caterer Jug | 6 June 1867 |
| 688 | Limoges Sceaux | 22 September 1864 |
| 723 | Reed Jug | 22 September 1864 |
| 744 | Cottage Shape Ewer | 25 March 1867 |
| 768 | Raleigh Tobacco Jar | 22 February 1869 |
| 851 | Bramble Flower Pot | 18 February 1868 |
| 855 | Trefoil Strawberry Dish | 3 July 1869 |
| 864 | Partridge Pie | 12 February 1868 |
| 1089 | Dragon Flower Pot | 11 October 1872 |
| 1104 | Aquarium Flower Pot | 11 October 1872 |
| 1115 | Dragon Flower Holder | 11 October 1872 |
| 1123 | Mask Matchpot | 2 July 1872 |
| 1139 | Double Mask Matchpot | 11 October 1872 |
| 1191 | Net Cigar Tray | 27 February 1869 |
| 1259 | Oriental Tea Set | 24 April 1871 |
| 1506 | Hyacinth Flower Holder | 10 July 1868 |
| 1659 | Hop Beer Set | 15 June 1875 |
| 1819 | Périssoire Stands | 2 February 1876 |
| 2304 | Cinquecento Candlesticks | 14 November 1876 |
| 2365 | Centennial Jug | 19 June 1876 |
| 2577 | Churn Butter | 27 June 1878 |
| 2646 | Sardinia Sardine Box | 23 May 1878 |
| 2657 | Punch Handle* | 27 June 1878 |
| 2674 | Matt Sardine Box | 30 April 1878 |
| 2746 | Fan Flower Pot | 3 February 1879 |
| 2761 | Fan Jug | 18 March 1878 |
| 2780 | Seaweed Oyster Tray | 30 April 1878 |
| 2820 | Gipsy Strawberry Tray | 18 October 1879 |
| 2832 | Ocean Sardine Box | 20 December 1879 |
| 3024 | Dolphin Oyster Tray | 24 May 1878 |
| 3040 | Fan Umbrella Stand | 25 May 1881 |
| 3074 | Kate Greenaway Umbrella Stand | 25 May 1881 |
| 3211 | St. Louis Jug | 23 June 1882 |
| 3273 | Chrysanthemum Jug | 13 December 1882 |
| 3292 | Chrysanthemum Bread Tray | 13 December 1882 |

Note: Pattern number is the first to appear in the Pattern Books.

*The Punch Handle was used on a variety of Punch & Judy wares.

The following rough estimate of patterns and their date of introduction can be made from the above:

| Pattern No. | Approximate Date of Introduction | Pattern No. | Approximate Date of Introduction |
|---|---|---|---|
| 1–200 | 1861 | 1351–1700 | 1873–1875 |
| 201–400 | 1862–1864 | 1701–2450 | 1876–1877 |
| 401–750 | 1865–1867 | 2451–3000 | 1878–1880 |
| 751–900 | 1868–1870 | 3001–3100 | 1881 |
| 901–1350 | 1871–1872 | 3100–3300 | 1882 |

## TYPES OF WARES

Wedgwood concentrated on the smaller ornamental and tablewares, with an increasing number of conservatory and garden-related items in later years. As late competitors in the market, it was necessary for them to underprice Minton wares, which were, even at that time, considered expensive. They wisely did not try to compete for the small élite market in large fountains and *animalier* pieces.

It is worthwhile to make a detailed analysis of the Wedgwood Pattern Books, because they are the most complete record we have of the majolica made by any factory. None the less, such an analysis is, necessarily, somewhat flawed as some entries are incomplete or illegible. Some entries cover only one shape to be decorated with the pattern indicated, others include several shapes, or just indicate 'wares', meaning all shapes in, for instance, Chrysanthemum pattern could be decorated in that colour combination. Furthermore, there is no record of the actual quantities of each pattern number produced. Thus, although there are only nine entries relating to spittoons, these few patterns may have been made in large numbers.

The nature of the Wedgwood majolica wares changed over the thirty-year period covered by the Pattern Books. During the later years, useful wares increasingly predominate. However, the following list of the approximate number of entries regarding the various types of wares does provide a profile of the factory's output.

| | | | |
|---|---|---|---|
| Flower Pots, Jardinières and Urns | 469 | Sardine Boxes | 45 |
| Jugs | 389 | Pickle Dishes | 45 |
| Vases and Spills | 294 | Lamps, Lamp Bases and Lamp Vases | 43 |
| Dessert Wares | 219 | Oyster Trays and Stands | 42 |
| Strawberry Baskets, Sets, Trays etc. | 165 | Trays (excluding bread, ice, pen, | 42 |
| Salads | 130 | jewel, cigar, ash, card, oyster, | |
| Tiles (Series M only) | 108 | strawberry) | |
| Pedestals and Columns | 107 | Candlesticks and Candelabra | 41 |
| Bread Trays | 102 | Toilet Wares | 39 |
| Teapots | 89 | Cigar Trays and Ash Trays | 36 |
| Butters | 80 | Cups, Mugs and Tankards | 32 |
| Cheese Bells and Stands | 75 | Ewers and Basins (not included | 30 |
| Baskets and Flower Baskets | 75 | elsewhere) | |
| Umbrella Stands | 64 | Kettles | 30 |
| Flower Holders | 63 | Salts | 27 |
| Garden Seats | 58 | Butters, Individual | 24 |
| Tobacco Jars | 52 | Brackets | 22 |
| Tea Wares (excluding Teapots) | 50 | Biscuit Boxes and Jars | 22 |
| Centres | 48 | Match Boxes and Holders | 21 |
| Jug Stands | 48 | Comports | 20 |

There are dozens of other items which were made in fewer patterns and, presumably, lesser quantities. The above, however, gives a fair idea of the items which were most common, and one can reasonably assume that a smoking set, for which only four patterns are recorded, was uncommon at the time, and is a very rare item for the collector today.

## CHARACTERISTICS

Wedgwood made such an enormous range of majolica patterns and wares that it is difficult to make general statements about them. Overall, there seem to have been few whimsical pieces, and a fortunate avoidance of the macabre. The wares were often recommended by contemporaries for their 'tasteful' appearance and use of colour. Some of these may appear rather dull and lifeless to the modern majolica collector. As mentioned above, the quality is highly variable. However, every majolica collector will find Wedgwood pieces to suit his taste, and they are still easy to find and affordable.

The following is a list of those patterns which were represented by the largest number of entries in the Pattern Books (when more than one item is specifically mentioned in an entry, each ware counts as a separate entry). The pattern numbers following each name are the first and last occurrences.

| | | | |
|---|---|---|---|
| Fan (2746/3971) | 90 | Primrose (1409/3679) | 34 |
| St. Louis (3202/3787) | 79 | Imperial (470/1721) | 33 |
| Grosvenor (3350/4095) | 79 | Tunbridge (3603/4076) | 31 |
| Italian (1309/4153) | 72 | Early English (2058/3922) | 30 |
| Luther (3450/4130) | 70 | Elizabethan (468/2984) | 29 |
| Ocean (2814/4018) | 57 | Dragon (1089/2442) | 29 |
| Lincoln (3086/4070) | 56 | Satyr (882/2650) | 28 |
| Magnolia (3531/4092) | 46 | Raleigh (768/2826) | 25 |
| Chrysanthemum (3273/3805) | 44 | Oak (1013/4069) | 25 |
| Fruit (2913/4189) | 44 | Reed (486/1646) | 24 |
| Griffin (317/4027) | 42 | Bamboo (765/2802) | 23 |
| Lowell (1961/4155) | 39 | Leopard 1082/3788) | 23 |
| Sunflower (1778/3927) | 39 | Leafage (647/3587) | 22 |
| Wicker (998/4051) | 36 | Stanley (644/2655) | 22 |
| Bramble (851/4131) | 35 | Lorne (1280/2428) | 22 |

## DESIGNERS, MODELLERS AND DECORATORS

The Pattern Books contain numerous references to designers and modellers who worked on particular patterns. The following list gives the pattern numbers associated with particular persons. (More information about these persons can be found in Appendix C.)

Thomas Allen

William Beattie (343, 354–7, 544, 693, 959, 988)

John B. Bebbington

John Bell (498)

Simon Birks (644, 841–2, 851, 1823, 2144, 2209, 2256, 2609, 2640, 3502, 3589, 4131)

Hamlet Bourne

Henry Brownsword

Albert Carrier de Belleuse

Theodore Deck (868, 2242, 2349, 2378, 2383, 2469–71, 2608, 2724)

Christopher Dresser (590–3, 595, 612, 623, 634, 636–7, 686, 974, 1186, 1244, 1246–7, 1286–7, 1331–3, 1356, 1423, 2504–8, 2512, 2536, 2628)

William James Goode

Thomas Greatbach

Emile Lessore (1052, 1195, 1723, 1734)

Rowland James Morris (675, 831, 915, 1264, 1425, 1585, 1774, 1901, 2131, 2282, 2438–40)

Hughues Protât (1089–90, 1220–1, 1350–1, 1398–9, 1503, 1684–6, 2291)

Frederick Bret Russel (638, 644, 674, 722, 738, 750–1, 841–2, 935–6, 964, 975, 1061, 1360, 1889, 1909, 2088, 2144, 2152, 2172, 2189, 2201, 2205, 2238, 2256, 2337, 2356, 2640, 2721, 2742, 3577)

Charles Toft (2972–3)

## MARKS AND DATE CODES

Most Wedgwood majolica is marked with a simply impressed WEDGWOOD. This may be accompanied by a painted pattern number, prefixed M or K (see Appendix D). Wedgwood began its system of date codes in 1860, so most majolica will bear the impressed three-letter code. The first letter indicates the month, the second the potter's mark and the third the year of production. This said, the system can be extremely confusing. There were four cycles. The first cycle began with the letter 0 for 1860, continuing to Z for 1871. The second cycle begins with A for 1872 and carries on to Z for 1897. The third cycle begins with A for 1898 and continues to Z for 1923. The fourth cycle begins with A for 1924 and continues to F for 1929. Thereafter, one usually finds the last two digits of the year impressed.

After 1907, the month code was replaced with a 3 or 4 to denote the cycle. Before that it is more difficult to determine the cycle used, and other evidence must be used to determine the most likely cycle. Pieces made after 1890 are marked 'England' and those after 1910, 'Made in England'. Charts of the month and year codes can be found in most marks books.

None the less, sometimes the code still cannot be deciphered. For example, the Stanley Butter Stand (Plate 39) is marked YZW. A chart tells us that Y was the code for the month of May between 1860 and 1863. Similarly we learn that W was the year code in 1868 and 1894, both years in which Y was not used as a month code. The piece is not marked England, so 1894 can be discounted. Geoffrey Godden has helpfully noted that the month code sometimes occurred second, rather than first. In this case, however, we find that Z was never used as a month code. This particular piece bears a diamond registration mark for 29 October 1867, so it is likely that the piece is from 1868, and we must leave the Y unexplained. It is also possible that the letters are completely

*38. Wedgwood leaf dish in mottled glazes. Impressed 'WEDGWOOD', date code for October 1867. Length 22 cm.* Author's collection

transposed: the Y standing for the year 1870, and the W for the month of August.

The Caterer Jug (Plate 35) has a diamond registration mark for 6 June 1867. The date code is CGY. Neither C nor G was ever used as a date code, and Y only used between 1860 and 1863. Given the registration mark, and the early pattern number 674, this was probably made in the Y year 1870, but the month code remains undeciphered.

*39. Stanley Butter Stand. Impressed 'WEDGWOOD', diamond registration mark for 1867, date code for 1868 (see right). Diameter 20 cm.* Author's collection

# CHAPTER FOUR

# OTHER MAJOR BRITISH MAJOLICA MANUFACTURERS

T he following firms have been chosen from some 130 British majolica producers because they are of special interest to the collector. Some produced especially fine-quality majolica, some enormous quantities and some, such as Copeland and Royal Worcester, are of particular interest because they seem to have made large quantities of majolica which they did not advertise at the time, and which are scarce today.

## JOHN ADAMS & CO.; ADAMS & BROMLEY

John Adams & Co. operated at the Victoria Works, Hanley, from 1860 to 1873. The 1861 census returns record John Adams, aged 27, as a china manufacturer employing 160 hands. Initially, he was in a partnership, Warren & Adams, which was dissolved in 1865. Adams must have died shortly after this, as the *Staffordshire Potters' Directory 1868* lists the executors of John Adams, china manufacturers, at Park Place and Victoria Works, High Street, Longton; as does the *Kelly Post Office Directory 1868*. The executors were Elizabeth Adams and John Lorenzo Johnson. In 1873, this partnership was dissolved and the Victoria Works were taken over by Adams & Bromley until 1886. The same line of wares, including jasper, majolica, *émaux ombrants* and green glaze, was continued. *Keates's Gazetteer & Directory 1875–6* lists 'Adams & Bromley, Victoria Works, jasper & majolica'. None the less, there seems to have been continuing confusion over the firm's name, as *Pottery and Glass Trades' Review* referred to them as Adams & Co. or John Adams & Co. during 1878.

The *Art Journal* in 1871 described their output as 'for the millions' – a phrase which at the time generally denoted large output at the expense of quality. This firm's wares were, however, usually of high standard. Jewitt wrote, 'the quality of the majolica is far above the average, and many of the designs are artistic; the workmanship in all cases is skillful and good.' He illustrates a corn garden seat and three jardinières shown at the Exhibition of 1871.

*Pottery and Glass Trades' Review* announced in May 1878:

Adams & Co., Hanley have recently commenced manufacture of teaware in majolica. The articles have rather a novel appearance and are well calculated to please. Only two designs at present have been got out, consisting of apple, fruit and foliage and pineapple, fruit and foliage. For choice, perhaps the former will be selected. This design has the most taking appearance and will no doubt find favour in the eyes of the ladies. The service, which is complete, is decorated with a very bright brown ground, pink lining with fruit and foliage in relief coloured naturally.

The firm successfully exhibited jasper, majolica and rockingham wares at the Paris Exhibition of 1878. *Pottery and Glass Trades' Review*, July 1878, reported, 'John Adams & Co. who excited the friendly enthusiasm of our French neighbours by the prompt setting forth of their exhibits at the Paris Exhibition, are also full of orders for their jasper and majolica.' *Crockery and Glass Journal*, 21 March 1878, described their Paris display as follows:

> The most conspicuous objects in the case are the majolica exhibits. Occupying the top of the centre is the British lion, about which we hear so much just now. The figure, which is coloured naturally, is about 2 feet high and 4 feet 3 inches long. It represents the king of beasts in a couchant attitude, but with head erect. Near this is a cupid fountain, 3 feet 2 inches high. At the top is a large brown and green basin lined with green, supported by a figure of cupid in white, and set off with quaint figures in green. The pedestal fountain, another magnificent specimen of majolica, is 4 feet high. The vase, or basin, at the top is supported on four female busts, terminating in lions' or dragons' claws. Below these is the perforated pedestal, decorated in colours, one of which is a very pretty shade of lilac. At the foot is a mottled plinth. All these three are modeled by Thomas. Jardinières, with garden seats to match, will also be shown. One has a ground of mazarine blue, decorated with oak leaves and acorns naturally coloured, and supported on three claws. Another is profusely decorated with ears of various kinds of corn. Other jardinières, such as mermaid, fern and dolphin, may be known by their names, which illustrate the style of decoration. In dessert ware, Messrs. Adams and Bromley come out strong, particularly in their well known stork, lily, and apple and pear sets. The acorn and fish teapots are great curiosities in their way, while the jugs, bread-trays, cheese dishes, and other domestic wares are sure to command admiration.

*Pottery Gazette*, January 1882, recommended Adams & Bromley's new teaset 'in a light green decorated with love birds and embossed leaves' and 'a set of jugs in the same light colour ornamented with Japanese subjects'. Adams & Bromley advertised majolica in *Pottery Gazette* during 1883 and 1884. The dissolution of their partnership was announced in *Pottery Gazette*, January 1886.

Some pieces from the John Adams period are marked J Adams & Co. or Adams & Co. Adams & Bromley pieces are marked Adams & Bromley, A & B or A.B. As relatively few marked pieces of majolica have been recorded, much of it was probably left unmarked.

## BROWN-WESTHEAD, MOORE & CO.

The history of the Cauldon Works is long and complex. The works were erected by Job Ridgway in 1804. His two sons, John and William, joined him in 1808. On Job's death in 1813, they carried on the firm together until 1830, when William left for the Bell Works. In 1854, John Ridgway took Mr. Bates as a partner, operating under the

*40. Brown-Westhead, Moore and Co., camel group, c.1870. Impressed mark 31, painted 1285. Width 40 cm. Sotheby's*

style, Ridgway, Bates & Co. In 1858, Ridgway retired and the firm became Bates, Brown-Westhead, Moore & Co. This early period of the works is discussed in detail in Godden's *Ridgway Porcelains.* Bates retired in 1861, and the firm became T. C. Brown-Westhead & Moore. Thomas Chappell Brown-Westhead supervised the administration and finance, while William Moore supervised the potting side of the business.

In 1866, William Moore, who had worked for Ridgway for many years, died. His brother James Moore took his place, managing the pottery. In 1872, the firm took over the Victoria Works from Thomas Cooper. It was here that the large-scale majolica pieces were produced, under the direction of Frederick T. Moore, James Moore's nephew. In 1875, James Moore was taken into the partnership.

The firm made an aggressive and successful attempt to sell to the American market. Their display at the 1876 Centennial Exhibition in Philadelphia included a great deal of majolica. The *General Report of the Judges* described:

> Modern majolica, colors bright, glazing rather overbrilliant. A pair of large vases, about 40 inches high, of modified classic form, are well potted; large garden-pots, seats, vases, etc.; pair of candelabra supported by Cupids, good in design and color; ...

*Crockery and Glass Journal,* 1 April 1878, described in detail the firm's exhibit at the Paris Exhibition, including 'some magnificent specimens of majolica which required considerable space' and which had been prepared at 'great expense':

The *chefs d'oeuvre* in the majolica section consist of a pair of candelabra and a double group of tigers. The candelabra are about nine feet high, with seven branch lights, one being perpendicular and central. The centre is like a column in shape, but tastefully proportioned from an enlarged base, which rests on six raised feet. The diameter of the base is three feet four inches. The colors in one are most beautifully brought out, there being no glaring contrast while the other being worked out in fashionable blue and white, the two form a pleasing contrast. They are the largest pieces of majolica the writer has ever seen, and in point of artistic beauty, as well as achievements in potting, we prophesy they will prove unequaled, even at the Paris Exhibition. They were designed, we believe by Mr. Joseph Brown, the head designer, and modeled by Mr. James Evans, the head modeler. The tigers are life-size and naturally colored, in groups of two each, the foliage of the jungle being introduced with good effect. Each group is five feet four inches long by three feet ten inches wide at the base, and as they will be placed in the centre of a stand specially devoted to them, the spectator will view a group of three tigers, from whichever point he looks at them. On the same stand there will be exhibited life-size swans, dogs, cats, and other animals. We must not omit to mention that Mr. Brown designed the tiger groups, and the animals were modeled from life studies at the Zoological Gardens, London, by Mr. Marshall of London. On this same stand will be flower boxes filled with natural flowers and plants, and decorated with Cauldon-place tiles. On the principal stand will be shown some magnificent vases in majolica. One pair of large vases are four feet high, bluntly oviform in shape, with embossed medallion heads, surrounded by chaplets of green foliage. The medallion ground is light turquoise, while that of the vase is a rich mazarine. Another pair, about the same height, are very rich specimens of majolica. They are decorated with panels, enclosing a group of flowers painted under glaze.

The firm had outgrown even the combined Cauldon Place and Victoria Works, and a major reorganization took place. Upon completion in 1882, the works covered eight acres, and included fourteen kilns and twenty ovens. Some 1500 hands were employed, making it the largest pottery in England. Their new showrooms were decorated with a series of majolica plaques painted by Léone Mallet, Bernard Edwards and others.

Unfortunately, James Moore died in 1881 and T. C. Brown-Westhead in 1882, before the completion of the new works. The firm was passed on to William Moore's sons, William Bailey Moore and Frederick T. Moore; the latter had been assisting his uncle for many years. The firm continued until 1920, when it became Cauldon Potteries Ltd.

The firm advertised majolica in *Pottery Gazette* throughout the 1880s. They registered 140 designs between 1862 and 1883. It cannot be determined from the records which of these were majolica, but those most probably made in majolica include:

| | |
|---|---|
| Drum Déjeuner Service | 2 June 1871 |
| Jardinière | 7 October 1872 |
| Bramble Tea Service | 19 September 1873 |
| Chestnut Garden Seat | 23 July 1875 |
| Wicker Bread Tray | 26 September 1876 |
| Potato-shaped Tureen | 19 October 1877 |

Majolica, which was not always marked, is most likely to bear one of the following impressed marks: B.W.M., B.W.M. & CO., T.C. BROWN-WESTHEAD MOORE & CO. or BROWN-WESTHEAD MOORE.

# WILLIAM BROWNFIELD & CO.

William Brownfield went into partnership at Cobridge Works with Noah Robinson and John Wood in 1837. Rodney and Eileen Hampson, who have written the most detailed account of the firm ('Brownfields, Victorian Potters'), believe that Brownfield had been a commercial traveller for Robinson and Wood during their partnership in Shelton (*c.*1832–7). Robinson died in 1837, and was succeeded in the partnership by his widow and father until 1841. Then Wood and Brownfield operated the works until Wood's retirement in 1850. Now the firm grew rapidly with Brownfield at the helm, and by 1861 they employed over 450 persons.

William Brownfield took his son William Etches Brownfield into partnership in 1871, at which time the style was changed to William Brownfield & Son. William Brownfield died very suddenly in 1873 leaving the business to his three young sons. The second son, Edward Arthur, was taken into partnership in 1876, and the style was changed to William Brownfield & Sons. In 1879 the third son, Douglas Harold, joined the firm. Despite the tremendous shock of William Brownfield Senior's death, the firm prospered. By the 1880s over 600 persons were employed at the factory.

Brownfield registered 127 designs between 1851 and 1883, mostly made in porcelain, relief-moulded stoneware or Parian, but many of the shapes were in majolica. Unfortunately, the design registrations do not specify which bodies and glazes were to be employed. For more information about Brownfield's porcelains see Godden's *Staffordshire Porcelain* and *Encyclopedia of British Porcelain Manufacturers*. Brownfield's relief-moulded wares are thoroughly discussed in Henrywood's *Relief-Moulded Jugs*.

After 1872, under the art directorship of L. Jahn (see Appendix C), the firm took, according to the Rheads, a 'leading if not premier place among the potters of the district. The best attainable modellers were employed, the bodies and glazes improved and many interesting experiments were made.' Both Carrier de Belleuse and Protât modelled for them (see Appendix C). Jahn remained at Brownfields until 1895.

It is not known when Brownfield began producing majolica wares, but they exhibited them at the London Exhibition of 1871. A shape book, *c.*1876, in the Spode Archives at the Keele University Library consists of sepia photographs of wares in the bisque state, and it is impossible to tell which were made in majolica and which in bone china. The following, however, are shapes known to have been made in majolica:

| | |
|---|---|
| Claude Garden Seat | Maple Cheese Bell & Stand |
| Vine Garden Seat | Chestnut Cheese Bell & Stand |
| Pillar Garden Seat | Tower Cheese Bell & Stand |
| Staffordshire Knot Garden Seat | Bamboo Cheese Bell & Stand |

| | |
|---|---|
| Man & Gourd Teapot (Registered 31 October 1876) | Fern Leaf Tray |
| | Fish Head Spittoon |
| Cocatoo Jug | Fish Teapot (Registered 31 October 1876) |
| Face & Pigtail Teapot | Boa Constrictor & Hare |

At the 1876 Centennial Exhibition in Philadelphia, the Brownfield exhibit included 'a few pieces of modern majolica', but it was the porcelains which were most highly praised. In *Pottery and Glass Trades' Review*, December 1878, a review of the Fine Art Exhibition at Stafford commended their 'noble lamp stands in majolica, jet and other wares'. The firm advertised majolica in *Pottery Gazette* and *Crockery and Glass Journal* from 1880 to 1885.

At the Sydney Exhibition of 1880, Brownfield was awarded a second degree of merit for their majolica which was, according to *Crockery and Glass Journal*, 8 July 1880, commended by the judges, 'Designs and workmanship of goods in majolica, very artistic. Designs and shades very fine.' The same journal described Brownfield's Sydney display in detail on 12 February 1880:

> The richness of coloring on the excellently-conceived and well-modeled objects cannot fail to please every admirer of this kind of ware. Particularly striking is a large snake in the act of dispatching its prey – a hare. Were this piece placed amongst grasses or ferns in a garden it would certainly strike terror to any passers-by by its life-like appearance. The design of two parrots also well represents their species. The birds are shown sitting with outspread wings on branches of bamboo, and looking at them one almost expects to be startled by their shrill screams, so natural and life-like is their appearance. Among the same class of goods are garden-seats, flower-pots, biscuit boxes, game-pie dishes, ornaments, fancy groups, etc. From the appearance of their earthenware exhibit, it is very evident that this firm mean to keep up their world-wide reputation for this class of goods, and, indeed, in the bodies, glazes, designs, and general execution they need fear no competitors. The variety and excellence of their shapes, patterns, and decorations show at once with what spirit they support their name.

The boa constrictor and hare, one of the most repulsive pieces of majolica ever produced, is thought to have been modelled by A. Carrier de Belleuse. It was first exhibited at the Fine Art Exhibition in Stafford, 1878. There it did not meet with the approval it found in Sydney. *Pottery and Glass Trades' Review* reported:

> There is also one disagreeable object: it is a group in majolica of a poor hare, life size, being crushed in the coils of a boa constrictor, the swallowing operation being just commenced at the nose of the victim, which has already disappeared in the gaping mouth of the serpent. This group has no use but to give the sensation, on leaving the stall, of having woke up from a hideous dream.

In 1883, W. E. Brownfield left the partnership. After 1892, the potting business was run as a co-operative, the Brownfield Guild Pottery, under the direction of Edward Arthur Brownfield. In 1898, it was taken over by Brownfields Pottery Ltd. This firm failed in 1900 and the pottery closed for good. Meanwhile, W. Brownfield & Sons continued until 1904, as potters' millers, under the direction of Douglas Harold Brownfield.

XI. Villeroy & Boch lilac plates, impressed mark for Schramberg, shape number 1241/7. Diameter 19 cm. *c.*1883–90.

XII. Minton Cockerel Teapot, 1877. Impressed mark, shape number 1909, and date code. Height 19.7 cm. *Sotheby's*

XIII. Egyptian slave-girl garden seat. *c.*1870. *Sotheby's*

Brownfield's majolica is often unmarked. Impressed marks used by the firm include from 1850–71: W. & B., W.B., W B in a Staffordshire knot; and after 1871, W.B. & S., W.B. & SON; and after 1876 W.B. & SONS.

## W. T. Copeland & Sons

The Spode works were established by Josiah Spode I in 1770. In 1797 they passed to his son Josiah Spode II, under whose guidance they became the premier manufacturers of blue and white tranfer-printed earthenwares and bone china. In 1826, the firm passed on briefly to Josiah Spode III, who died in 1829. The history of the Spode factory is dealt with extensively in Leonard Whiter's *Spode*. In 1833, the factory was purchased by William Taylor Copeland, who with his father had been running the firm's London showrooms since 1811, under the style of Spode & Copeland. He ran the firm with a partner, Thomas Garrett, under the style Copeland & Garrett until Garrett's retirement in 1847.

W. T. Copeland ran the factory alone until he took his four sons into partnership in 1867, trading as W. T. Copeland & Sons. The firm remained in the Copeland family until 1966. In 1970 the name became Spode Ltd on the 200th anniversary of the works' foundation. The Copeland firm was best known for its Parian wares and bone china. None the less, they continued to produce the blue and white transfer-printed wares of the Spode era, as well as utilitarian wares and tiles.

*41. Copeland garden pot and stand. Impressed mark, date marks for 1881 and 1879. Height 23.5 cm.* Sotheby's

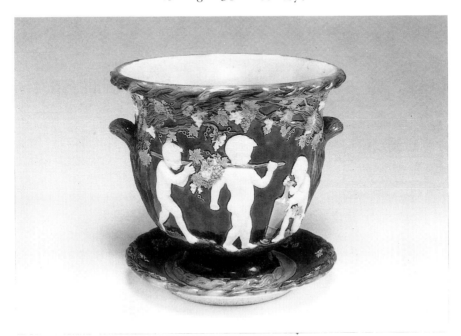

*42. Copeland centrepiece. Impressed mark. Height 29.2 cm. c.1865.* Sotheby's

Copeland made a fair amount of majolica from 1869 to 1880. These dates are only approximate, based on the Majolica Fixing Book in the Spode Archives, and the registration dates of recorded pieces. Although, as one of the greatest potteries of the period, they advertised widely, none of these advertisements mentions majolica. Nor is majolica mentioned in the descriptions of their displays at the various international exhibitions. Given the fragmentary nature of the surviving records, however, one can assume that the 200 patterns listed in Appendix D represent a very small proportion of the patterns produced.

*Crockery and Glass Journal,* 13 December 1877, described the majolica on display at J. M. Young & Co. of New York: 'Copeland is represented largely by a number of richly decorated specimens in Renaissance style. These are among the choicest shown.' Copeland issued a number of Parian wares with majolica glazes, most notably the 'French Fidler' and companion; 'Irish Wolfhound'; 'Setter Dog'; 'Bloodhound'; 'Falstaff in a Basket'; and a jug with dragon handle. Although Copeland registered a good many designs over the years, it is impossible to tell from the registers which designs were made in majolica. The only recorded pieces of majolica with a registry mark are the Birds & Bamboo Teapot (registered 21 January 1874) and the Lotus Jug (registered 2 July 1877). The teapot was also made in stoneware and china bodies.

Copeland made a great deal of majolica, and yet today pieces are rarely seen. Copeland was quite meticulous about marking their wares (even the lowly sanitary wares), so it seems unlikely that the answer is that their majolica was unmarked. Fortunately, an Ornament Book which includes some majolica, a Majolica Fixing Book and hundreds of sepia photographs of Copeland shapes, some with contemporary handwritten notations indicating that they were made in majolica, are all within the archives at Royal Worcester Spode in Stoke-on-Trent. From these documents this author has compiled the list of patterns found in Appendix D.

The mark used on Copeland majolica is COPELAND impressed in very small letters. This mark can sometimes be quite faint, even on bone china, and the thick majolica glazes would tend to further obscure it. Most pieces after 1870 will also bear a two-digit date code, corresponding to the last two digits of the year. This is surmounted with a single-letter month code.

## SIMON FIELDING

Simon Fielding established himself at the Railway Pottery on Sutherland Street, Stoke-on-Trent, in 1870. He had already established himself as an authority and judge of dogs and poultry at the Duke of Sutherland's estate, Trentham Hall. The pottery was not successful, and rather than let bailiffs take possession, Simon Fielding's son Abraham paid off the debts and took over in 1878. Abraham had been a partner in a colour mill in Cresswell.

*43. Copeland pedestal. Height 61 cm.*
*c.1875.* Sotheby's

With his training in that field, he was well prepared to tackle the booming majolica market. Within a very few years, he had established an international reputation for his majolica. Already on 8 January 1880 they were advertising in *Crockery and Glass Journal:*

> MAJOLICA, ETC., In a large and varied assortment of shapes and patterns done in the Old Styles or in the new imitations of Beryl, Amethyst, and Segrifito stones, consisting of useful and ornamental goods, such as Ash Trays, Candlesticks, Ice Creams, Oyster Trays, Beer Sets, Cruets, Jugs, Pickles, Bread Trays, Cuspadores, Lamp Vases, Salad Bowls, Flower Baskets, Dessert Ware, Leaves, Tea Ware, Butters, Butter Pats, Garden Seats and Pots, Match Holders, Umbrella Stands, Etc.

The firm also made tiles. *Crockery and Glass Journal,* 13 April 1882, described a number of Fielding productions:

> Their 'Hare' umbrella stand is a remarkably fine piece of work, vigorously modelled and beautifully colored. Their 'Foxglove' jardinière, 'Stork' garden seat, and a new toilet pattern 'Indian' on the Sutherland shape, will add to their reputation. The 'Indian' design is thoroughly characteristic, and is adapted to various other articles with good effect. They are also making a special line of jugs, hexagon in shape, with flowers embossed on a diaper ground. The same artistic design is reproduced in fruit sets, dessert services, jardinières, and umbrella stands, etc. We were favored with a view of several novelties, including a pair of umbrella stands formed by the trunk of a tree, against which is the figure of a skating girl just starting off on the ice. The 'Goat' umbrella stand gives promise of extraordinary merit. The general finish of their goods is excellent, and the color is remarkably good.

Fielding introduced argenta wares around 1879, registering the design for the Daisy & Fan Comport on 16 June 1881. Although Fielding has sometimes been credited with the invention of the argenta colouring, it had been used by Wedgwood since 1878. An advertisement in *Crockery and Glass Journal,* 8 January 1880, read, 'ARGENTA WARE, The new decoration applicable to every kind of embossed goods which we have succeeded in obtaining with scarcely any sign of crazing.' Fielding's most succesful argenta patterns were Shell & Net, Ribbon & Leaf, Ribbon & Blossom (introduced in 1884) and Daisy & Fan. *Crockery and Glass Journal,* 22 December 1881, reported:

> Their latest success, the 'Fan' dessert, a remarkably elegant Japanese design in 'argenta' colors, has induced them to carry out the same excellent idea through the whole range of their special manufactures. This design now extends to dessert services, tea and coffee sets, fruit, ice cream and fish services, vases, jardinières, cuspadores, jugs, teapots, and umbrella stands. These stands are marvels of good taste. The blending of the colors in sweet harmony is very successful. The purity and delicacy of the turquoise tone is very remarkable in all their numerous productions. Their strawberry set is very appropriate. In adddition to their other novelties, Messrs. Fielding & Co. have just finished an entire new design (which they are carrying out in the same thorough manner as the Fan pattern) in umbrella stands. This stand is hexagon in form, with a background of 'Japanese key diaper,' with bamboo canes running up the angles, the diaper ground acting as a foil to the decoration of raised flowers, lotus, lilies and sunflowers, exquisitely modeled after nature. The same

design is carried out in dessert ware, jugs, cuspadores, oyster and fish sets. They are bound to add to their reputation and business. Another new umbrella stand is formed by the trunk of a tree, on which hangs a hare and duck, vigorously modeled (life size). This fine piece of majolica will rival the 'stork' stand of Minton's.

On 10 August 1882, *Crockery and Glass Journal* reported that Fielding & Co. had brought an unsuccessful action against Hawley & Co. for infringing the 'Fan' design. 'Owing to some technical oversight, Messrs. Fielding & Co. were unable to secure a verdict', although they were 'morally the victors'. Fielding & Co. had registered ten designs between 1881 and 1884, mostly for moulded jug forms. By the end of 1882, they had a large range of argenta wares available. *Crockery and Glass Journal*, 21 December 1882, noted:

> The 'Shell and Net' salad, a net suspended round the bowl and foot of the salad, with some trophies from the deep – shell, coral, and seaweed – faithfully modeled, is a most exquisite specimen of the service they have in hand. This design, and the 'Ribbon and Leaf' another novelty, Messrs. Fielding & Co. are carrying out through the whole range of articles made of majolica. The jugs to both services are very capacious, and the 'Shell and Net' jug more particularly is very graceful. We have seen the plates, comports, tea and saucer, and salads to both these services, and can highly recommend them to our readers. The 'Greenaway' umbrella stands are very graceful and useful ornaments for the hall. The figures – on panels – are Spring and Autumn respectively. A lady's hat framed into a basket is a pretty receptacle for flowers or as a bracket.

It is interesting to note that a Kate Greenaway Umbrella Stand had been registered by Wedgwood in 1881. That umbrella stand is hat shaped, however, as opposed to the Fielding version with a hat flower basket attached.

Jewitt also recommended their majolica wares:

> One of the distinctive features of the majolica produced by Messrs. Fielding & Co. was the masterly and effective way in which they introduced, on some of their best pieces, hand modelled flowers and foliage. Modelled and coloured true to nature in every minute detail, and thrown in graceful negligence around the bodies of the vases, they became such perfect reproductions that it was difficult to divest the mind of the idea that the roses were not fresh gathered from the tree and temporarily twined around the vase for its adornment.

The firm made major expansions in 1881, 1884 (after a fire had gutted the works) and again in 1892. During the 1890s majolica was phased out and the firm specialized in Vellum Ware. By 1890, the firm's advertisements did not mention majolica. None the less, *Pottery and Glass Record*, January 1914, advised 'Majolica, Flower Pots, Pots & Pedestals and Grotesque ware in self and shaded colors, give a wide choice to buyers of this class of goods.' The firm continued to be successful into the twentieth century, using the name Crown Devon. Simon Fielding died in 1906, and Abraham in 1932. Their Salad Ware, moulded in the form of lettuce leaves and embossed tomatoes, had been selling well for twenty years in 1949. It was coloured green, primrose and red. Although it was not majolica, it can be regarded as a twentieth-century descendant. The pottery was destroyed by a fire in 1951, but was rapidly rebuilt. The firm remained in family hands until the 1980s.

Fielding majolica is often impressed FIELDING. In many cases this impression is quite faint and difficult to read, especially when obscured by the thick majolica glazes.

## THOMAS FORESTER

According to Jewitt, Thomas Forester established his first business at the Blythe Works (Newtown Pottery), High Street, Longton, in 1877. He soon took additional premises in Church Street. These he promptly demolished to make way for the new Phoenix Works, completed in 1879. He soon purchased the adjoining china factory – a truly extraordinary expansion in a period of only six years. In 1883, Thomas Forester took his two sons into the business, under the style Thomas Forester & Sons (Ltd). This firm should not be confused with the firm of Thomas Forester & Son, subsequently Forester & Hulme, at the Sutherland Pottery, Fenton. In 1887, Forester considerably expanded his capacity by purchasing the majolica works of Samuel Lear in Hanley. The Hanley address is not mentioned in any subsequent advertisements or documents, however, so it is not certain when he may have disposed of them.

This firm was a regular advertiser in the *Pottery Gazette* between 1881 and 1895. Jervis wrote, '… by catering to the multitude, [they] have, from a very humble beginning built up quite an extensive business.' In fact, Forester was a very aggressive businessman, who made a special effort to capture the American market. He advertised 'artistic and useful majolica' extensively in the *Crockery and Glass Journal* during the 1880s. On 1 January 1883, the *Pottery Gazette* noted:

> Mr. Forestor [sic] in his 'American' style of business seems to be rushing in where others fear to tread. His productions are being planted in every state in America, and his premises are filled with busy hands working early and late to keep down his increasing trade. Others are keenly competing for the American favours, and it will be interesting to watch the struggle for supremacy.

Overall, the Forester pieces cannot be judged to have been of a very high standard, despite contemporary praise. Jewitt remarks, 'The quality of Messrs. Forester's majolica was remarkably firm and good in body, the colouring well managed and the glaze very satisfactory, as was the modeling of the floral decoration.' Be that as it may, they also made some very poorly modelled robin on branch jugs, with sloppily painted glazes, though these, marked 'Foresters England', are of later production.

In 1882, Forester introduced raised flower decoration, in what was wrongly called the barbotine style, to his majolica. This was mostly in ornamental wares such as baskets and vases. An advertisement in the *Pottery Gazette*, 1 February 1883, featured a pull-out colour lithograph of the following pieces (pattern names author's own, unless in quotes):

| | | | |
|---|---|---|---|
| 73 | Apple Blossom Jug | 75 | 'Rose' Plaques, 3 sizes |
| 74 | Bird Jug | 76 | 'Stork' Jug |

| | | | |
|---|---|---|---|
| 77 | 'Bramble' Jug | 88 | Wild Rose Teaset, 3 pieces |
| 78 | Partridge Lid Teapot | 89 | Waterlily Sardine Box, cobalt ground |
| 79 | 'Bramble' Coffee Pot, 3 sizes | 90 | Apple Blossom Cuspadore |
| 80 | 'Japanese Garden Seat' | 91 | Wild Rose Strawberry Server with |
| 81 | Rose Coffee Pot and Stand, cobalt | | Sugar and Cream |
| | ground | 92 | Waterlily Covered Butter, cobalt |
| 82 | 'Jumbo' Teapot (elephant) | | ground |
| 83 | 'Rose' Jardinière | 93 | Artichoke Covered Butter |
| 84 | 'Rose' Vase | 94 | Bird and Bamboo Cabaret Set |
| 85 | Bird Jardinière, cobalt ground | 95 | 'Stork' Stilton Cheese Stand, 5 sizes 'in |
| 86 | Owl Jug (figural) | | various patterns' |
| 87 | 'Flag Iris Scent Jar' | 96 | Apple Blossom Teaset, 3 pieces |

It is to be hoped that some of the above-listed pieces were marked with the numbers designated in the advertisement. Other patterns mentioned in an article in *Crockery and Glass Journal*, 27 April 1882, are 'Egyptian', 'Doric', 'York', 'Reed', 'Lily', 'Begonia Leaf', 'Strawberry' and 'Bamboo'. In fact, all of the standard patterns of a large majolica producer of the time. An article in *Crockery and Glass Journal*, 19 October 1882, also mentions the 'Ribbon', 'Berry' and 'Hawthorn' Stilton Cheese Stands, as well as the 'fine' Cupid Umbrella Stand and the Stag Candelabra, 'which only has to be seen to be admired'. Forester won a silver medal at the International Exhibition at Calcutta in 1884. A two-page photographed advertisement in *Pottery Gazette*, June 1887, mostly represented the applied flower pieces, but also what was possibly Forester's ugliest design – a melon teapot with a frog crouched upon it.

By 1889, the firm's advertisements no longer mention majolica, although they continued to make it for many years. On 1 February 1895, the *Pottery Gazette* observed of their majolica:

> This firm claims to be the largest in the world for turning out art flower pots, their capacity running to a thousand dozen per week, one machine being able to produce two per minute. When we consider the artistic shape and design of these pots, such an output as this truly marks the development of the age as regards machinery in the application to art.

The firm was, in fact, one of the last in Staffordshire to make majolica. *Pottery and Glass Record* reported in 1914:

> Every time we call, there is something new, something which by its real artistic merits appeals to one immediately. For a long period the firm has been famous for vases and pots and pedestals in majolica and decorated. They put out a fine line at attractive prices and they give good value for money every time. We are pleased to be able to show in this issue one of their latest pedestals and pots, which is one of the best they have made, in our opinion. It has been well-modelled and treated in a most effective fashion, and we say without hesitation that it would be an ornament to any room. They have a fine range of majolica glazes which are in every sense of the word, art colours, and the popularity of these tints is undoubted.

When marked, Forester majolica may have a printed or impressed mark T.F. & S. Later pieces may bear a printed mark 'Foresters England'.

# JOSEPH HOLDCROFT

After working for Minton for eighteen years, Joseph Holdcroft set up in a works in St. Martin's Lane, Longton. *Keates's Gazetteer 1875-6* lists him at that address, specializing in silver lustre. Joseph Holdcroft probably established the Sutherland Works at Daisy Bank, Longton, in 1877. The firm made Parian and silver lustre wares, but its chief production was majolica. The firm continued until 1930, operating under the style Joseph Holdcroft Ltd from 1907.

*Pottery and Glass Trades' Review*, October 1878, reported:

> Mr. Holdcroft has been making majolica with great success for many years, and, being originally from Minton's he has himself now become the Minton of Longton so far as majolica is concerned. Some of his pieces are very large and important. His last production is a fine Greek Tripod stand for elevating vases or statues, in halls or conservatories. It is 38 inches in height and 28 inches across the base. Its three feet are bull's feet, about natural size, and from three ram's heads, at the upper part, are pendant festoons of fruit and flowers. The colouring of the plain parts is chiefly malachite, royal blue, and deep orange. It is a very noble pedestal, and surmounted with either his 'Stork' or 'Heron' flower holder, which are each about 33 inches high, the effect is very fine. That this manufactory turns out good majolica work is evidenced by the fact that during all the late bad times, Mr. Holdcroft has been quite busy in executing orders from Paris, Rome, Naples, and other such places where a pretty thing is known when seen, and an ugly thing likewise.

The Stork and Heron Flower Holders were illustrated in an advertisement in *Pottery Gazette*, January 1885. Holdcroft advertised majolica regularly in the *Pottery Gazette* during 1885-7. Holdcroft continued to specialize in large pieces, alongside his wide range of useful wares. *Crockery and Glass Journal*, 2 November 1882, described his 'Stork' fountain:

> It stands three feet six inches in height, the base being formed by a majestic stork standing at rest against a cluster of bulrushes and ferns, with lotus leaves and flowers modeled in high relief at its feet. On the top of the pillar of reeds, etc., supporting

another basin, in the middle of which is a nude figure holding a shell, from the centre of which the jet of water ascends. The stork, foliage and figure are skilfully modeled, and the brilliant colors make the fountain one of the finest we have ever seen. Mr. Holdcroft & Co. have a larger fountain having three basins, standing over nine feet, in preparation, in addition to many other large pieces in the same good style.

*44. Joseph Holdcroft Bramble Stilton Cheese Stand. Impressed 'HOLDCROFT'. Base diameter 29 cm.* Collection of Don Kelly and Warren Fitzsimmons

*45. Joseph Holdcroft umbrella stand. Height 82 cm. c.1875.* Sotheby's

Stork and Crane garden ornaments were illustrated in *Pottery Gazette*, January 1885. The services of especially competent designers and modellers were required for such large pieces. Sadly, we know little about the factory's employees. Marks in *Second Series Majolica* illustrates a rustic umbrella stand which is signed 'T. Fay Scupltor'. It is possible that Fay may have been responsible for some of the other above-mentioned pieces, but nothing else is known of him. Holdcroft copied many designs from Minton and George Jones, particularly apple blossom and pond lily. His best pieces often bear a very clear turquoise glaze. His green and brown glazes were also very good. Many of his pieces are characterized by a celadon-coloured base. Jervis described him as 'a manufacturer of majolica of an imitative rather than original description, though the pottery is good'. Some twenty-seven of his pieces are illustrated in Marks's two volumes. The pieces vary considerably in quality, some being very finely modelled and carefully glazed, and others quite the opposite. It seems that Holdcroft increasingly turned his attention to a lower class of wares as the 1880s progressed. *Pottery Gazette*, January 1886, reported:

> [Holdcroft] has been making alterations and additions to his pottery, with a view to increased business and has laid himself out specially for cheap and ornamental majolica in all branches. He is dealing largely just now in the Moss, Mottled and Alligator goods, and is introducing a variety of new shapes for the coming season.

The Alligator Wares mentioned have grounds moulded to represent alligator skin. Marks, *Second Series*, illustrates a cheese keeper and a fruit set in this style.

Holdcroft registered a number of his majolica designs:

JOSEPH HOLDCROFT'S REGISTERED MAJOLICA DESIGNS

| | |
|---|---|
| Bird & Leaf Ornament | 4 October 1870 |
| Ornamental Tray, Bird Handle | 22 March 1872 |
| Two Ornamental Trays, Bird Handles | 6 April 1872 |
| Bird & Oak Wall Pocket | 19 June 1876 |
| Jug | 7 June 1877 |
| Rustic Tea Service | 29 November 1877 |
| Bird Nest Breakfast Cruet | 1 December 1877 |
| Melon Teapot | 1 December 1879 |
| Shell Form Bonbonnière | 3 March 1880 |
| Moulded Jug | 4 November 1882 |
| Moulded Teapot | 5 February 1883 |

Although his advertisement did not mention majolica, Holdcroft was listed as a majolica manufacturer in *Pottery and Glass Record*, November 1914.

When marked, Holdcroft majolica bears an impressed J HOLDCROFT or an impressed J and H monogram in a circle.

## GEORGE JONES

The majolica of George Jones vies with that of Minton and Wedgwood for the place of the best majolica ever produced. Although this was a major firm, whose productions spanned ninety years, there is very little information about the firm's early years. Some of the firm's records are in the Wedgwood Archives, but these deal with the twentieth century. Fortunately, however, a majolica shape book with sepia photographs, copiously annotated, and part of a catalogue survive. They are, unfortunately, incomplete and quite late. They probably date from the 1880s, as the latest pattern number is No. 5276. Thus, they include only 31 patterns from the first

*46.* Left: *George Jones leaf dessert plate. Diameter 21 cm.* Author's collection

*47.* Right: *George Jones leaf dessert plate. Showing typical tortoise-shell glazing and pattern number in reserve.* Author's collection

1000–1999 series of majolica pattern numbers; 82 patterns from the 2000–2999 series; and 178 patterns from the 3000–3999 series. The 4000 series was bone china, followed by the 5000 series which was majolica. Only 31 of the 5000 series numbers are included. The 6000 series were ivory ware, followed by the 7000 series which were bone china. From these the list of pattern numbers in Appendix D has been constructed.

Unlike other manufacturers, George Jones annotated most of their design registrations 'China, Majolica & Earthenware', so that we can ascertain which designs were meant to be produced in majolica. The factory's abundant production is evident in the very large number of pieces still to be found by the collector. These are, none the less, expensive, as they are usually of the very highest quality.

George Jones, a former Minton employee, founded his firm at the Old Bridge Works, Stoke-on-Trent in 1861. Their first products were white granite, but success led to the construction of the Trent Works, which enabled them to produce a full line of wares. He was assisted by W. Candland, who eventually became a partner, and was still with the firm as late as 1902. George Jones was later joined by his three sons. Frank Jones-Benham was, according to Jervis in 1902, 'now regarded as perhaps the best potter in Staffordshire'. Horace O. Jones studied art at South Kensington, followed by a world tour, which included a stay at Trenton, New Jersey, to view the potteries, 'with which he expressed much satisfaction', according to *Crockery and Glass Journal,* 9 September 1880. Eventually, he was placed in charge of design at the works. The youngest brother, G. H. Jones, handled the financial and sales side of the works. Jervis said that his 'geniality has done much to build up an extensive business'. George Jones died in December 1893, and his sons, with W. Candland, carried on the business with continuing success.

*48. Pair of George Jones vases. Height 47 cm.* Sotheby's

Soon after founding his firm, George Jones established himself as a maker of fine-quality majolica and Palissy wares. The firm first won a medal at the Paris Exhibition in 1867, and also exhibited successfully in London 1871, Vienna 1873, and Sydney 1876. In 1872, they began producing a very fine-quality bone china. *Pottery and Glass Trades' Review*, December 1878, reported on Jones's display at the Paris Exhibition:

> Messrs. Geo. Jones & Sons, of Stoke-on-Trent, make a remarkably good display of majolica, which is scattered about the Hall in several very effective groups of vases, tazzas, pedestals, wine coolers, dishes – in fact, things for use and ornament in the house, the garden, and the conservatory – in great variety. A pair of dishes in this ware, painted by A. Gravier are very good.

The firm advertised majolica in *Pottery Gazette* from 1881 until early 1886. Perhaps George Jones's most successful pattern was Apple Blossom, which has been mistakenly called Dogwood by many writers. The first Apple Blossom piece was registered in 1873 (No. 3303). Eleven shapes were made in this pattern: Stilton Cheese Stand, Jug, Covered Cheese Dish, Tea & Coffee Tray (with tea and coffee pots, cream, sugar, cup & saucer), Covered Butter Dish, Honey Pot, Jug Stand, Mug, Cabaret Set, Dish with Two Birds and Cake Plate. This last has a pattern number of 5238, indicating that the pattern was popular and continuously produced for a long time. It is most commonly found in turquoise ground, but was also made in dark blue. Recently Phillips New York offered a very rare covered cheese dish with a green ground.

*49. George Jones Sardine Box in bone china. Diamond registration mark for 16 February 1862. Length 22 cm.* Author's collection

*50. George Jones Hen Teapot. Length 28 cm.* Sotheby's

Overall, the Jones's production was fairly typical. The pattern list in Appendix D, which is, of course, incomplete, shows 58 jardinières, urns and flowerpots, 26 jugs, 25 vases, 17 tiles and 7 dessert sets. The most sought-after pieces today are the Stilton cheese stands, sardine boxes and game pie dishes. The pattern list shows 14 game pie dishes, 12 Stilton cheese stands and 5 sardine boxes.

*51. George Jones jardinière. Impressed mark. Height 69 cm. c.1880.* Sotheby's

GEORGE JONES REGISTERED MAJOLICA PATTERNS

| No. | Description | Date |
|-----|-------------|------|
| 2542 | Pineapple Teapot | 27 June 1870 |
| 2763 | Salmon Dish | 29 August 1871 |
| 2782 | Camel Centrepiece | 23 December 1871 |
| 2796 | Ornamental Tray | 1 December 1871 |
| 3207 | Africa Centrepiece | 16 February 1872 |
| 3230 | Elephant Vase | 4 March 1872 |
| 3303 | Apple Blossom Jug | 25 March 1873 |
| 3304 | Apple Blossom Tea & Coffee Tray | 29 April 1873 |
| 3331 | Tortoise Spittoon | 25 August 1873 |
| 3341 | Tower Stilton | 25 August 1873 |
| 3371 | Hare Game Pie Dish | 27 December 1873 |
| 3382 | Pine Flower Stand | 9 May 1874 |
| 3384 | Wren Flower & Card Holder | 28 March 1874 |

| 3401 | Oyster Plate | 15 September 1874 |
| 3409 | Stork Jug | 8 December 1874 |
| 3436 | Butterfly Spill Case | 23 February 1875 |
| 3441 | Pelican Sardine Box | 12 March 1875 |
| 3465 | Monkey Tea Set | 26 June 1875 |
| 3467 | Wild Rose Jug | 13 September 1875 |
| 3468 | Punch Punch Bowl | 13 September 1875 |
| 3470 | Crocus Vase | 18 September 1875 |
| 3490 | Terrier Ash Tray | 22 January 1876 |
| 3491 | Cat Ash Tray | 22 January 1876 |
| 3562 | Drum Tea Ware | 25 January 1877 |
| 3557 | Barrel Caviar Set | 2 May 1877 |

George Jones's majolica is frequently marked. Some otherwise unmarked pieces may be identified by the pattern numbers painted in a reserve in the glaze.

*impressed (1861-73)*    *impressed (1861-73)*    *impressed (1873-1924)*    *moulded and applied pad (1861-73) 'N' followed with painted pattern no.*

## JAMES WARDLE & COMPANY

James Wardle first potted at Hope Street in Shelton *c.* 1854. Between 1859 and 1863 he was in a partnership, Wardle & Ash, at James Street, Hanley, where he made majolica. From 1865 until 1881 he operated from William Street, off Broad Street, Shelton. He then moved to his new Washington Works, Victoria Street, Hanley.

Wardle & Co. made enormous quantities of mediocre majolica. They advertised majolica in *Keates's Directory 1867*. The firm registered fifteen designs between 1868 and 1883, most of them apparently for majolica wares. As will be seen by the following list, even their registered designs were hardly original.

| Monkey Chestnut Dish | 28 August 1871 |
| Bamboo Flower Pot | 6 August 1879 |
| Sunflower Salad Bowl | 19 July 1882 |
| Bamboo & Fern Teaset | — — |
| Bird & Fan Jug | — — |

Wardle advertised majolica extensively in *Pottery Gazette* during the period 1881-6. A typical advertisement in January 1884 proclaimed:

Messrs Wardle & Co. have just completed the whole range of their new works, in which the most approved principle of oven and the best known means of drying have been introduced; and the quality of the work already finished surpasses that which had already gained for them substantial support from the chief trading centres of the world.

Jugs, Teapots, Sugars, Creams, Teas, Bread Trays, Cheese Trays, Butters, Dessert Sets, Tea Sets, Sardines, Tobacco Jars, Flower Vases, Flowerpots, Flower Baskets, Candlesticks, Spittoons, Cuspadores, Egg Baskets, Salad Bowls, Spills, Smoke Sets, Cruets, Umbrella Stands.

Their most popular designs were Bamboo & Fern, Pineapple and Sunflower. *Crockery and Glass Journal*, 21 April 1881, reported, 'Another American combination of a tea-set, consisting of teapot, box, and cream, in several shapes and styles of decoration – Japanese and octagon, in dark blue and turquoise, made by Messrs. Wardle & Co., of Hanley.' In fact, *Pottery Gazette*, January 1890, stated that their chief trade was in America. *Crockery and Glass Journal*, 21 December 1882, described their latest goods at length:

> The 'Sunflower' jug is very quaint; their 'Stork' jardinier is a fine piece, as is also the umbrella stand. The 'Swallow and Marne' vase, the 'Gondola' basket and flower vase, 'Blackberry' jardinier, brackets, and small vases decorated with hyacinth blossoms and other flowers are brightly tinted, the colors being transparent; more particularly their yellow, which has a very pure tone, and turquoise. Their dark brown is soft, yet rich, and the mazarine blue ground on the large 'Blackberry' jardinier is as full and rich as a cobalt ground on china.

In 1910, the works were purchased by Harold Taylor Robinson, who traded under the style Wardle Art Co., Ltd until 1935.

A great deal of Wardle majolica appears to have been unmarked. Marked specimens bear an impressed WARDLE.

## ROYAL WORCESTER

The first porcelain was made at Worcester in 1751, by Dr. John Wall and William Davis. Over the next hundred years the factory was owned by a number of persons. In 1862, the Royal Worcester Porcelain Company was founded by Edward Phillips, William Litherland and others. Richard William Binns, who had been a partner of Kerr & Binns, the previous owners of the factory, was the Art Director of the new firm until his retirement in 1897. The Royal Worcester factory and its wares is discussed in detail in Henry Sandon's *Royal Worcester Porcelain*.

Today Royal Worcester majolica is rare, and it has been assumed that little of it was made. This author's study of Worcester's London showroom Sales Journals for the period 1868–72 has shown that it was actually made in large quantities. It can only be conjectured that much of the firm's majolica was unmarked, as were many of their useful wares during the Kerr & Binns period. Royal Worcester did not advertise their majolica, and habitually downplayed their earthenware production. R. W. Binns, in his history of the firm's second hundred years, mentions only a pair of majolica vases prepared by the factory for the Paris Exhibition in 1878:

> ... scenes from the manufacturers of the sixteenth century were selected. The design was in the style of the Italian Renaissance and the subject suggested by drawings in the famous work of the Cavaliere Picolpasso were worked out in deeply sunk panels or recesses, the figures being in *alto rilievo*. On the first vase portrait-busts of Luca della

*52. Pair of Royal Worcester posy vases. Impressed mark. Height 14.5 cm. c.1876–91. Sotheby's*

Robbia and Maestro Giorgio were planned on the handles and the panels represented the potter at the wheel and the modeller respectively. Similar heads of Michael Angelo [sic] and Raphael appeared on the second vase and the panels contained groups illustrating the painter and fireman.

The two latter portraits were selected as representing men of the highest type of modeller and painter, and the two former as being those of the representatives of the sister arts as applied to pottery.

Opportunely, at this time Longfellow's beautiful poem 'Keramos' was published and was reprinted by the Worcester Directors as an appropriate explanation of the vases.

These vases decorated by Thomas Botts, and a few other pieces of majolica, may be seen at the Dyson Perrins Museum, Worcester. Worcester did display some ordinary majolica wares at this exhibition. *Crockery and Glass Journal*, 19 August 1878, decided, 'The "fern jugs" (from the Royal Worcester factory) are among the most charming pieces of majolica shown in this market.' In general, it must be said that the Royal Worcester majolica was not of a very high standard. Many pieces were coated in a mottled grey and brown glaze, which may have been considered tasteful at the time, but holds no charm for the collector today. The turquoise glaze is not as good as that of Minton, Wedgwood, George Jones or Holdcroft, being rather dark. In general, the glazes were quite opaque.

Between 1861 and 1872, the factory's shapes were numbered consecutively within ten classes. Classes One and Two, busts and statuettes over eight inches in height, were not generally made in majolica. It appears, however, that nearly every

*53. Royal Worcester 'Asheley' wall brackets. Impressed mark. Height 24.5 cm
c.1880.* Sotheby's

shape in the remaining classes was made in polychrome majolica glazes during the 1860s and in what the firm called 'turquoise coloured majolica' during the 1870s. The classes are as follows:

Class 3    Candlesticks, tapers, etc. (Nos. 1–46)
Class 4    Centres, baskets and dessert ornaments (Nos. 1–108)
Class 5    Brackets, plaques, pedestals (Nos. 1–34)
Class 6    General (Nos. 1–236)
Class 7    Small figures, match boxes, and extinguishers (Nos. 1–113)
Class 8    Flower pots etc. (Nos. 1–22)
Class 9    Butter tubs, honey pots, etc. (Nos. 1–32)
Class 10   Inkstands, caskets, spill pots etc. (Nos. 1–75)

At some point during the recording of shape numbers, items rightfully belonging in the other nine classes were assigned to Class 6. From 1872 the items were numbered consecutively and chronologically, beginning with No. 237, where Class Six had ended. A complete list of all the shapes produced by Royal Worcester from 1862 to 1969 is to be found in Henry Sandon's *Royal Worcester Porcelain.* The shape numbers were impressed, incised, printed or written on the bases of the objects. If, as has been supposed, Worcester majolica is not so much rare as unidentified due to lack of marks, some more pieces may come to light, identified by the shape marks.

Majolica candle extinguishers are nearly unique to Royal Worcester (Copeland is the only other firm known to have produced them). Sandon illustrates a number of these, although made in porcelain rather than earthenware.

It has been put forward that a good deal of Worcester majolica may have been unmarked. It may also be that the marks have not been recognized. Worcester majolica which is marked will bear an impressed rather than a printed mark, as the latter would have required an enamel firing. The intricate Worcester mark does not come up very well when impressed, and thus some marked pieces may not be recognized. Impressed shape numbers should be easier to read, and it is to be hoped that more Worcester majolica may come to light through this method of identification.

*impressed*
*(1862–75)*

# CHAPTER FIVE

# AMERICAN MAJOLICA

*Air: 'Little Brown Jug'*

*If I had a love that would give to me*
*Porcelain, majolica, and potterie,*
*I'd 'spoon' him in the gushingest way*
*And kiss him a million times a day.*

Chorus:
*Ha! ha! ha! wouldn't I hug*
*If he'd give to me a majolica jug?*
*Majolica jug, he! he! he!*
*Little brown jug, oh, I love thee.*

The verse above, which appeared in *Crockery and Glass Journal*, 4 July 1878, is indicative of the ridiculous heights to which the majolica craze rose in the late 1870s and early 1880s. *Crockery and Glass Journal*, which was published between 1875 and 1905 in New York, chronicled the craze in great detail.

Majolica came to America quite late in relation to its popularity in England. Initially, the wares were considered to be harbingers of an improvement in public taste. *Crockery and Glass Journal*, 22 April 1875, said of the majolica wares then being imported:

> It will require a taste for arts and beauty to appreciate the most ingenious designs, and the artificial coloring of the more expensive articles in this line, and which are more calculated to adorn the palaces of Fortuna's favorites, than to appear in the houses of the middles classes. However, there is any variety of useful, and at the same time, ornamental articles which are within the reach of almost everybody . . .

*Pottery and Glass Trades' Review*, September 1877, commented:

> Three or four years ago Majolica, Parian, Tiles, Chinese or Japanese Porcelains would very rarely be found outside of New York, Boston or Philadelphia, where as now, every dealer in a town of any importance finds it necessary to carry a fair stock of such goods and finds a ready sale for them. The more we get of artistic goods, either home or foreign, the more they will be appreciated and sought after, and thereby the art taste of the masses increased.

These arbiters of public taste soon began to have misgivings. By 26 May 1881, when majolica had been the rage for several years, *Crockery and Glass Journal* opined:

> If there ever has been a distinct line of goods that had what is called a good run it must be majolica. For twelve months past, if not a longer time, the cheaper majolicas have

been displayed in great profusion and in all degrees of excellence, and the people have bought them without stint. Some of the designs are none too sweet, but perhaps they sell better for that, as witness the fish-shaped jugs with gaping mouths and tails turned up for handles. Thousands of such atrocities have been and continue to be sold with questionable taste on the part of the buyer.

On 14 July 1881, the same journal mourned:

> It must be confessed that the native taste for majolica goods is extremely bad, when we contemplate the thousands of pieces which go to adorn our households. They are simply monstrous in form and conception... The producers and dealers are in no wise to blame for this or that abomination. On the contrary, they are quite right in bringing out what is demanded. We could wish, however, that the demand was for better things with more money in them.

On 13 October 1881, the journal announced: 'Majolica still reigns supreme.' Two years later the situation had not improved, for the journal reported on 24 May 1883:

> I know of shelf loads of Wedgwood's finest work lying dust covered and immovable in the big warehouses of New York, while the gaudy majolicas come and go in ship loads. The aboriginal rage for glaring glazes seems to affect the American mind, and they are willing to have their pottery 'any color so she's red'.

On 6 September 1883:

> How many times have we heard it said: 'Majolica is played out,' 'Majolica is passé.' And yet it keeps on coming – the bulk of it in the same well-known patterns that have made majolica recognized wherever seen, and some of it in a style that would not be accepted as majolica, but with no other name to fit it.

On 12 February 1885:

> It was predicted two years ago that majolica had seen its best days, and so far as good prices are concerned it probably has passed its palm. At present, however, there is nothing that adequately takes its place as a cheap and showy class and as far as we are able to judge, the large traders have not lost faith in it as an article for which there is still a fair demand. We notice with pleasure that the majolicas now coming into the market are very much superior to some of the trashy abominations of shape and color which contributed largely to the sudden decline which broke prices on this class of goods when the demand was at its highest point.

And finally on 13 May 1886, the obituary:

> Majolica as known to the ancients of three years ago is now no more. Towards the end of its career it degenerated into the cheapest of all cheap forms of pottery, and eventually reached such a low ebb that it could not be given away, even at wholesale.... Some of the things made then were in shocking bad taste, the making of which was a crime against the laws of artistic simplicity.

## MAJOLICA AND AMERICAN POTTERY

Although one might call majolica an English 'invention', the Americans were very soon imitating it. Through the medium of the international exhibitions staged throughout Europe and the United States during the second half of the nineteenth century, new ideas and techniques were spread more quickly than ever before. It must be said that to a very large degree American majolica was imitative of the English originals. Modellers freshly emigrated from the English potteries were very much sought after, and it cannot be disputed that in many cases their models were direct copies of English manufactures. It will be seen again and again in the accounts below and in Appendix B, that such English potters were instrumental in American majolica production.

The American potters were not necessarily to blame for their mimicry. An article, 'American vs. English Crockery' in *Crockery and Glass Journal*, 9 January 1875, explained: 'The main cause of that [copying], however, was doubtless the necessities of the business, the trade demanding patterns identical with foreign, and the consumers wishing the same thing.'

In January 1875, when the first national association of potters was formed in Philadelphia, they agreed. 'We should not in future, as we have been doing in the past, copy all or nearly all of our patterns from foreign manufacturers. We have sufficient talent in this country to originate new designs, more elegant and more suitable to the wants of the American people.'

This is not to say that the American manufacturers had not already turned out some very fine designs or that some of their work was not of good quality, for they did create some original and even 'elegant' work. However, it must be remembered that the American pottery industry was in its infancy during these decades. In 1884, in her article 'Pottery Old and New', Jenny Young explained:

> The fact is, that with a family of something like 50,000,000 to provide with household crockery, America has had comparatively little time to think of ceramic art. Its attention was first turned to competing with the manufacturers – chiefly French and English – who kindly volunteered to supply the household needs aforesaid. A high tariff kept down the average quality of the imported goods and a high rate of wages led the American manufacturer to content himself with equalling the cheap foreign goods he found in the market. After the Civil War, the industry rose with the rapidity characteristic of the country, and Trenton and Cincinnati contended for the proud title 'Staffordshire of the West'.

By 1876, there were nearly 800 potteries in the United States. These were mostly concentrated at Trenton, New Jersey; East Liverpool, Ohio; Cincinnati, Ohio; and at Flushing and Greenpoint, Long Island, New York. The remainder were scattered throughout the country.

None the less, even by 1884, the American trade was at a distinct disadvantage. *Crockery and Glass Journal*, 31 May 1883, reported that *all* professional colours were still being imported from England or Germany. Similarly the Americans were still importing significant amounts of clay. English potters who emigrated complained bitterly of the quality of the clays available locally. There was a great prejudice against American goods, which were said, perhaps with great justice, to be prone to crazing. The Americans evaded this prejudice by putting spurious English marks on their wares. An article in *Pottery and Glass Trades' Review*, November 1877, claimed that, 'more white ware dishes, made in Cincinnati and

Trenton, New Jersey, are sold as imported English ware than are sold under the name of imported ware.'

Speaking specifically of majolica, John Ramsay summed it up, 'American potters rarely attempted the large and complicated pieces made in England, but confined themselves to tableware, pitchers and mantel ornaments in vegetable, floral, animal, and even fish forms, and many of these are impossible to distinguish from imported ware.' Perhaps it is true that the best-quality American potters were as good as the mediocre English wares, but with few exceptions the American goods can be distinguished for their weak modelling and colours.

The first pottery in Trenton was established by Taylor and Speeler, who produced yellow and rockingham wares. They also unsuccessfully attempted porcelain and Parian manufacture. Eventually white granite was produced. In 1853, William Young & Sons made the first cream-colour ware. By 1878, there were nineteen potteries in the city. Majolica manufacturers here included Carr & Clark, Eureka Pottery, Mayer Bros., Willetts Manufacturing Co., and William Young & Sons.

East Liverpool became a pottery centre because of the large deposits of clay and kaolin found on the banks of the Ohio river between East Liverpool and Wellsville. The pottery could be easily transported by flatboat on the river. By the middle of the nineteenth century, this was a centre for the manufacture of useful wares and three-quarters of the inhabitants were English. English social traditions were maintained in the home, the community at large and, most importantly to us, in the potteries. By the Civil War, there were nearly ninety potteries in the vicinity. James Bennett, eldest brother of Edwin Bennett, is said to have established the first pottery in the district in 1839. Manufacturers of majolica included Cartwright Bros., William Colclough, Holland Manley, McDevitt & Moore and George Morley. Buckeye leaf and corn patterns were particularly popular in Ohio. Today this once-flourishing centre is commemorated at the East Liverpool Museum of Ceramics, established in 1980.

One hundred years after the Declaration of Independence, the first national association of potters declared their intent to create original designs and ones more suited to American needs than English wares. They also committed themselves to creating a truly impressive display at the Philadelphia Centennial Exhibition. Sadly, contemporary accounts seem to have dismissed the American exhibits, as they were inferior to the English ones. *The Illustrated History of the Centennial Exhibition* remarked:

> On the south side of the hall, near the eastern end, was a display of American pottery and porcelain. It was creditable on the whole, but did not compare with the display made by either of the leading European nations, or by China or Japan. The exhibits in this line were, therefore, modestly placed in a corner.

However, majolica was at the height of its American popularity, and a good deal of it was displayed. Indeed, it is only from the listing of exhibitors at this and other exhibitions that we can say with some certainty that some firms did in fact make majolica, largely if not always unmarked.

## GRIFFEN, SMITH & HILL

Certainly the best-known American majolica manufacturer was Griffen, Smith & Hill, of Phoenixville, Pennsylvania. Their Etruscan majolica is popular with collectors, not only for the relatively wide range of shapes and patterns which they produced, but because these pieces were so often well marked with the firm's official trademark and/or a pattern number. Artists' numbers may also be found. Their 1884 *Catalogue of Majolica*, reprinted in 1960 by Brooke Weidner, is an invaluable guide to their wares. The reprint, however, lacks the final three pages of illustrations, which include the much-sought-after Shell pieces (often called 'Shell & Seaweed'). A complete facsimile of the catalogue along with price list is reproduced in Arthur E. James's .*The Potters and Potteries of Chester County, Pennsylvania.*

The Phoenix Pottery was built at Starr and Church Streets in 1867 by the Phoenix Iron Company at the urging of W. A. H. Schreiber, who became Secretary and General Superintendent of the new venture, styled the Kaolin and Fire-brick Company. Although Phoenix Iron's chief interest was in manufacturing fire-bricks for their iron furnaces, their kilns were also designed to burn white ware, rockingham and yellow ware. (Phoenix Iron's property was adjacent to the new pottery.) In 1871, the pottery began to manufacture terracotta wall ornaments shaped like the heads of boars, stags and dogs.

On 31 August 1872, Mr. Schreiber and John E. Baum leased the pottery from

*54. Etruscan Begonia Leaf Pickle Dish. Length 22.5 cm.* Author's collection

*55. The underside of the pickle dish in Plate 54, showing typical impressed 'GSH' monogram.* Author's collection

Phoenix Iron. Mr. Baum withdrew almost immediately and his place was taken by J. F. Betz. Moulds and models from the American Porcelain Manufacturing Co. of Gloucester, New Jersey, which had closed in 1857, were purchased. The New Jersey firm had been best known for its soft-paste porcelain decorated with floral designs in relief. Their attempts had been largely unsuccessful, due to difficulties in firing their kilns. Few examples survive, but Ellen and Bert Denker illustrate a relief-moulded pitcher with a chinoiserie design. Parian ware was now produced using these moulds and models, burning them in the fire-brick kiln. The local paper reported that the firm was experiencing financial difficulties on 12 October 1875. On 11 February 1876, Mr. Schreiber left the firm and David Smith took over.

On 1 January 1877, Levi Beerbower and Henry Griffen leased the pottery. Henry Griffen was still studying engineering at Rensselaer Polytechnic Institute, so he was, presumably, financed by his father, John Griffen, then Superintendent of Phoenix Iron. In June 1877, Henry joined the business, on his graduation. At the end of 1878, Mr. Beerbower left the firm, and on 1 January 1879, the pottery was leased to Henry Griffen, his brother George (who had been working as an engineer for the Grand Tower Mining, Manufacturing and Transportation Co., Grand Tower, Illinois), David Smith and William Hill, trading as Griffen, Smith & Hill. David Smith was an English potter who had worked at Stoke-on-Trent, New Glasgow in Nova Scotia and Trenton.

*56. Etruscan Punch Bowl. Impressed 'GSH' monogram. Diameter 30 cm.*
Chester County Historical Society

In 1880, Mr. Hill left the firm, which then traded as Griffen, Smith & Co., although they continued to use the mark which is a monogram of Griffen, Smith & Hill. The firm continued to make cream-coloured ware, white earthenware, yellow ware, rockingham ware, Parian and ornamental terracotta.

The firm must have begun production of majolica sometime in 1878, for the *Daily Local News*, 7 April 1879, reported that the firm 'has recently engaged in the manufacture of majolica ware, which is already acquiring an extensive reputation'. The same source announced on 9 January 1882 that the firm 'find the majolica business increasing so rapidly that they have been obliged to increase their facilities for its manufacture'. *Crockery and Glass Journal*, 25 January 1883, reported that they had 'been successful with the manufacture of majolica, and their ware is very favorably looked upon wherever exhibited'. On 1 February 1883, the same journal reported: 'The firm give their entire attention to the line of majolica.'

The firm won a Gold Medal for two majolica vases and a jug, at the World's Industrial and Cotton Centennial Exposition at New Orleans in 1884. *Crockery and Glass Journal,* 17 April 1884, commented: 'The majolica manufactured by Messrs. Griffen, Smith & Co., at their works at Phoenixville, Pa., finds its way to distant parts of the country, and is found at all the leading jobbing houses. The patterns and the tint are always improving.' During this era, their majolica was given away as premiums by the Atlantic & Pacific Tea Company (A&P grocery stores).

The factory more than doubled their capacity by the addition of two new kilns and buildings in 1885. In September of that year, they employed 140 hands, including 60 apparently lively female decorators. The *Phoenixville Messenger,* 28 May 1881, reported:

> On Monday afternoon last the majolica young ladies of the Phoenixville Majolica works, took half a day off and went over to Mt. Clare, where, in Thompson's Grove, they had a high old time all to themselves, which must have made the boys mad, for they say all kinds of funny things about that frolic, and among the rest, that, running out of pennies, the girls had to row themselves back across the river. Of course envy prompts this sort of thing.

Apart from the amusement value of this account, it reminds us that the potteries of this period employed a good many children. The *New York Herald,* 24 March 1883, reported that in the census year 1880 there were employed in the pottery industry: 7,205 males above sixteen, 943 females above fifteen and 1,341 children.

The 'majolica girls' were paid considerably less than male decorators would have been. None the less, the expense of this hand decoration for such a low-priced ware made its profitability dubious. Early in 1885 china ware manufacture was

*57. Etruscan Daisy Salad Bowl. Diameter 23 cm.* Chester County Historical Society

introduced and Albino ware a few months later. It was hoped that the reduced amount of decoration required would make this latter line more profitable than the ordinary majolica. *Crockery and Glass Journal*, 11 March 1886, announced that the firm 'in addition to their sales of majolica are doing well with a handsome line of ivory-bodied goods decorated in colors'. None the less, the *Daily Local News*, 12 August 1886, quoted David Smith as saying that, 'the demand for majolica ware is not so great as it was a few years ago, although they are still making it in considerable quantities to supply orders.' Only twenty of their fifty decorators were still engaged in majolica decoration. However, on 23 May 1887 the same paper wrote that the firm 'also continue to manufacture large quantities of majolica ware'.

Henry Griffen left the firm in 1888, and established Griffen Bros. & Miller, manufacturers of enamelled brick. This became, subsequently (1894–6), Griffen Enameled Brick Co. He then went on to work for the American Terra Cotta Co., Illinois (1896–1903).

In 1889, Mr. Smith sold out, in order to erect levigating mills at Toughkenamon, Pennsylvania, where they ground kaolin from nearby beds into a fine powder for industrial use. J. Stuart Love, Henry Griffen's father-in-law, now joined the firm, which traded as Griffen, Love & Co. They advertised majolica in *Pottery and Glassware Reporter* from October 1889 to April 1890. During this period they employed 150 workers.

After a serious fire on 3 December 1890, the pottery closed until April 1891. It reopened as the Griffen China Company, its creditors becoming stockholders, with George Griffen as Secretary. This firm produced only white porcelain table ware. The pottery shut down again in 1892. George Griffen died on 27 January 1893. His brother Henry died in 1907.

Many of the Etruscan designs were copies of English majolica patterns. Barber commented, 'The modeling of some of the pieces, such as *compotières* with supports composed of three intertwined dolphins, boudoir flower-shells or jewel cups, and other fancy shapes, was refined and artistic, the designer being an English artist of the name Bourne.' This could have been Hamlet Bourne (see Appendix C), although the name Bourne was a common one in Staffordshire.

Barber also noted the similarities to Belleek, 'Some of these designs bear a striking resemblance to the Irish belleek ware, not only in conception but in the extreme thinness of body and the tinted nacreous glazes which cover them.' This is an exaggeration, for the Etruscan body is very heavy in comparison with better-quality English or Continental majolica, and those wares are very heavy in comparison to the Belleek Parian body. None the less, Etruscan Shell wares are lighter and more crisply potted than their other wares. The glazes have a translucence and iridescence which are also lacking in other Etruscan wares. These pieces must have been more expensive to produce, for the 1884 *Catalogue* lists Shell teacups at $3.00 per dozen, whereas Bamboo or Cauliflower teacups were only $2.00 per dozen. These wares are immensely popular with collectors today, and modern reproductions of cups, saucers and eight-inch dessert plates are being sold in the United States by Carolyn Horchou. These should be distinguishable by their heavier body and the lack of iridescence in the glazes.

The Cauliflower Teapot (Pattern E13) was, of course, an imitation of Wedgwood's cauliflower ware introduced in 1759. The Wedgwood ware was creamware, however, not majolica, and featherlight in comparison to the majolica imitations. Another design copied from Wedgwood was the Baseball Jug (Pattern E6). The Etruscan version of Wedgwood's 'Athletic Jug' (Nos. 2836, 2972-3) substitutes baseball for the cricket in the original.

The Corncob Jug (Pattern E12) is an exact copy of that registered by T. C. Brown-Westhead, Moore & Co. on 21 April 1864. The Geranium pattern (Pattern C7) was made in both green and majolica glazes by a number of English manufacturers, but the only marked piece known to this author is a green glazed dish by Hope & Carter (1862-80).

Most Etruscan majolica is marked with either an impressed backstamp or a pattern number (see Appendix D). Decorator's marks may also be found.

## HAMPSHIRE POTTERY

This pottery was established on the premises of a former clothes pin factory in Keene, New Hampshire, in 1871 by James Scollay Taft (1844-1923). He was soon joined by his uncle James Burnap. The location was ideal because of the large deposits of feldspar and blue clay in nearby Troy. In 1874, the purchase of a nearby pottery, Chamberlain & Baker (formerly Starkey & Howard), greatly increased their capacity. Originally established for the manufacture of redware (mostly flower-pots), they had later made a variety of wares, including stoneware. Now Taft made redware exclusively at the newly acquired plant, freeing the Hampshire pottery for other wares.

Although majolica production had begun the previous year, it has often been written that Taft's majolica was the result of the efforts of Thomas Stanley, an Englishman who began to work for Taft in 1879. Stanley was certainly active as a turner and modeller of majolica. After 1891, the Hampshire Pottery specialized in art pottery, with an opaque white body, in a variety of glazes. During this era, they employed forty workers, half of whom were decorators. Taft's brother-in-law Cadmon Robertson joined the firm in 1904 and was responsible for over 900, mostly matt, glaze formulae, while in charge of all manufacturing. His death in 1914 created problems for the firm and Taft sold out to George Mortman in 1916. Closed during the First World War, Mortman reopened briefly to manufacture hotel china. During 1919-23, the Hampshire Pottery made mosaic floor tiles. The firm closed in 1923.

*Pottery and Glass Trades' Review*, December 1878, announced, 'a firm in New

Hampshire have commenced the manufacture of majolica, principally in flower pots and vases, and have produced some very fair specimens.' An article in the *Keene Evening Sentinel* in 1971 by D. R. Propter quotes an 1882 account, 'Millions of articles in majolica ware are manufactured here annually, including almost every known article or ornamentation, the variety being almost bewildering and past enumeration in our limited space.'

The majolica had a white body, glazed with green, yellow, blue and brown. The pieces this author examined at the Colony House Museum in Keene were indistinctly moulded, with the bodies showing many impurities which mar the surface. The glazes were unevenly applied, and showed great unevenness of colour. Small specks of undissolved colour in the glaze further disfigure the pieces. Relief-moulded jugs, vases and jardinières were made in many designs, most of which are copies of the efforts of other factories. A very popular item was a 'majolica' marmalade server in the shape of an orange. However, upon examining an example, this author found it to be painted in opaque colours, rather than majolica glazes. A dolphin sweetmeat server was very like the Etruscan Dolphin Comport (Pattern L–2), which was in turn made by countless British firms.

The New England Astor tea and dessert services are the most popular and original pieces of Taft majolica. They are particularly admired for the delicate tints of blue and pink. Marks (1983) illustrates a cake stand in this pattern. Items produced in the ubiquitous Corn pattern included large jugs, teapots, jampots and salt and pepper shakers. Blackberry, Bamboo and Bamboo & Bow were also popular patterns.

58. Left: *Hampshire Pottery jardinière with green and brown shaded majolica glazes. Height 18 cm.* Colony House Museum, Historical Society of Cheshire County, Keene, New Hampshire

59. Right: *Hampshire Pottery basket, yellow with pink lining. Height 15 cm.* Colony House Museum, Historical Society of Cheshire County, Keene, New Hampshire

The Colony House Museum of the Historical Society of Cheshire County in Keene has a few pieces of Taft's majolica on display, among their very large collection of Hampshire Pottery wares. Most of the majolica pieces are illustrated in *Hampshire Pottery* by Joan Pappas and A. Harold Kendall. Much of the majolica was unmarked, but some pieces may be impressed J. S. TAFT & Co., KEENE, N. H.

## EDWIN BENNETT

The Bennett family originated in New Hall, Derbyshire. Edwin Bennett was born there in 1818, and, probably at the age of twelve, was apprenticed to the firm of Harrison & Cash, in nearby Woodville. Woodville, also known as Wooden Box, near Burton-on-Trent, was a busy pottery centre during the early part of the nineteenth century. The inhabitants were mostly potters and colliers. Godden's *Jewitt* lists seven potteries which had been established here by 1840. One of these was the Wooden Box Pottery, established in 1817, by Thomas Hallam. This was successively worked by Mr. Robinson, Harrison & Cash, Hallam & Co., Watts & Cash and Thomas Nadin. The Cash family also controlled the Woodville Potteries.

Bennett's oldest brother, James (1812–62), a master potter in Woodville, emigrated to America in 1834. He first worked as a master turner for the American Pottery Manufactory Company in Trenton, New Jersey. Founded as the Jersey City Porcelain & Earthenware Company in 1825, this firm was to be the first stop in American for many English potters. In 1837, James joined Ralph Clews's short-lived firm in Troy, Indiana. Abandoning Troy after a bout of malaria, James settled in East Liverpool, Ohio, founding the first pottery in the region in 1839. James sent for his three younger brothers, Daniel, Edwin and William, in 1841. In 1844, shipping problems and the encroachment of the Ohio River caused them to move to Birmingham, Pennsylvania, now part of Pittsburgh.

Although Edwin did not establish his own pottery at Canton Avenue in Baltimore, Maryland, until 1845, he was living there as early as 1844. So it seems that he never worked at the Birmingham pottery. Baltimore offered convenient sources of local clays, and more importantly, a port. The first productions were of caneware, queensware and rockingham ware. In 1848, he was joined by his brother William, and the firm became E. & W. Bennett. The firm received a number of awards and was said to be the first quality pottery south of the Mason-Dixon line.

In 1855, William left the firm to join his brother Daniel at the Birmingham pottery. (James Bennett, in failing health, had retired the previous year.) During the Civil War, Bennett moved his family to safety in Philadelphia, partially suspending his business in order to visit them frequently. In 1864, the pottery experienced a severe fire, but business was resumed in 1865. In 1869, Edwin established a whiteware plant, for the production of china. He hired Philip Pointon to manage this new enterprise. In about 1876, Bennett established a roof tile manufactory – the first in Maryland.

In 1887, Bennett acquired the Chesapeake Pottery, formerly D. F. Haynes & Co. (see below). In 1890, the firm incorporated as Edwin Bennett Pottery Co. In 1890 and 1891, Edwin Bennett was the President of the United States Potters' Association.

By this time he was popularly regarded as the 'Father of the American Pottery Industry' (for which title there are several other contenders). He continued actively in the business until his death in 1908, at the age of ninety. The firm continued in operation until 1936.

The firm's rockingham wares with mottled green, brown and blue glazes have often been miscalled majolica. Barber mentions pieces of 'majolica' made by Bennett during the 1850s: 'a majolica bust of Washington ... a pair of mottled majolica vases, two feet in height with raised grape-vine designs and lizard handles ... an enormous octagonal majolica pitcher, with blue, brown, and olive mottled glazes ...'

These early pieces were modelled by Charles Coxon, their chief designer and modeller for at least a few years early in the decade. Coxon came from England, with a 'Fortune Teller' relief-moulded jug, dated May 1849, which he displayed as an example of his skill. This would have been the 'Hecate' jug, with a fortune-telling or cup-tossing scene, published by Edward Walley, Villa Pottery, Cobridge, in May 1849. According to R. K. Henrywood, this scene was derived from a painting by N. J. Crowley, which was engraved by C. W. Sharpe and published under the title 'Cup Tossing' in the *Art Union* for April 1846. Henrywood illustrates both the jug and the engraving. Thus, Coxon may have worked for Walley in Cobridge.

The famous Marine Pitcher designed by Coxon falls into the category of a relief-moulded jug, rather than majolica. So far as can be determined, this piece was an original Coxon design. Coxon left Bennett sometime in the 1850s. He managed the Swan Hill Pottery at South Amboy, New Jersey, for about a year and a half *c.*1859. Sometime after 1863, he established Coxon & Co., in partnership with J. F. Thompson in Trenton.

The actual majolica production of the Bennett pottery began much later. In 1878, Philip Pointon, who had left Bennett to work in Canada in 1870, returned to make trial glazes and firings with the aim of producing majolica similar to 'ancient wares'. The popular Sunflower pattern, which was given away as premiums by the Price Baking Powder Co., was patented in the U.S. in 1873 (a jug is illustrated in Marks, 1983). Although the Sunflower pieces are generally regarded as majolica, they were apparently not considered such by Bennett. In fact, the pieces seem to be painted with enamels, rather than majolica glazes. Some ten years later, *Crockery and Glass Journal*, 6 December 1883, reported, 'We saw at this pottery two or three sets of fancy jugs, one ornamented with a sunflower, another with a rose in relief, intended for decoration after the manner of the very popular Avalon ware of Messrs. D. F. Haynes & Co.'

Jervis reported that they made 'an excellent reproduction of the cauliflower teapot'. which might be regarded as majolica. An exhibition held by the Maryland Historical Society in 1973 included the following pieces of majolica:

*Cigar Holder.* Majolica glaze, net, fish, and foliage with basket, wood trunk, and brick box for holding cigars and matches. Penciled on base: 'Nov. 6, 1884'. Stamped on base: '100'.

*Jardinière and Pedestal.* Light blue majolica glaze, scalloped-rim jardinière with all-over scroll design in relief, pedestal with three scroll feet and beading. *c.*1879–80.

XIV. Minton pedestals, one with impressed mark, shape number 2227 and date code 41880. Height 95.3 cm. *Sotheby's*

XV. Passion flower dish, Salopian Art Pottery. Diameter 35.5 cm. Clive House Museum, Shrewsbury. *Photo by Richard Bishop*

XVI. Terrarium, Salopian Art Pottery. Height 45.5 cm. Clive House Museum, Shrewsbury. *Photo by Richard Bishop*

*Pitcher and Bowl.* Multi-coloured majolica glaze bas-relief decoration, wheat and leaves, yellow twisted rope at rim and base, pitcher glazed blue on interior, bowl glazed pink. Pitcher marked on base: 'B'.

*Jardinière.* Majolica salmon-colored glaze, decoration in relief, flowers and scrolls, scalloped rim, originally had pedestal. *c.*1869–80.

*Griffin Fern Stand.* 'Robin's Egg Blue' majolica glaze on white clay body, trefoil planter with liner on pedestal base, three scroll feet, elaborately modeled griffins mounted on each foot, embossed repeating motif at rim, decorative treatment throughout. *c.*1898. Designed by Mr. Herbert M. Beattie. Exhibited at the Louisiana Purchase Exposition, St. Louis, April 2, 1904 through December 1, 1904.

However, regarding this last piece, in 1893, Barber wrote, 'One of the most striking pieces of his more recent work, is a large majolica jardinière, three feet in height consisting of a trefoil basin supported by three griffins. This was designed and modeled by Mr. Herbert W. Beattie of Quincy Mass., and is produced in robin's-egg blue, lemon and other colours.' This would place the date of the piece a little before 1893. It is intriguing to conjecture whether or not this Herbert Beattie might have been a relative of William Beattie, who designed and modelled majolica for Wedgwood (see Appendix C).

None of the pieces listed above is clearly marked, but that may be because they were pieces handed down within the family, rather than pieces that had actually been prepared for the market. However, the Sunflower pieces are marked BENNETT'S PATENT, sometimes with the date JAN. 23, 1873. The firm had several other marks which were associated with ivory wares or stone china.

After 1893, the firm started the production of art pottery. The Brubensul line was introduced the following year. It consisted of highly glazed majolica art pottery with flowing glazes of brown, orange, red, crimson and green. The name is a combination of Brunt, Bennett and Sullivan, the foremost figures at the pottery. Large items such as pedestals and jardinières were specialities. Brubensul pieces were generally marked with a paper label, featuring a globe run through with a sword.

## D. F. HAYNES

The Chesapeake Pottery was established in Baltimore in 1880 or 1881 by John Tunstall, Henry Brougham and Isaac Brougham, three Englishmen who had been working in American potteries for some years. They made yellow ware and rockingham glazed ware. David Francis Haynes, who had for many years been very successful in the business of jobbing crockery and glass, purchased the pottery in 1882. *Crockery and Glass Journal*, 5 January 1882, reported that the partnership between Haynes and George H. Miller, special partner, had expired, and that a new partnership had been formed. Haynes's new partners were Nelson Ramsay and, again, George H. Miller, who contributed $80,000 to the partnership. This massive sum was soon put to use, for two weeks later the same journal announced the purchase of the Chesapeake Pottery by Haynes.

## NEW WARES
# CHESAPEAKE POTTERY,
### BALTIMORE, MD.

Cheap and Beautiful.

Entirely New Decorations.

BRAMBLE LEMONADE BOWL —Five Sizes.

**Clifton Ware, Avalon Ware, Ivory Ware, Cecil Ware, Parian Ware.**

The high degree of success attained in the manufacture of these Wares has never been equaled in the history of American Potting.

**SEND ORDER FOR SAMPLE LOT.**

## D. F. HAYNES & CO., SOLE PROPRIETORS.

Haynes immediately enlarged the works to six kilns, and installed improved machinery, doubling its capacity. As he would often do over the years, he enlisted the services of English experts. Lewis Toft, for many years with William Brownfield in Cobridge, and with Ott & Brewer since arriving in America, took charge of the bodies, glazes and kilns. Frederick Hackney, formerly of Wedgwood and then proprietor of his own firm, F. Hackney & Co., which specialized in majolica (see Appendix A), took charge of the artistic department. *Crockery and Glass Journal,* 20 July 1882, reported:

> Mr. Frederick Hackney … has for months been preparing his molds for the various lines of ware, experimenting with colors and materials, and putting things in shape to show some new and beautiful goods as soon as matters are fully under way.

The article was also at pains to point out that Mr. Haynes had 'personally prepared many of the designs for fancy ware which will be made by the firm'. On 14 September 1882, the same journal reported, 'At the Chesapeake the men were hard at work, drawing the first glost kiln and the majolica painters busy putting on the fancy touches to a great variety of jugs, vases and sets intended to make a display in the trade procession of the Oriole festival.' (The oriole is the state bird of Maryland.) The firm met with great success, and *Crockery and Glass Journal,* 13 May 1883, explained:

The long experience of this firm in jobbing goods, combined with the good taste of the senior partner who designs and also personally supervises the production of all the new patterns, enables the Chesapeake to produce something that will sell and that the public wants every time.

Until 1887, they operated under the style of D. F. Haynes & Co. In that year, due to financial difficulties, the pottery was put up for sale, and purchased by Edwin Bennett (see above), operating under the style Chesapeake Pottery Co. In 1890, Bennett sold his interest to his son E. Huston Bennett and D. F. Haynes. They operated as Haynes, Bennett & Co. The younger Bennett retired in 1895, selling his interest to Frank R. Haynes, son of D. F. Haynes. In 1896, the firm changed its name to D. F. Haynes & Son. D. F. Haynes died in 1908, and his son carried on the firm until it closed in 1914.

Their most famous lines of ware were Clifton Decor, Avalon Faience and Calvertine, although they made many other wares, such as Cecil, a combination of two bodies, dry and white; and Parian. The Clifton and some of the Avalon wares surpassed the Wedgwood majolica argenta wares they copied. Clifton patterns included Blackberry and Fruit. They made push-up tobacco humidors for Sunny Tobacco made by Spaulding & Merrick of Chicago, presumably to be given as premiums. They made advertising wares for a number of other firms as well.

Avalon was one of the titles of Lord Baltimore, and the name of an estate held by him in Nova Scotia. The name was chosen because the Avalon ware was produced entirely from materials found in Maryland. *Crockery and Glass Journal*, 31 August 1882, reported:

> The color of the ware is a very light cream or ivory tone, the body dense and compact, and free from all impurities or discolorations, and the glaze so well suited to it as to be a part of it. It will be worked only in embossed patterns showing strong relief and admirably suited to the rich and striking decoration that will be worked on the whole line of ware. Six sizes of bramble jugs, teapots and sugars of the same design, cake plates and pickles of very attractive shapes, a very handsome line of vases, comports, salads and lemonade bowls, and many other useful and beautiful articles are coming through and will be added to continually, as the pottery has had three first-class modelers at work, with a large staff of mold makers, and will have something new on the tapis all the time.

On 14 September 1882, the same reporter wrote:

> … stole a good look at a large rustic lemonade bowl just finished, which sent visions of family gatherings and cooling beverages floating through his brain. This bowl was in their ivory body, with rustic ground, embellished with a rich cluster on each side of blackberry leaves and fruit in neutral colors warmed up with rich autumnal tints, and finished at top and bottom with a knotted stick border in like shades, making a very beautiful effect.

Lemonade bowls were, in fact, punch bowls, but in response to the pressures of the temperance movement, the industry had rechristened them.

As described previously, the majolica craze waned during the 1880s. In 1886, Haynes introduced Buttercup ware. Their advertisement in *Crockery and Glass*

*Journal,* 5 August 1886, explained, 'This ware while designed to take the place of Majolica does not resemble it in any way.'

Most Chesapeake majolica seems to have borne printed marks as follows:

## JAMES CARR

James Carr was born in Hanley, Staffordshire, in 1820. He began working in the potteries at the age of ten, serving his apprenticeship to John Ridgway at the Cauldon Place Works, Shelton. He then worked for James Clews at Cobridge. James Carr emigrated to America in 1844. For the next eight years, he worked for the American Pottery Manufacturing Co. at the Jersey City Pottery, as had James Bennett before him (see above). During Carr's tenure there, they made yellow ware and rockingham wares, flint and buff stonewares, white earthenware relief-moulded jugs, cream earthenware with sponged decoration and transfer-printed earthenware. However, they only produced white earthenware from 1850 to 1854, and this limited repertoire may have been an inducement for Carr to leave them in 1852.

In that year, he entered partnership with Thomas Locker and Enoch Moore at the Swan Hill Pottery in South Amboy, New Jersey. The Swan Hill Pottery had been established in 1849 by Sparks & Moore, who manufactured rockingham ware and yellow ware. In 1850, the venture was taken over by Hanks & Fish, who soon abandoned it. James Carr then rented the pottery from Charles Fish. Carr later described it as 'a little pottery' which 'had only one small ten foot-six kiln' (*Pottery & Porcelain of New Jersey*). The pottery burnt down on 9 August 1854, but was rebuilt. By this time, Locker had left the partnership. Carr left in December 1855. Two pieces attributed to James Carr during his sojourn at South Amboy are a fish-shaped buff stoneware foot warmer and a tall buff stoneware candlestick, both with reddish brown and mottled yellow rockingham glaze. The Swan Hill Pottery was particularly known for druggists' ware, including blue dome-top jars.

In December 1855, Carr moved to New York City, where he remained (barring a brief hiatus in Trenton during 1879, described below) until 1888. In 1856, he formed a partnership with Morrison. The partners built a pottery on 442–452 West 13th Street, not far from Ninth Avenue, in 1856. Ketchum says the firm was first known as Carr & Smith and then as Morrison, Carr & Smith, and finally as Morrison & Carr. After Morrison left in 1871, Carr continued as sole partner. In any case, he had always been the driving force in the partnership. Apparently there were rumours of difficulties in September 1883, because *Crockery and Glass Journal* reported:

A note from Mr. James Carr informs us that he has not left his old pottery on the Astor estate, in this city, but remains in full blast, and expects to continue. He further stated, 'It is true that I bought an interest in a small works for one of my sons, but things not being as satisfactory as I would like, I expect to sell said interest.'

Unfortunately, nothing more is known about this small works. Carr continued to run his business until 1888, when he retired. The *Crockery and Glass Journal* published his memoirs in 1901. He died, much honoured and frequently called the 'Father of American Pottery', in 1904.

Originally, Morrison & Carr made only white wares, but Carr had a passionate interest in developing new bodies and glazes. According to Ramsay, majolica was manufactured from 1858, which is very early for an American potter. Although it has been written that Carr discontinued majolica production after the departure of Morrison in 1871, he exhibited a representative sample at the United States Potters' Association exhibition at the Philadelphia Centennial in 1876. He also exhibited Parian ware, pâte-sur-pâte, granite ware and painted plaques. According to J. G. Stradling, majolica exhibited at the Centennial included:

> ... garden vases and seats in majolica. These vases are in the shape of immense water lilies, colored in the richest hues, and the seats are ornamental on the sides with boys bird-nesting in the regular school-boy style ... The garden seats and pedestals are also very handsome. The former are appropriately 'rustic', while the latter are eminently patriotic, being decorated with the celebrated scene of Washington Crossing the Delaware.

There was a furore when Carr did not win a medal, and an appeal resulted in his being awarded a gold medal after a reassessment by Judge Arthur Beckwith. Among other laudatory remarks, Beckwith commended, 'The majolica is well fired and coated with an excellent glaze of great hardness and transparency.'

In 1877, Carr received a gold medal at the American Institute Fair. *Crockery and Glass Journal*, 4 October 1877, described the majolica in his display:

> In majolica there is a great profusion of specimens, such as pedestals, pitchers, vases, etc. The prevailing style in the majority of these is 'rustic', and their coloring and finish is very little, if at all, inferior to the imported goods of the same kind. One quaint jug or pitcher attracts considerable attention. The handle is formed by an inebriated-looking individual in a white hat, who gazes longingly into the depths of the interior. What is he looking for is explained by a white label on the body of the pitcher, bearing the mystic word 'Whisky' ... Two of the small majolica vases show a successful venture into the field of humor, their bodies being each upheld by a row of energetic bull-frogs. These may be said to be in the French style.

Carr also exhibited at the Paris Exhibition of 1878. A Cauliflower Teapot was among the items he exhibited, winning a silver medal, the highest prize given to any American manufacturer. In 1879, Jennie Young said that his majolica 'is made into a great variety of forms – jars, pedestals, seats, boxes, and cups, the leading colors of which are a clear deep blue, yellow and green.' Aside from the Cauliflower ware, Carr is known to have produced Shell pattern, similar to Wedgwood's. The Carr examples are distinguished by iridescent seaweed and pink, yellow and brown edged shells. The JC monogram with which he marked some of his wares could conceivably be confused with George Jones's mark.

In 1879, James Carr bought the International Pottery Company (the Old Speeler Pottery) in Trenton, New Jersey, and took in as partners Edward Clark, newly arrived from Burslem, and John and James Moses. They traded as the Lincoln Pottery Company, but were also known as Carr & Clark. A few months later, the pottery was purchased by William Burgess and John H. Campbell, who once again traded as the International Pottery Company. *Crockery and Glass Journal*, 17 June 1880 reported that Clark returned to England 'with the expressed intention of returning to this country for the purpose of manufacturing china from American materials.' Upon his return to New Jersey, Clark formed a partnership with John Tams. Carr continued his business in New York.

Although Carr & Clark made primarily cream-coloured and white granite wares, they appear to have made some majolica: an unmarked pitcher with brown glaze and a rose lining, 'slightly concave cylindrical form, rustic handle; relief decoration of leaves and flowers in greens and pinks', attributed to them was displayed by the Newark Museum in 1947, a gift of Mrs. M. E. Clark and her brother Mr. Carr. It is highly unlikely that any Carr & Clark majolica would be marked.

# CHAPTER SIX

# CONTINENTAL MAJOLICA

A lthough certain pieces of majolica imitated Italian Renaissance wares, Palissy wares and the lead-glazed French wares of the early nineteenth century, the majolica wares as a genre were a new melange of styles and techniques. After Minton's resounding success with majolica at the London Exhibition of 1862, the race was on amongst the continental manufacturers to produce their own majolica. As in England, the manufacturers ranged from the large, established firms who included it as just one more range of wares among many, to smaller potteries who specialized in this new genre.

The Italians have more or less consistently produced maiolica based closely on the Renaissance wares down to the present day. However, in the middle of the nineteenth century, they experienced an enormous resurgence in demand for their traditional wares, which they made in profusion. An account of the Italian National Exhibition in Milan in *Crockery and Glass Journal*, 4 August 1881, reports:

> Of late the Florence potters have taken to the manufacture of imitation antiques, and they are turning out lots of goods in this line ... The imitation is so perfect that I fancy a collection of bogus goods labelled well back from the nineteenth century would pass without question for a collection of veritable antiques.

With this large and lucrative trade, the Italians felt no need to experiment with the English-style majolica. Reproduction maiolica was exhibited at the Philadelphia Centennial Exhibition in 1876 by G. Ascione & Son, Naples; Benucci & Latti, Pesaro; Jafet Torelli, Florence; Torquato Castellani, Rome; The Farina Company, Faenza; and Cesare Miliani, Ancona. A. Castellani of Rome also exhibited a 'valuable, interesting, and instructive collection of early lustred wares and Italian majolica, systematically arranged, commencing with the Sicilian-Arab period and continuing until the time of the Abruzzi painted wares.'

Bernard Palissy is discussed in detail in Chapter One. It is mentioned there that during the second quarter of the nineteenth century there were a number of potters reviving his style and techniques. The most notable of these was Charles Avisseau. Other makers of nineteenth-century French Palissy wares included Victor Barbizet, George Pull, Thomas-Victor Sergent, Auguste Chauvigne and Alfred Renolleau.

Quite a few French firms also made imitation maiolica, but apparently majolica really took Paris by storm in the 1870s. A reporter for *Crockery and Glass Journal*,

23 September 1880, recounted:

> A few days ago I took a walk around the 'Exposition des Arts Decoratifs', at the Palais
> de l'Industrie, which is now open, although not fully installed, and I was surprised to
> find that the ceramic art was represented in very little else but majolica, of which the
> display is splendid – the work being artistic, and the effects produced very striking.

For the most part, however, the continental manufacturers imitated the English majolica which they had seen at the international exhibitions. These wares sold particularly well in the American market, where it was rightly recognized that they offered exceptional quality for less cost than the English wares did.

The largest continental producers were Sarraguemines, and Villeroy & Boch. Because these two continued to produce majolica in the twentieth century, their majolica wares are sometimes dismissed as modern. In fact, both firms took up the challenge in the 1860s and produced a great variety of high-quality majolica during the nineteenth century. Their lead was followed by a great many smaller manufacturers throughout Europe. As in Britain, many of these lesser factories left their wares unmarked in the hopes that they might be mistaken for those of the major firms, or at the behest of retailers who wished to affix their own marks or labels.

As we saw in Chapter One, British majolica was greatly inspired by the historical wares from the continent. Surprisingly, the continental firms largely ignored their own historical precedents to copy British copies of continental wares. This explains to some degree the lack of vigour and originality usually associated with the continental majolica. It also explains the lack of regional differences among the continental wares. Another explanation for the homogeneity of the continental majolica is that both Sarraguemines and Villeroy & Boch made majolica at more than one factory. Most notably, Villeroy & Boch produced majolica at factories in Septfontaines, Schramberg, Wallerfangen, Mettlach and Dresden.

Continental majolica can be seen as a stylistically coherent group of wares, not just a designation of geographical convenience. Overall, it can be said that the wares were well potted, crisply moulded and the glazes good, tending to be thick and glossy. The colours are generally clear and a shade darker than those of British wares. There is a distinctive yellow of the sort today called 'gold', which is often found on continental majolica, especially that of Villeroy & Boch. As the briefest glance at an historical map of Europe will show, borders shifted, and several of the potteries here discussed have changed nationality. To lessen confusion, the potteries are discussed according to their nationality at the present time.

## GERMANY

**VILLEROY & BOCH** (also Luxembourg and France)
This partnership was established in 1836 to co-ordinate the operation of the creamware factories of Nicolas Villeroy and Jean-François Boch. During the course of the next 150 years, the firm would acquire several more factories and produce an astonishing array of high-quality wares.

Villeroy had been making creamware at Vaudrevange (later to become Wallerfangen) since 1787. After 1815, they had specialized in transfer-printed utilitarian wares. As the century progressed the factory became ever more prominent, but suffered when the town stopped being served by rail in 1860.

Boch had been making creamware at the Septfontaines, Luxembourg, factory since the eighteenth century. During the nineteenth century, the factory declined in importance, as Mettlach and Vaudrevange became the primary Villeroy & Boch operations. Earthenwares which have since been termed majolica were made at the Septfontaines factory between 1840 and 1875. Judging from the wares of this factory included in the catalogue of the exhibition *Villeroy & Boch, 1748–1930* at the Rijksmuseum, Amsterdam in 1977–8, these wares properly belong to the class of lead-glazed French earthenwares which had influenced early English majolica. They are very different from those produced at the Schramberg factory, for instance.

Boch had also been making creamware at the factory at Mettlach in the Saar basin since its establishment in 1809. During the nineteenth century, Mettlach became the most important of the Villeroy & Boch factories, best known for their stoneware. The factory at Dresden was opened in 1856.

The Schramberg factory in south-western Württemburg, which had been operating since 1820, was acquired by Villeroy & Boch in 1883. It seems to have been the largest majolica producer. The vast majority of Villeroy & Boch pieces found today bear the Schramberg mark. Those marked 'Made in Germany' date from after 1888. The factory closed in 1912. An article about the factory in *The Artist*, 1 October 1883, states: 'The manufacture of majolica ware has of late been taken up, and the goods produced have great artistic merit.... The models used in the majolica embrace Renaissance as well as modern styles.' None the less, majolica had been made at the factory during the time of Uechtritz and Faist (see below). As late as 1904 (at the St. Louis Exhibition), Villeroy & Boch were still exhibiting majolica.

The Villeroy & Boch majolica is well potted and crisply moulded. The glaze is thick and seldom crazed, although it is not unusual to find signs of wear on the raised surfaces. For the most part the colours are clear and true, with botanical subjects naturalistically coloured. Thus, many pieces are appealing even to those who do not care for most majolica.

Commonly found patterns include lilacs, hazelnuts, buttercups, leaves, lilies of the valley, violets, waterlilies, marsh plants and sunflowers. The Lilac pattern (Plate XI) is one of their most beautiful designs. *Japonisme* is evident in the Bamboo Fan with Butterfly design (Plate 7) which can be found in both polychrome and green glazes.

The two leaf dishes illustrated in Plate 60 are of particular interest. The small pickle dish was made at Septfontaines by Boch Bros. *c.*1813–25. It is a beautifully moulded, light creamware with gold, green and cobalt glazes. The larger dish was made by Villeroy & Boch at Schramberg during the 1880s. A similarity of shape can be seen, but the later piece is heavily potted, and is, in all, less attractive. This, then, is a majolica leaf copied not from an English example, but from a Boch creamware leaf, which was in turn, a copy of eighteenth-century English creamware.

*60. Two Villeroy & Boch leaf dishes. Right: Impressed Schramberg mark, shape number 20/3. Length 23 cm. Left: Impressed 'BOCH A LUXEMBOURG' around the letter 'T'. Length 18 cm.* Author's collection

A good deal of Villeroy & Boch majolica is marked. Most pieces have the impressed Schramberg mark. Later pieces (*c.*1888–1910) have MADE IN GERMANY impressed in a circle around the mark. It seems that all Villeroy & Boch majolica bears an impressed pattern number. These are usually fractional pattern numbers, such as 1241/7, but some pieces have been noted with four-digit numbers alone. The pieces most frequently found are dessert wares, especially plates. Comports and two-handled dishes are not uncommonly seen as well.

*(c.1883–90)*

### GEORG SCHMIDER

The firm of Georg Schmider at Zell Harmersbach, Baden, is still in operation, but their current pottery designs do not fall within the majolica genre. The history of the Schmider firm is confused by the fact that there are, in fact, two factories, known

*61. Georg Schmider Waterlily Plate. Impressed 'S' and shape number '806'.
Diameter 23 cm.* Author's collection

respectively as the *Obere Fabrik* and the *Untere Fabrik*. The *Obere Fabrik* was first established in 1794. After 1842, this was a porcelain works, and it was purchased by Georg Schmider, son of the Zell Postmaster, in 1907. The history of the *Untere Fabrik* begins in 1859. In 1890, Georg Schmider became a partner in this pottery, and by 1898 he was the sole owner. It was here that the majolica was probably made.

The Schmider majolica thus probably dates from the 1890s, although it is quite possible that he was continuing patterns introduced by the former owners of the works. The author has found four patterns to date. All have impressed pattern

*62. Georg Schmider Art Nouveau Waterlily Plate. Printed mark. Diameter 23 cm.* Author's collection

numbers: Dandelion (722), Waterlily (988), Iris & Tulips (723) and Waterlilies (2474). This last is an Art Nouveau design, which dates from the twentieth century. No doubt there are many, many more patterns to be identified. The mark illustrated here appears on the Art Nouveau plate along with an impressed 2474. The other pieces bear only a large incised S, along with pattern numbers.

(1930–)

108

*63. Georg Schmider Dandelion Plate. Impressed 'S' and shape number '722'.
Diameter 23 cm.* Author's collection

## UECHTRITZ & FAIST (Schramberg)

The Schramberg factory was probably the largest German producer of majolica. The factory was established in 1820 by Isidor Faist. Originally making ordinary chinaware and stoneware, the production of porcelains was added in 1856; and majolica by 1880. According to *Crockery and Glasss Journal*, 21 December 1882: 'The models used in the majolicas embrace many of the Renaissance as well as modern styles...' At this time the firm was known as Uechtritz & Faist, Faist being a nephew of the founder. On 31 March 1882, the same journal reported:

In the [majolica] productions of this factory there are many new effects on the color of the enamels that create a balanced confusion in the eye, and impress one with the idea that they are more costly than they are.

Yet on 8 February 1883, the journal announced:

Mechtritz [sic] & Faist, manufacturers of majolica, Schramberg, Wurtemberg, Germany, whose failure was announced more than a month ago, appear to be in a bad way. It is reported in a recent German print that some of the members of the firm have been arrested for alleged fraud and their books and papers have been taken posession of by the courts. The amount of the liabilities is placed at 500,000 marks, and it looks as if next to nothing would be realized.

In 1883, the factory was acquired by Villeroy & Boch, who continued to produce majolica there (see above). There are no recorded marks.

## OTHER GERMAN MANUFACTURERS

J. VON SCHWARZ of Nuremberg is said to have made charming majolica from 1880. In 1902, Jervis described him as:

... a manufacturer of fine majolica, whose artistic treatment has done much to restore the disrepute into which majolica had fallen. Some of his color schemes are equally beautiful and/or grand, the colors often of technical difficulty, realized with a brillancy which is truly wonderful. Dr. Richard Lindhurst is the director.

Unfortunately, nothing else is written about the firm and their wares are unknown to the author. It is to be hoped that the illustration of the firm's mark will bring some to light.

*J. von Schwarz (c.1880)*

The porcelain and stoneware factory at HORNBERG, Baden, was established in 1832, and according to Danckert, was still in operation as late as 1880. In 1906, the SCHWARZWALDER-STEINGUTFABRIK was established. The author has seen any number of majolica plates with marks from both the earlier and later concern. These are undistinguished but of fairly good quality, most often bearing the Greek key bordered leaf & fern pattern (Plate 3). One of the several elaborate marks often found on Hornberg majolica is this printed one.

*Hornberg (1906–)*

According to Danckert, OTTO HERMANN SPINDLER made majolica at Frauenwald, Thuringia.

## FRANCE

### SARRAGUEMINES

The Sarraguemines pottery was established in 1784 by Nicholas-Henri Jacobi and André Fabry, a tobacco dealer in Strasbourg. After Jacobi's death his brother took over with dismal results. In 1798, Fabry regained control and summoned Francis-Paul Utzschneider, an old colleague from Strasbourg, to his assistance. At the time of Utzschneider's arrival the faiencerie had only two employees; within a year, it

*64. Typical Sarraguemines Berry Bowl. Diameter 18.5 cm.* Author's collection

had over 100. Between 1836 and 1859, the faiencerie was run by the Baron A. de Geiger, and then by his son. In 1860, Auguste Jaunes, former Director of Vaudrevange (see Villeroy & Boch above), became Director at Sarraguemines, assisted by his three sons. In 1874, as a result of the Treaty of Frankfurt, after the Franco-Prussian War, Sarraguemines became German territory and the factories at Digoin and Vitry-le-François were established in order to maintain the firm's claim to French nationality.

*The Pottery and Glass Trades' Review,* November 1877, noted that Utzschneider & Company employed 4–5000 hands at the manufactories at Sarraguemines, Limoges and Digoin. They also reported:

65. *Sarraguemines covered jug.* Friends of Time Antiques, Madison, Conn.

> Their designs in majolica are frequently original, but also reproductions of classical subjects, and present some specimens of bold modelling and moulding. Mazarine blue is a difficult colour to govern, but this firm has reproduced it on earthenware and majolica in an almost faultless manner. We believe goods in this branch of faience are now sold by English makers at much reduced prices; but we imagined that they had a very serious opponent to contend with in this eminent house … This firm has long held a front rank for its designs in trinket sets, flowerpots and vases, which are by no means of such trivial importance as might be supposed…. The bric-a-brac pieces in majolica and earthenware are numerous and well suited for china dealers during their approaching season.

Sarraguemines's most popular pattern was relief-moulded fruit on a background of yellow leaves (Plate 64). This was made in both fruit and dessert sets well into the twentieth century. Tureens formed as baskets of strawberries or pansies are also frequently seen. Sarraguemines was well known for character jugs, which displayed either the full figures or the heads of the subjects. They also produced elaborate pieces such as inlaid table tops. In 1902, Jervis noted that they produced majolica, 'principally in large pedestals and vases'.

Sarraguemines majolica usually bears an impressed SARRAGUEMINES or SARRAGUEMINES MAJOLICA. FRANCE was added after 1890. One can also find a wealth of other impressed information, presumably pattern and shape numbers, and a painted decorator's mark.

### H. BOULENGER

H. Boulenger et Cie., Choisy-le-Roi, Seine, made a large variety of majolica. There

XVII. Majolica columns designed by James Gamble and executed by Minton, Hollins & Co. in 1867. The Gamble Room, Victoria & Albert Museum. *Tony Herbert*

XVIII. Craven, Dunnill bar front. The Red Lion, Erdington, Birmingham. *c.*1890. *Tony Herbert*

XIX. *Left:* Maw & Co. tile from the billiard room at 12 Kensington Palace Gardens. *c.*1864. *Right:* A replacement tile *c.*1982. Note how the lead glazes on the original are richer and more lustrous than the lead-free glazes on the modern reproduction. *Tony Herbert*

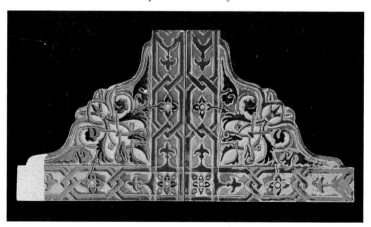

XX. Maw & Co. majolica tile. 23 cm square. *Tony Herbert*

XXI. Maw & Co. majolica tile panel. *c.*1875. *Tony Herbert*

was a porcelain factory established here in 1785, but pottery was not made until 1804. In 1836, the factory was taken over by H. Hautin and L. Boulenger. In 1863, the firm became H. Boulenger (presumably Hippolyte Boulenger was the son of the previous owner). Lesur reports that in 1869 there were four kilns working and the firm employed 250 men and 50 women. Boulenger was particularly known for the schools, savings banks, mutual benefit societies, etc., which he founded for his workers. His display at the Paris Exhibition of 1878 received two gold medals, one diploma of honour, one medal of progress and a special proposition from the jury for a higher compensation. From 1887 to 1907, Ernest Chaplet made art pottery in a studio at the factory, but this does not fall into the genre of majolica. In 1902, Jervis noted:

> Messrs. H. Boulanger [sic] & Co. have a large factory there under the control of the Comptoir Céramique, and produce a large variety of decorated earthenware which is favourably known in this country. The large fountain they exhibited at the Paris Exhibition attracted deserved attention, as did also some beautifully painted tile panels. Many of their colored glazes are really charming.

In the early years their lead glazes were soft and easily chipped and crazed. They later introduced borax into the glazes, which became harder. Boulenger was one of the factories to buy the *émaux ombrants* moulds from the Rubelles factory on its closure in 1867. The most commonly seen *émail ombrant* pieces are turquoise glazed tiles with japonesque designs, such as flying cranes. It is likely that the moulds for these designs were made by Choisy-le-Roi themselves, as *japonisme* did not really take hold until the 1870s. In *trompe-l'oeil*, they made a speciality of asparagus and oyster plates. They also made pots in the form of ducks and pigs, Palissy ware and an abundance of the more ordinary majolica, such as leaf dishes and rustic flower pots. The pieces are often marked H B & Cie CHOISY LE ROY or with a variation on the following:

## GIEN

The faiencerie at Gien was founded in 1821 by an Englishman, Thomas Antoine Edme Hulm, known as Hall, who was already proprietor of the faiencerie at Montereau. Gien was an attractive spot due to the proximity of the forest of Orleans for fuel, and the Loire, whose waters provided transport and whose banks provided clay. Hall's plan was to make creamware to compete with the English products flooding the French market. He was not successful, and the firm was dissolved in 1826. Over the next fifty years, the pottery would be owned by five successive partnerships. The definitive history of the factory, *Gien Faience* by Roger Bernard and Jean-Claude Renard, recounts these in detail.

The pottery is best known for its reproductions of eighteeenth-century French faience, but they also made some majolica. Michele-Cécile Gillard's *Faience de*

*Gien: Formes et Décors,* and Bernard and Renard illustrate a number of pieces of majolica, mostly influenced by Italian maiolica. They exhibited some of these, influenced by Faenza and Urbino, at the Paris exhibition in 1855, winning a bronze medal. The most spectacular piece of 'modern' majolica Gillard illustrates is the Elephant Clock modelled by Ulysse Bertrand. Resting on a Chinese fretwork stand in cobalt blue, the elephant bears a clock mounted in the howdah on his back. At his side, stands a Nubian, who pulls at the tail of a monkey perched on the elephant's head. This piece personifies all that is best in majolica, stunning true coloured glazes, exquisite modelling and a bit of whimsy.

The firm used a number of variations on this printed mark:

## OTHER FRENCH FIRMS

EMILE GALLÉ (1846–1904) is best known today as one of the principal figures of the French Art Nouveau movement, and founder of the Nancy school in 1901. This style is generally dated from 1884, and Gallé specialized in glass, and later, furniture. He was, however, trained as a potter at his father's faiencerie at Nancy, and quite a number of signed pieces from this period survive. *Crockery and Glass Journal,* 23 September 1883, described his display at the Exposition des Arts Décoratifs: '[E. Gallé] confines his attention principally to Barbotine ware, which consists of a majolica body, upon which are painted in enamel subjects of various styles, in a most artistic and effective manner.' Pieces may be signed E. Gallé.

BOURG-LA-REINE, Hauts-de-Seine, established in 1772, is best known as a centre of soft-paste porcelain manufacture, but it also produced large quantities of faience. Laurin took over the factory *c.*1850, and was joined by Ernest Chaplet in 1853 or 1857. In 1872, they produced a renowned barbotine, as well as painted earthenware. By painting with coloured slip, Chaplet hoped to imitate the effects of oil painting on pottery. However, probably due to the mediocrity of the painting, the barbotine was not successful, and Chaplet left to join Haviland in 1874. Chaplet decorated some pieces in the style of the Italian Renaissance, but it was after his departure that Laurin made most of its majolica. These pieces are heavy and crudely decorated, but have their charms. The factory closed in 1910. Marks used are variations on B. la R.

Majolica was also made at the POTERIE CAFFIN in Cauderan, Bordeaux. In fact, it appears to have been the sole product from the works' establishment in 1882 until Victor Caffin was succeeded by Grenier, who closed in 1913. Caffin used this mark:

(c.1882)

The factory at LUNÉVILLE, Meurthe-et-Moselle, has a long and distinguished history. There was a pottery at Lunéville as early as 1605, but the present concern dates back to about 1723, when it was established by Jacques Chambrette. The factory passed through many hands during the next 250 years, but during the majolica period it was under the directorship of Germain Thomas and, subsequently, his son. Majolica played only a very small part in their productions, but they do seem to have made a fair amount of it, especially pieces such as asparagus plates, which the author has seen several times in the Paris flea market.

This author believes that the majolica figural jugs marked FRIE ONNAING are probably the work of the FABRIQUE MOUZIN FRÈRES ET CIE., at Onnaing (Nord). The factory was taken over by Mouzin about 1850, and specialized in transfer-printed creamware with relief-moulded borders. Mouzin controlled the firm at least as late as 1867. In the twentieth century the Faiencerie Onnaing was run by the Société Anonyme de la Faience.

Like the Lunéville factory, who produced much the same sort of wares, SAINT CLÉMENT has a long and distinguished history as a maker of traditional French faience. The factory was, in fact, established in 1758 by Jacques Chambret as a branch of the Lunéville concern. At the end of the nineteenth century they produced masses of majolica decorated with relief-moulded fruit. This ware is now being reproduced by the Société des Faienceries Guérin using the original moulds. They also made asparagus services. The early pieces are marked:

Majolica dessert services impressed SALINS are fairly commonly found. Bourgeois, Page et Cie. established a pottery at Salins, Jura, in 1876. However, it seems that they did not mark their goods. Therefore, it is likely that this majolica is the product of their successors RIGAL ET HAMELINE. The Société de Faiencerie de Salins has owned the pottery since 1950. The patterns are naturalistic, e.g. birds in a peach tree, or fruit scattered on basketweave. Salins also made figural jugs, most notably owls.

THOMAS-VICTOR SERGENT of Petit Montrouge, Paris (c.1870–85?), is best known for his imitation Palissy wares. These closely resembled the originals, but the glazes were thicker and glossier, and less prone to crazing. He exhibited at the International Exhibitions at Vienna in 1873 and Paris in 1878. He also exhibited a species of majolica at the Exposition des Arts Décoratifs in Paris in 1883. *Crockery and Glass Journal,* 23 September 1883, describes these:

> The body is majolica, and is decorated with raised flowers, most delicately modeled, considering the rough material employed; these are colored naturally, and produce a most effective appearance. It has a perfect command of the market, and fills the greater part of the windows of all Parisian shopkeepers.

## BELGIUM

An article in *Crockery and Glass Journal*, 12 August 1880, quotes an article in the *Staffordshire Advertiser* on Belgian ceramics: 'Our ceramic artists and earthenware manufacturers have nothing to fear from those of Belgium.' The author did go on to say that the Boch Bros. (see Villeroy & Boch above) proved an exception to this statement.

The same article describes the wares of 'the principal exhibitor of majolica ware', VICTOR PETERNICK of Tournai. '… [T]he ordinary earthenware of this firm like all the rest of the exhibition, is more or less of a character that shows disadvantageously with respect to form, finish, lightness and gracefulness by the side of our English products.' Peternick was probably a descendant of the Peternyck family who had been potting in Tournai since the Treaty of Aix-la-Chapelle in 1748. F. J. Peternyck, founder of the dynasty, also owned a factory in Lille, where he made soft-paste porcelains of the same sort he was to make in Tournai. After his death, in 1799, his son sold his interest in the porcelain works and acquired a newly established earthenware manufactory. Chaffers says of this works, '… although successful as a business enterprise, nothing of consequence from a collector's point of view has been produced.' This implies that the factory was still in operation at the time of writing (1863). Whether this is the same factory to which the 1880 account above alludes is not known.

LECAT ET CIE., Nimy-les-Mons, was a royal manufactory at the end of the nineteenth and beginning of the twentieth century. They seem to have made a wide variety of majolica including jugs, dessert services and fish jugs. An article in *The Pottery and Glass Trades' Review*, May 1879, said that they also produced white granite, porcelain, clay pipes and fire-proof articles. Their produce was principally sold in Belgium, but they also exported 'considerable quantities' to France, Germany and Holland. The author has seen pieces in England and in Zurich.

## CZECHOSLOVAKIA

Although countless pieces of majolica marked Czechoslovakia or Made in Czechoslovakia can be found, many made up to the present day, the author has only been able to identify five Czechoslovakian majolica manufacturers.

It seems that Bodenbach (now Padmokly) was a centre of majolica production. In 1902, Jervis noted that 'Messrs. Schillers & Sons and several other manufacturers of majolica are situated here.' However, this author has been unable to discover the names of the other manufactories. Founded *c*.1820, this firm was successively known as Schiller & Gerbing, F. Gerbing and, finally, W. SCHILLER & SONS. Originally a stoneware manufacturer, they seem to have made increasing amounts of majolica later in the nineteenth century. They also made white porcelain. The firm used a variety of marks incorporating WS & S.

A pottery was established in Kremnice, Körmöczbánya, then in Hungary, in 1800. After 1868, it was owned by JANOS KOSSUCH. The dish illustrated in Plate 66 is of exceptionally fine quality.

In 1883, C. RIESE founded a factory for porcelain, terracotta and majolica at Dux

*66. Körmöczbánya leaf tray. Impressed mark and shape number '6424'. Length 25 cm.* Author's collection

*Kremnice, Körmöczbánya, impressed (c.1868–90)*

(now Duchov), Bohemia. The firm displayed majolica at the St. Louis Exhibition of 1904. This firm should not be confused with the other factory at Dux, owned by E. Eichler, which made only porcelain, including the Royal Dux figures which are much collected these days.

H. E. PISTOR of Harda and Steinschönau, Bohemia, advertised in *Pottery Gazette* during 1883 as a 'manufacturer and importer of all kinds of glassware, china,

*67. Josef Steidl leaf plate. Impressed mark. Diameter 17.5 cm.*
Author's collection

majolica, fancy goods &c.' It is not known whether majolica was one of the goods he manufactured, or if he only imported it. No marks have been recorded.

The plate illustrated in Plate 67 is marked 'Josef Steidl, Znaim'. There seem to have been a number of potteries in Znaim (now Znojmo), but no other information about JOSEF STEIDL has been found. The plates are heavily potted, but crisply moulded. The combination of rich brown, green and cobalt glazes is particularly successful.

ALOIS KLAMMETH, also of Znaim, exhibited at the Centennial Exhibition in Philadelphia, 1876. The judges decided, 'The imitation majolica is of soft body and the decorations rather pale in color.' No mark has been recorded.

## HUNGARY

There were probably several majolica manufacturers in Hungary. According to Danckert both THEODOR HÜTTL at Budapest and WEISER & LÖWINGER at Iglo made majolica among their other wares. Gyorgy Domanovsky says that at one time there was a majolica manufactory at Tata. The craftsmen employed there were imported from Holics, a faience centre in the north, and elsewhere.

IGNAZ FISCHER founded his Budapest workshop in 1866. He had previously worked at the Herend porcelain works for his father-in-law, M. F. Fischer, one of the firm's founders. Ignaz Fischer's works are best known for their cream-coloured earthenware, imitating that produced at Herend. However, *Crockery and Glass Journal,* 13 May 1880, said that he 'produces the most charming majolicas of sacred and etruscan designs. The fireplaces, stoves and fountains of majolica are masterpieces of taste and originality.' There are no recorded marks.

## OTHER CONTINENTAL MANUFACTURERS

The GOLDSCHEIDERSCHE PORCELAIN WORKS AND MAJOLICA FACTORY in Vienna was founded in 1885 by Friedrich Goldscheider, and carried on by his widow. They made porcelain and pottery (both majolica and faience) and were known for their majolica mosaic tiles. In 1920, his sons took over the factory. They continued there until they fled Austria for the United States, at the time of the Second World War. They manufactured pottery figurines in Trenton, New Jersey, between 1943 and 1950.

There were several majolica producers in Switzerland during the nineteenth century, according to an article in *The Pottery and Glass Trades' Review,* June 1878. 'The production of Heimberg is a species of majolica, the glaze of which . . . is of a very friable nature. The designs are in most instances crude, although some specimens now exhibiting in Paris shew that the Switzer can produce some very creditable and artistic pieces when he is so inclined.' The three firms listed were EYER, CHRET; BENEDICHT KUNZI and T. SCHENK-TRAIHSEL.

MANUEL CYPRIANO GOMEZ MAFRA established a pottery at Caldas da Rainha, Portugal, in 1853. The firm later included Mafra's son, Cipriano Gomez Mafra, who took over in 1897. They made Toby jugs, figural jugs and Palissy ware. The Palissy ware is very well modelled, and glazed in characteristic golds, greys, blues, greens and browns. The backs are usually covered with mottled glazes. The *General Report of the Judges* for the Philadelphia Centennial Exhibition described his wares:

> A considerable collection of vases, dishes, baskets, animals, imitation Palissy pieces, etc. Well modeled from nature. A large circular dish, with various fish, etc., in full relief, is very good and cheap; also an oval dish with cray-fish is remarkably well modeled and manufactured; small imitation wicker-work baskets, very delicately and minutely executed. This exhibition is of original character, with good expression in the work. The prices are very low.

Pieces often bear this mark, which is sometimes almost indistinct. After 1890, pieces were marked with a printed PORTUGAL which may be difficult to read against the coloured glazes.

José Alves Cunha of Caldas, Oporto exhibited Palissy ware, figures, basket-work and grotesque teapots in '[d]esigns peculiar, sometimes humorous and attractive' at the Philadelphia Centennial Exhibition in 1876. These too were very cheap. The judges mention in their report that these Portuguese pieces were so cheap because the workers' wages were so low: 'men, from 30 to 60 cents per diem, the women, 10 cents; and the children 6 cents'.

Majolica, in imitation of the English wares, was made in Sweden by two manufacturers, both renowned for their porcelains. The Gustavsberg factory near Stockholm made majolica and Palissy ware from the 1860s. Per Palme illustrates two pieces from the Gustavsbergs Museum: a bowl on a leaf-shaped stand and a bedouin on camelback figure. He says that the Swedish factories made dessert and fruit services, bowls, vases and figures. The Rörstrand Porslins Fabriker concentrated on large exhibition type pieces, such as vases with modelled decoration in the Minton style.

68. *Rörstrand vase, cover and stand. Printed and impressed marks. Height 178 cm.* c.*1880.* Sotheby's

# CHAPTER SEVEN

# MAJOLICA TILES AND ARCHITECTURAL CERAMICS

B ritain's small tile industry was revolutionized by Richard Prosser, a Birmingham engineer, when he patented a method of dust-pressing tiles in June 1840. The clay was ground into a fine powder with a fixed moisture content, before being pressed into shape and fired. The speed (up to 1800 tiles per machine per day) and simplicity of this technique made for cheap tiles. Moreover, they were of consistently good quality. By the end of the nineteenth century Britain had the largest tile industry in the world.

In September 1878, *Pottery and Glass Trades' Review* exclaimed:

> To what uses cannot tiles be put? Cornices and chair-mouldings, door-frames and windows are set with them; hearths outlined or made wholly from them, doors inlaid, and staircases decorated with tiles let into the ends of the stairs or laid as the steps themselves; summer houses are gay with them, and summer vestibules, for the tile is always fresh and cool-looking in its bright designs, while nothing is warmer or more admirable for winter rooms than the dark earth-coloured ones.

The writer went on to scorn the use of tiles in furniture, but to no avail, for washstands and hall stands with inset tiles continued to be popular into Edwardian times. Tiles were also frequently used to decorate flower boxes.

Tiles were not confined to the Victorian home, they were used in churches, town halls, railway stations, hospitals, shops and pubs. Special tiles were made for butcher shops and dairies, where their use allowed for a new standard of cleanliness. Indeed, tiles were to become so ubiquitous that people ceased to notice them, and during the twentieth century many fine examples were lost during demolition or renovation of old buildings. Majolica archways, columns and fireplaces were also made in considerable numbers, although these are very rarely found today. It is this author's hope that some of these may yet lurk under coats of 'tasteful' white paint, awaiting discovery, but most have probably been destroyed.

It was not long after the introduction of majolica that manufacturers recognized how attractive relief-moulded tiles decorated with majolica glazes could be. They became a standard product made by many, if not most, large tile manufacturers. For the most part, they were more subdued than other majolica wares, and as such, survived well into the twentieth century. Monochrome majolica tiles increasingly found favour towards the end of the nineteenth century.

Majolica tiles were usually relief-moulded, most often in low relief, but sometimes in dramatic high relief. Some were tube-lined (the application of slip through a nozzle to form raised outlines on the surface of the tile), but more often on closer examination one discovers that they have been moulded to appear tube-lined, in order to reduce costs. The relief-moulding or tube-lining acted as a guide to the artist, considerably simplifying his task.

Majolica tiles made their début, like the other majolica, at the Great Exhibition in 1851. A tiled stove designed by A. W. N. Pugin for the Medieval Court contained 158 majolica tiles in five different designs. It was an enormous stove of the type one commonly finds in the French châteaux, as well as in Austria and Switzerland, differing only in that it is encased in an elaborate wrought iron cage. The tiles were yellow, pale blue, green, pink and white. They were relief-moulded; and those at the top were perforated to facilitate the escape of the heat. The tiles were designed by Pugin and some of the drawings for them in the Minton Archives are signed by him. Minton also included majolica tiles in their display at the World of Science, Art and Industry Exhibition at Crystal Palace, New York, in 1853.

Majolica tiles suited the warm and cosy look sought so often by the Victorians in their homes. An article in *Pottery and Glassware Reporter*, 29 October 1885, 'Art Tiles in Decoration' explained why relief-moulded majolica tiles were so successful in this regard:

> ... till within the last few years it would have been impossible to find in the United Kingdom any apartment which was covered from floor to ceiling with glazed pottery. ... future ages may wonder why its general employment was so long delayed, but amongst the reasons are two which are palpable at present to all. In the first place the appearance of tiles is uncomfortable in a wet and cold climate, and in the next, they are not so cheap as paper and paint.
>
> ... Now, however the use of coloured glazes is general and the chilliness of appearance is reduced to the reflecting surface of the glaze. This is also in a measure overcome by the employment of uneven sufaces of different grains which blunt and diffuse the light ...

Majolica tiles made an easy transition into Art Nouveau style, and indeed the bulk of those found today are in that style. The Art Nouveau designs were tube-lined, or more often relief-moulded so as to give the appearance of tube-lining (which was cheaper). The colours were carefully painted within the lines, and then fired flat to prevent any blending.

Herbert Minton began his production of encaustic floor tiles in the mid 1830s. In 1835, Minton issued their first catalogue for encaustic floor tiles. During these early years Minton was clearly the leader in the tile industry. Herbert Minton acquired rights in Prosser's patent, and began production of dust-pressed tiles in August of 1840.

In 1845, the production of wall tiles was taken over by Minton, Hollins & Co., a partnership between Herbert Minton and his nephew Michael Daintry Hollins, who ran the firm. Hollins carried on alone after Herbert Minton's death in 1858, until 1863, when he was joined by Robert Minton Taylor. Taylor left in 1868, to set up his own tile works in Fenton.

Meanwhile, Colin Minton Campbell, another of Herbert Minton's nephews, who ran Minton's china business, had begun tile production there. In 1875, he bought out Robert Minton Taylor, whose Fenton works briefly manufactured under the style Minton Brick & Tile Co., and subsequently as Campbell Brick & Tile Co. After 1882, the style changed to Campbell Tile Co. Minton China continued to manufacture tiles until 1918; Minton, Hollins & Co. was also absorbed by H. & R. Johnson-Richards Tiles Ltd in 1962; and Campbell Tile Co. was absorbed by H. & R. Johnson-Richards Tiles Ltd in 1968. If all this is confusing, it must be added that relations between the Minton firms were not always cordial and there was a long, involved lawsuit over the right to use the Minton name on tiles. More information about the Minton tile factories can be found in *Minton Tiles: 1835–1935*, a catalogue of an exhibition held by the Stoke-on-Trent City Museum and Art Gallery in 1984 and in Terence Lockett's indispensable *Collecting Victorian Tiles*.

Most of Minton's majolica tiles were dust-pressed, relief-moulded tiles. These were sometimes in high relief, but usually low. Minton also decorated some encaustic tiles with majolica glazes.

Jewitt particularly recommended Minton, Hollins's majolica tiles for flower boxes, but the firm's greatest effort was the Gamble Room at the South Kensington Museum. Their contributions included the wall tiles, designed by James Gamble; majolica columns and a frieze of putti, also designed by James Gamble; and a majolica inscription designed by Geoffrey Sykes, but probably modelled by James Gamble. These items cost, in 1867, £257 for the columns, £987 for the walls and £465 for the wall tiles.

Minton, Hollins exhibited wall and floor tiles in white and coloured glazes, embossed majolica, enamelled, tessellated, encaustic (glazed and unglazed) and art tiles at the Philadelphia Centennial Exhibition in 1876. The judges described the tiles, 'The colored body very hard and glaze good, the white body softer and glaze good.'

The Campbell Brick & Tile Company made majolica tiles from the time they were established in 1875. They advertised majolica tiles in *Keates's Gazetteer 1875–6*; and later in *Pottery Gazette* from 1880 to 1895. They displayed majolica tiles at the 1876 Centennial Exhibition in Philadelphia and at the Paris Exhibition in 1878.

Wedgwood, who had not made tiles since the eighteenth century, began to produce majolica tiles during the 1870s. The first tile in the Pattern Books is No. M629, the Trophy Tile, which would have been introduced about 1865. This was apparently unsuccessful, for it was never repeated and the next tile in the Majolica Pattern books is No. M1430, a Tremblay Tile, introduced about 1873.

After having gone to enormous expense to develop the *émail ombrant* technique and to purchase moulds and glaze formulae from the bankrupt Rubelles factory (see Chapter Three), Wedgwood wanted to make as many different shapes as possible. Unfortunately, the technique did not lend itself to curved surfaces, so tiles, which all their rivals had been making successfully for some time, were a

**MANUFACTURERS OF**

**TILES** OF ALL KINDS FOR
FLOORS, WALLS,
FIREPLACES, STOVES,
BATH ROOMS,
WINDOW BOXES, &c.

**THE CAMPBELL TILE CO.**

TRADE

MARK

MOSAICS.

MAJOLICA TILES
For **DADOS**,
IN NEW ENAMELS,
A **SPECIALITE**.

**DECORATIVE FAIENCE,**
AS EXECUTED AT THE MUNICIPAL BUILDINGS, GLASGOW,
AND NATIONAL PROVINCIAL BANK, PICCADILLY, LONDON.

**STOKE-UPON-TRENT.**
London: 340, GRAY'S INN ROAD, W.C.          Wm. MASTERS, Agent.

logical application. The tiles were very successful. Sixty-five Tremblay tile patterns were introduced during the next five years.

It was about 1876 before any more non-Tremblay majolica tiles were made. The first patterns were Nos. M1712–17, patterns for the Passion Flower Tile, Narcissus Tile, Anemone Tile and Square Tile. Most of these designs were repeated many times in different colour combinations. (All of the majolica tile patterns are listed in Appendix D.) Wedgwood's tiles represented a fairly minor portion of their majolica production, however. Of some 4000 patterns only 106 are for tiles. The Tremblay tiles made up the majority of these designs. Of the others, the Passion Flower Tile seems to have been the most popular, having been introduced in six different versions between 1876 and 1880. The Majolica Pattern Books include, however, only a small proportion of Wedgwood's tiles. There is a blank page headed 'SERIES V – TILES' and a 'SERIES Q – TILES' which only lists Nos. Q421–44.

Sherwin & Cotton produced a wide range of colourful majolica tiles with flower and animal patterns. They also produced George Cartlidge's *émail ombrant* portrait tiles. Cartlidge modelled these from photographs with such precision that they are sometimes mistaken for photographic tiles. These tiles bear Cartlidge's signature or initials. At Sherwin & Cotton since 1882 as an apprentice, then painter, modeller and decorator, he perfected the technique *c.*1896–9, and worked freelance for Craven Dunnill as well. Subsequently, his designs were produced by Adams & Cartlidge and J. H. Barrett. After the First World War he settled in America, apparently in Newport, Kentucky, but this author has been unable to discover any tile works in that vicinity.

Ironbridge Gorge, Shropshire, became the second major centre for British tile production during the 1870s. The combination of high-quality local clays and cheap coal for firing kilns made it an ideal location for the tile industry. The two tileworks, Maw and Craven Dunnill, competed with Minton for the market in encaustic, transfer-printed and majolica tiles.

George and Arthur Maw moved to Ironbridge Gorge in 1852 from Worcester, where they had been producing tiles since 1850. They established the Benthall Works at Broseley, where they remained until 1883. They expanded to works in Jackfield in 1882, where they remained in business until 1962. During the 1880s they were the largest tile producers in the world.

*69. Chimney piece of majolica tiles in stone executed by Maw & Co. for the 1862 Exhibition. From* The Builder, *29 March 1862.* Tony Herbert

At the Exhibition of 1862 in London, they received a prize medal for a mosaic and for a chimneypiece, which was Maw's 'first attempt in architectural application of enamels and majolica'. Over 100 tints were used in this chimneypiece. The majolica glaze was devised by George Maw, and he and his brother also devised the range of colours. Maw made the tile pavement and the majolica lunettes for the Gamble Room at the South Kensington Museum in 1867. On 30 October 1872, they registered a design for a terracotta and majolica fireplace. They exhibited their majolica tiles at the Centennial Exhibition in Philadelphia in 1876.

Their 1888 catalogue included 'Majolica Tiles. Moulded in relief and painted with enamels of various colours, after the manner of the Italian, Della Robbia ware and ancient Moorish examples.' George Maw was a great scholar and he travelled throughout Europe and the Middle East, sketching tiles. Some of his sketches are at the Ironbridge Gorge Museum Trust Library, as are all the catalogues to which this text refers. The 1888 catalogue also included:

> Architectural Majolica Enrichments, including columns, pilasters, capitals, panels, friezes, medallions, ballusters, hemispherical and ornamental bosses for insertion in oven or stove work. The designs are modelled in high relief and covered with enamels. … Special designs in this class of work can be executed, but as such involve the expense of moulds they are necessarily charged at a higher rate. Where, however,

several copies are required, the cost is much less than of similar decoration in carved stone and the material is not subject to injury by the action of the weather.

Between 1880 and 1899, they produced Art Nouveau tube-lined majolica tiles. Their 1890 catalogue included majolica tiles, and 'architectural majolica columns, bosses, panels, fenders, edging &c.' However, their 1902 catalogue made no mention of majolica tiles.

Craven Dunnill took over the Jackfield tileworks of Hargreaves and Craven in 1871. These works were old and dilapidated, so the new firm decided to establish a purpose-built tileworks. Craven Dunnill's new tileworks were built near the Maws

*70. Craven, Dunnill* émail ombrant *tile.* c.*1890.* Tony Herbert

factory between 1871 and 1874. Catalogues at the Ironbridge Gorge Museum Trust Library, dated 1879 and 1905, list majolica tiles among the wares. Their price lists for 1885 and 1888 offer majolica tiles:

> Having the ornament embossed, coloured in various rich or low toned colours to suit individual tastes, are not designed for floors. They are applicable for the decoration of walls, ceilings, reredosses, dados, pilasters, friezes, sides and linings of fireplaces and cabinet work.

It is interesting to note that the tiles were priced according to the number of colours employed in the decoration: one colour, 18–27 pence; two colours, 21–32 pence; 3 colours, 24–35 pence; and 4 or more colours, 27–32 pence. (The tiles were priced by the foot and so the lower price was for larger tiles, and the higher for smaller tiles. Four-colour tiles were not made in the smallest size.) None the less, the firm's advertisements in *Pottery Gazette* during the 1880s do not mention majolica tiles. Towards the end of the century the firm made a great many Art Nouveau majolica tiles.

There were two major American producers of majolica tiles. The American Encaustic Tile Company in Zanesville, Ohio, established as Fischer & Lansing in 1874, was one of the first American firms to produce floor and wall tiles. Previously, all tiles had been imported. The firm floundered for two years, before Gilbert Elliot arrived from England to superintend production. The quality then improved, but in order to persuade architects to use American tiles, the firm had to lay and guarantee the tiles themselves. This was successful, and the firm expanded rapidly, finishing six more kilns by 1879. Glazed tiles were introduced in 1880, and embossed tiles in 1881. By the time of the grand opening of their new plant, the largest tileworks in the world, in 1892, the firm employed 1000 men. Herman C. Mueller was responsible for many of the relief-moulded designs, which would have been majolica glazed, between 1887 and 1894. Portrait tiles using an *émail ombrant* technique were also produced.

The United States Encaustic Tile Works was founded in 1877 by several Indianapolis businessmen inspired by the tiles they had seen displayed at the Centennial Exhibition at Philadelphia the previous year. Their specialities were encaustic floor tiles and 'High Art Maiolica Tiles', which were relief-moulded and dipped in monochrome majolica glazes. Designs included birds, charming children and, especially, flowers. Between 1881 and 1883, Robert Minton Taylor was connected with the firm. In 1884, they claimed to have the largest tileworks in the world, with six kilns and eight muffle kilns. They employed 300 people, and had a capacity of 2,000,000 square feet per year.

In Germany, Villeroy & Boch made Art Nouveau majolica tiles at the turn of the century.

## MANUFACTURERS OF MAJOLICA TILES & ARCHITECTURAL CERAMICS

Between 1870 and 1920 there were more than 100 British firms making tiles. It is likely that the majority of these made at least some majolica glazed tiles. The following list, which includes only those known for certain to have manufactured majolica tiles and/or architectural majolica, probably only represents a small fraction of the firms which could be included. (Firms followed by an asterisk have been discussed elsewhere in Chapter Seven.)

Adams & Cartlidge, Vine Street, Hanley, c.1900-10.*

American Encaustic Tile Co., Zanesville, Ohio, c.1875–1935.*

Anchor Art Tile & Pottery Co., Longton. This firm advertised majolica tiles in *Pottery Gazette*, June 1890.

Barrett, J. H. & Co., Booth Works, Stoke-on-Trent, c.1896–1924.*

Boote, T(homas) & R(ichard), Ltd, Burslem, c.1842–1963. Their *Catalogue A: Suggestions for Inexpensive Wall & Dado Tiling* at the Stoke Reference Library illustrates quite a number of majolica tiles.

Booth, Thomas & Sons, New Hall Pottery, Hanley, c.1845–80; Church Bank Factory, Tunstall, c.1850–1948. (See Appendix A.)

Camm, T. W., Frederick Street, Birmingham, c.1866–70.

Camm Bros., Frederick Street, Birmingham, *c.*1870–80. This firm won an Honourable Mention for majolica panels at the Paris Exhibition in 1878.

Campbell Brick & Tile Company, Stoke-on-Trent, *c.*1875–82.*

Campbell Tile Co., Stoke-on-Trent, *c.*1882–present day.*

Carter & Co. (Ltd), Poole Pottery, Dorset, *c.*1873–1921. An incomplete catalogue in the Ironbridge Gorge Museum Trust Library lists majolica tiles as one of their products.

Copeland, W. T. (& Sons Ltd), Spode Works, Stoke-on Trent, *c.*1847–present day.

Craven Dunnill, Jackfield, Salop, *c.*1872–1951.*

Crystal Porcelain (Pottery Co., Ltd), Tile Works, Elder Road, Cobridge, *c.*1882–90.

Gibbons, Hinton & Co., Brierly Hill, South Staffordshire, *c.*1883–1950. This firm's catalogue at the Ironbridge Gorge Museum Trust Library includes designs for majolica tiles and panels.

Jones, George (& Sons), Trent Works, Stoke-on-Trent, *c.*1861–1951.

Lee & Boulton (Lee of Tunstall), High Street, *c.*1896+.

Malkin Tile Works Co., (Malkin, Edge & Co.), Burslem, *c.*1866–1902. A price list in their catalogue at the Ironbridge Gorge Museum Trust Library includes 'Embossed Majolica Tiles in a large variety of designs'.

Maw & Co., Worcester, *c.*1850–2; Benthall Works, Broseley, Salop, *c.*1852–83; Jackfield, Salop, *c.* 1883–1969.*

Minton, Stoke-on-Trent, *c.*1793–present day.*

Minton, Hollins & Co., New Road, Stoke-on-Trent, *c.*1868–1962.*

Pilkingtons Tile & Pottery Co., Clifton Junction, Manchester, 1893–present day. This firm produced art nouveau majolica tiles, some by John Chambers.

Porcelain Tile Co., Cobridge, *c.*1890+.

Sherwin & Cotton, Vine Street, *c.*1877–1911.*

Simpson, W. B., St. Martin's Lane, London, *c.*1833-present day. Decorators known to have made majolica fireplaces and registered a design for a majolica pilaster on 22 September 1884. They used Maw's and Minton Hollins's blanks, and probably decorated majolica tiles as well.

Taylor, Robert Minton, Fenton Tile Works, *c.*1869–75.*

Timmis, Charles & Co., Sheaf Works, Longton, *c.*1890–1900+. This firm advertised majolica tiles in *Pottery Gazette* during 1890.

United States Encaustic Tile Works, Indianapolis, Indiana, *c.*1877–1939.*

Villeroy & Boch, Mettlach, Germany et. al., *c.*1836–present day. The firm made Art Nouveau majolica tiles *c.*1900.

Wade, J. & W., Burslem, 1890–1900+. *Email ombrant* tiles.

Wedgwood, Josiah & Sons, *c.*1759–present day.*

Zanesville Majolica Company of Ohio, Zanesville, Ohio, *c.*1882–3. Made relief-moulded tiles with mottled, orange, cream and olive green glazes.

# CHAPTER EIGHT

# COLLECTING AND IDENTIFICATION

## COLLECTING

I t has been frequently said that majolica was unloved, unappreciated and ignored by collectors until the 1960s. While it is true that majolica prices have risen precipitously since then, it is not true that it was ignored by the collector before that time. *Hobbies ... The Magazine for Collectors*, March 1939, featured a 'Majolica Round-Up' with articles titled 'Reminiscences in Collecting Majolica', 'Majolica, Like Gold Is Where You Find It', 'I, Too, Collect Majolica', 'Majolica, Links the Past and Present' and 'A Dessert Service Started It'. One collector stated, 'It is not a very difficult task to secure a nice collection of majolica. I have completed a service for twelve within the past three years without any particular effort, and I did not make an intensive search but merely bought such pieces as I happened to run across.'

Such will not be the experience of the collector today. None the less, majolica is not hard to find, and not necessarily expensive. A good selection of continental plates can be found for between £7 and £12 apiece, the cheaper ones usually having some small damage. On the other hand, a collector will pay thousands for large pieces such as *animalier* figures and garden seats. Price guides are highly unreliable, and it cannot be stressed too much that a piece is worth only as much as someone will pay for it. Two collectors may battle fiercely over a piece at auction, driving its price to double the estimate; on the other hand, if one of them had a flat tyre on the way to the sale, the same piece at the same sale on the same day might well have sold for half its estimate. Similarly, one may pay a premium for a piece purchased from a dealer who specializes in majolica, as opposed to a dealer who just happened to find a piece or two by chance. One must take into account, however, that a visit to a specialist will almost certainly result in a purchase or two, whereas one may spend a fortune in petrol visiting dozens of general dealers without finding a single piece of interest. It is also true that a general dealer may put a very high price on a very ordinary piece, knowing only that it is majolica and thinking that it must, therefore, be worth a good deal. Many collectors are intimidated by auctions, but the auction house can be an invaluable resource. At a viewing, the collector will be able to handle and carefully inspect pieces at his leisure. The timid collector might plan to attend an auction or two as a spectator, carefully following the sale with a catalogue in hand. When bidding, the best policy

*71. Fish bread tray, badly battered. Length 34 cm.* Author's collection

is to determine one's top bid before the sale and to drop out at that point *no matter what*. In short, the dedicated collector will investigate all avenues, and find each one has its advantages and disadvantages.

The novice collector must above all be honest with himself. If one is a magpie, who cannot resist anything which looks interesting, it is no good deciding to collect only mint specimens of Minton majolica. If one is concerned about the investment value of the collection, then pieces in prime condition with reliable attributions or marks should form the bulk of the collection. A study collection may include severely damaged pieces, purchased for their mark and pieces which are either representative or, conversely, atypical of a class of wares. The collector may concentrate on the work of one factory, one shape, e.g. oyster plates, or even one pattern.

The question of damage is one which each collector must settle to his own satisfaction. Some collectors will be haunted by the fact that the third plate on the right has a chip to the rim, while others will enjoy the piece as it is, and even forget that it is damaged. The investor will be wise to avoid any damaged pieces, whereas the collector who is primarily interested in interior decoration may be delighted to find a cheap damaged piece which will create the desired effect at little cost. Price is a very important factor here. There is no reason why the average collector should reject damaged pieces, but they should be appropriately priced. It is true that majolica is fragile, and many pieces have suffered over the years, but it is also true that damaged pieces are worth considerably less than those in good condition.

It is important to inspect all pieces carefully in good light. Restorations will frequently show up, because the enamels used lack the lustre of the original lead glazes. Restoration may also be revealed by running a finger carefully over the surface of the piece. If the restoration has been properly carried out, there will be no ridge between the filler and the original ceramic. None the less, the texture of the restored surface will often feel slightly different. One should, of course, ask the dealer if the piece has been restored, but if the restoration has been skilfully carried out, the dealer himself may not have recognized it. A poorly restored piece is worth much less than an unrestored damaged piece, because reversing old repairs is time-consuming. One will have to pay for this, as well as the restoration. One should beware of very dirty pieces, that look as though all they require is a good cleaning. The dirt may obscure stains and damage. One should ask oneself why, if cleaning is all that is required, the dealer did not take the trouble to do it.

Frequently, one will find firing cracks or even chips which occurred at the factory, and were glazed over at the time. These are not regarded as damage, and do not affect the value of the piece as severely as does damage. They do affect the value to a certain extent, however. There are any number of advertisements in contemporary journals for crates of 'cheap seconds', and just as those pieces were cheap at the time, they should today certainly be cheaper than goods that left the factory perfect.

Restoration is another complex issue. Some collectors want every piece in their collection restored to its original condition, whereas others will be satisfied with minimal cosmetic restoration. Experts generally concur, however, that when it comes to restoration, less is better. It is usually a mistake to attempt to make a piece look like new. Some pieces must be restored in order to preserve them, for example if the glue on riveted pieces has deteriorated, the join loosens and the edges will grind against one another, causing further damage. Riveted and soldered repairs in good condition can be safely left untouched. Usually if a piece has been subject to an old repair, it is wise to have it unstuck, cleaned and reglued. Old glues are often unsightly, but more important, the piece may fall apart quite suddenly as the glue dries out, particularly if you have central heating. Not only may the piece come apart and break badly, but its pieces may fall on other objects, damaging them in turn. In many cases it is best to have the piece repaired, but not painted. The colours and textures of majolica will hide the faults of a well-glued piece on display, but less than perfect painting will catch the light and show up across a room.

Because the glaze is prone to crazing, one often finds badly stained pieces. In most cases this staining just darkens the gay majolica colours, making them appear sombre or muddy. In the case of argenta wares, staining frequently defaces pieces seriously. The only really safe method for removing stains, which the collector can attempt himself, is by soaking in sterilizing solution, of the sort used for baby bottles. The piece should be soaked in plain water for 24 hours both before and after this bleaching. It is best to start with a mild solution, and if after several days there is no improvement, the concentration can be increased slowly. Be warned, however, that soaking in water will soften and deteriorate the plaster that holds rivets in place. Amateur repairs made with inappropriate glues and fillers may also dissolve.

Cleaning majolica can be a very dangerous exercise, for it chips easily and bits in high relief are very susceptible to damage. Always wash one item at a time in a plastic basin. Never hold a piece under the tap to rinse it: the slightest miscalculation will result in a chip. While washing, move the tap back out of the way, or remove the plastic basin from the sink. Never soak a repaired or restored piece in warm or hot water unless you want to risk reversing any old repairs. Never use steel wool or any abrasive cleansers; majolica glazes scratch easily, and fine scratches will dull the glaze. Needless to say, your majolica does not belong in your dishwasher. Flatware in storage should be stacked with squares of cloth, felt or thick paper between them, to protect the raised surfaces from wear. Never flick over your pieces with a dust cloth or feather duster. To dust remove every item from the shelf, front items first, and dust each item carefully.

Any serious collector needs to cultivate a good relationship with a professional restorer. The collector should never attempt restoration himself, unless he is a skilled restorer. There are not many ceramics restorers around, and the services of a good one will be expensive. One must also be prepared to wait weeks, or even months, for the restoration. Many restorers will not even attempt to restore majolica. Unless the restorer has an extensive knowledge and you have seen examples of his work *on majolica*, never trust a valuable piece to him until you have tried him on an unimportant piece. Matching the iridescent sheen of majolica is nearly impossible, and a poorly matched or blended colour will decrease the value and your enjoyment of the piece.

There are three types of restoration, often called invisible, museum and useful. This is the way these types of restoration are carried out at one major London restoration studio. An invisible repair is airbrushed with stoving enamels to render it nearly imperceptible. A museum repair is glued, filled with tinted filler and painted cosmetically with ordinary enamels. Museums want this kind of repair because airbrushing necessarily obscures some of the original surface. Stoving enamels are not used as the heat required to fire them discolours the unpainted filler. A useful repair is glued, filled with tinted filler and then cosmetically painted with coloured glue, diluted with cellulose thinners. There are as many different methods of restoring as there are restorers, so ask your restorer what types are available and how they would be carried out.

When commissioning a repair or restoration, get an estimate with a full description of the piece involved and the work to be performed. If, as sometimes happens, the restorer finds that the work is more difficult and so more expensive than expected, he should call the owner before proceeding with the work. Make it clear that you expect to be notified under these circumstances. Upon completion of any work, get a receipt describing the work carried out, particularly if an important piece is involved. The description should include the names of any adhesives or fillers used, for the benefit of anyone who may work on the piece in future.

According to the decorating magazines, it is fashionable to use antique ceramics with gay abandon. In fact, there is very little antique majolica which can or should be used for its original purpose. This is, quite simply, because most old pieces display some degree of crazing. A crazed piece should not be used for food as the juices will penetrate the glaze and stain the piece, to say nothing of the sanitation hazards. Similarly, it is never wise to leave flowers and water standing in a vase or jug, as this will also cause stains and/or hard-to-remove mineral deposits. Instead, place the flowers in a smaller glass or, preferably, plastic container inside the majolica vase. Plastic baby bottles are ideal for this purpose as they are slender, and if your fingers should slip as you set one into a vase, there will be no breakage. Likewise, plants and soil should be placed in a plastic pot with saucer or watertight liner, within a majolica jardinière (or any other piece you might be using as a planter). Restored pieces should never be subjected to normal use, unless the restorer has carried out a 'useful repair', as described above. Restorers dislike carrying out useful repairs, because they are usually unattractive, and the customer is disagreeably surprised when he receives the completed work.

Part of the charm of majolica is that it lends itself to informal display. It looks especially well clustered in small groups of contrasting shapes and colours. Plate stands should be the sturdy sort with a cross-piece at the back. Care should be taken to use a large enough size, to prevent a piece of flatware from overbalancing. It is wise to order these by the dozen from a specialist wholesaler, as it is economical, and if one has the correct stand at hand one will not be tempted to endanger a new piece by propping it up in some other way 'just for a few days'.

It is absolutely essential to use only plastic-coated plate hangers. The metal sort will scratch the glaze and, in an amazingly short time, will rust and discolour the plate. Once again it is important to use the correct size, as overstretched springs will lose their tension and send the plate hurtling to the floor. These too can be ordered by the dozen from a specialist wholesaler. Never glue rings for hanging onto the back of plates (there are, unfortunately, some sold for that purpose); and *never* glue plates directly to the wall, as recommended recently by one popular decorating magazine.

## IDENTIFICATION AND MARKS

Marks are not foolproof, but unless you are familiar with the body, glaze, shape and decoration of a piece, they are your best guide. The collector will want to refer to Geoffrey Godden's *Encyclopaedia of Pottery and Porcelain Marks* and J. P. Cushion's *Handbook of Pottery and Porcelain Marks*, the latter including European marks. Both of these are available in the reference sections of most public libraries. Lois Lehner's *Encyclopedia of U.S. Marks on Pottery, Porcelain and Clay* is the most complete reference on American marks. There are a number of other specialist mark books listed in Appendix E.

Beginning in 1891, makers had to mark pieces with the country of origin if they planned to export to the United States. Needless to say, many small local concerns did not institute the system, but a large number did. Therefore, most ceramics made after 1891 are marked, but not all. Many pieces were (and are today) marked with paper labels which are removed by owners. Some makers only mark one piece of a set (say a teapot), or saucers and not cups. So one must not assume that every unmarked piece is pre-1891.

In 1921, further United States legislation encouraged makers to mark their wares 'Made in xxx'. However, to this day some makers still mark their wares 'England' rather than 'Made in England', so 'England' (or France etc.) does not mean that the piece was made before 1921. Furthermore, both Wedgwood and Mintons began to mark pieces 'Made in England' in 1910.

The registration mark system was instituted in Great Britain in 1841. Between 1841 and 1883, a diamond registration mark was used. The letters and numbers in the corners of the diamond can be deciphered to reveal the date of registration, the place of registration, the parcel number (record number) and the maker. Needless to say a clearly printed or impressed mark is more valuable for this purpose. Impressed diamond marks are often too indistinct to read. Having determined that

## DIAMOND REGISTRATION MARKS

KEY

|  | 1842-67 |  | 1868-83 | |
|---|---|---|---|---|
| a | class | a | class |
| b | year | b | day |
| c | month | c | bundle |
| d | day | d | year |
| e | bundle | e | month |

YEAR CODE

| 1842 | X | 1848 | U | 1854 | J | 1860 | Z | 1866 | Q | 1872 | I | 1878 | D |
|---|---|---|---|---|---|---|---|---|---|---|---|---|---|
| 1843 | H | 1849 | S | 1855 | E | 1861 | R | 1867 | T | 1873 | F | 1879 | Y |
| 1844 | C | 1850 | V | 1856 | L | 1862 | O | 1868 | X | 1874 | U | 1880 | J |
| 1845 | A | 1851 | P | 1857 | K | 1863 | G | 1869 | H | 1975 | S | 1881 | E |
| 1846 | I | 1852 | D | 1858 | B | 1864 | N | 1870 | C | 1876 | V | 1882 | L |
| 1847 | F | 1853 | Y | 1859 | M | 1865 | W | 1871 | A | 1877 | P | 1883 | K |

MONTH CODE

| January | C | April | H | July | I | October | B |
|---|---|---|---|---|---|---|---|
| February | G | May | E | August | R | November | K |
| March | W | June | M | September | D | December | A |

NOTES

(i) In 1857 the letter R was used 1–19 September.
(ii) In 1860 the letter K was used for December.
(iii) From 1–6 March 1878 the following mark was issued:

instead of

your teacup was registered in 1871, however, does not mean that it was made in 1871. Although the registered design was only protected for three years, many makers continued to use the registration marks for many years – particularly in cases where the mark was part of the mould.

In 1884, Great Britain switched to a simplified system which started with number one and proceeded onward. The table here will enable the collector to determine the year in which a design was registered, but further information must be gleaned from the Public Record Office. As with the diamond registration marks, makers continued to use the registration marks for many years.

| Year | Registration Numbers | Year | Registration Numbers |
|------|----------------------|------|----------------------|
| 1884 | 1–19733 | 1897 | 291241–311657 |
| 1885 | 19734–40479 | 1898 | 311658–331706 |
| 1886 | 40480–64519 | 1899 | 331707–351201 |
| 1887 | 64520–90482 | 1900 | 351202–368153 |
| 1888 | 90483–116647 | 1901 | 368154–385499 |
| 1889 | 116648–141272 | 1902 | 385500–402499 |
| 1890 | 141273–163766 | 1903 | 402500–419999 |
| 1891 | 163767–185712 | 1904 | 420000–446999 |
| 1892 | 185713–205239 | 1905 | 447000–470999 |
| 1893 | 205240–224719 | 1906 | 471000–493999 |
| 1894 | 224720–246974 | 1907 | 494000–519499 |
| 1895 | 246975–268391 | 1908 | 519500–549999 |
| 1896 | 268392–291240 | 1909 | 550000– |

The Registry of Design is of limited usefulness when researching majolica. There are two sets of records – the representations and the registers. The registers list the registered number, exact date of registration, maker's name and address and occasionally a description of the design. All but the last can be found in Cushion's *Handbook of Pottery and Porcelain Marks*. The type of design, when mentioned, may just be earthenware or jug. For the most part, however, Wedgwood, George Jones and Worcester designs are named by pattern and shape, e.g. Sardinia Sardine. What must be remembered is that the *design* was registered and it may have been manufactured in any number of bodies and glazes. As we have seen in the preceding chapters, many manufacturers used the same design for several different types of wares.

The representation registers consist of scrapbooks of drawings and occasionally sepia photographs of the shape or design. It cannot be determined from these alone whether or not the design was carried out in majolica. The illustrations are usually only marked with the design registration number.

After 1883, the wares were not entered into the records by class. All classes of wares are listed chronologically, descriptions are usually brief, e.g. Shape of Jug or For the Pattern. This makes any search for majolica much more arduous.

Manufacturers sometimes dated their wares, always in code. Some, such as Copeland, just impressed the last two digits of the year. Wedgwood used this system after 1929. Previously they had used a three-digit code which can be deciphered when clearly impressed. Minton uses a small impressed symbol which has varied every year since 1840. It should be pointed out that the impressed date codes refer to the date on which the piece was made, not the date on which it was decorated. Wares sometimes sat in warehouses for several years before being decorated.

The small numbers painted on the bottoms of pieces, most often pieces of dinner, tea or dessert services, are usually pattern numbers. A specialist book on the factory involved (or perhaps Appendix D) will be able to tell you when that pattern was introduced and, sometimes, when it was discontinued. Other marks found on majolica are usually decorator's marks. These were used in tallying the decorator's production (they were paid by the piece), as well as a measure of quality control.

It is essential to know how to identify pieces using the marks involved, but the collector will find relatively few bargains that way. The way to find real bargains is to study a particular maker and learn to identify unmarked pieces with certainty. For example, the George Jones dessert plate illustrated in Plate 46 was purchased recently by the author for £3. It is not marked George Jones, but the pattern number is painted in a reserve, and the pattern itself was a familiar one, not known to have been made by anyone else. Moreover, the George Jones colours were recognizable both on the face and the back of the plate. The author recently saw a marked example for £65.

In the final analysis the only absolute way to determine date and maker is by body, glaze, shape and decoration. Looking at pictures and at items in museum cases can be helpful, but the only way to finally know is by handling as many pieces as possible, in shops, at fairs and in private collections. There is a great deal of reproduction majolica being made, all of which should be marked as such. Marks can be effaced, but these wares are so different from Victorian majolica in weight and glaze that they should not deceive the collector. The principal manufacturers are the American firms Mottahedeh and Fitz & Floyd.

# APPENDICES

# MINOR BRITISH MAJOLICA MANUFACTURERS

This Appendix attempts to list all the known British makers of majolica not covered in the preceding chapters. Some retailers are included as their marks have been found on majolica, and confused collectors. Contemporary accounts are cited extensively, because they give one a new perspective about majolica, and indeed the entire nineteenth-century ceramics industry. It should be pointed out that in most cases the firms described in the trade journals were principal advertisers and thus the accounts tend to be extremely positive, if not obsequious.

Where one firm succeeds another, the succeeding firm is given a separate entry if they are known to have made majolica. Asterisks in the text indicate firms which have independent entries, which should be consulted for related information.

**George Ash**, Broad Street, Hanley, c.1865–82.
Jewitt states that Ash occupied these premises as a Parian and majolica manufactory. This is confirmed by entries in the *Staffordshire Potters' Directory for 1868*, and *Keates's Gazetteer 1875-6*. There are no known marks, although Ash registered seven designs between 1868 and 1875, and some pieces may thus be identified by the diamond registration mark. Ash was formerly a partner of Wardle & Ash,* which partnership was dissolved 25 January 1865. These may have been the Havelock Works subsequently operated by Mrs. Mary Massey* c.1882. Grove & Cope* operated the works c.1884. Lidstone's *Londoniad* (1866) recited:

> What dazzled mine eyes with lightning flash?
> The remarkable works of Mr. Ash.
>
> ...
>
> Now, their Majolica engages
> All the attention of the immortal Nine,
> For which in later times a Raffaelle did design
> And which to highest point of excellence attained
> When learned Dukes in glad Urbino reigned.

**W(illiam) & J(ames) A. Bailey**, Alloa Pottery, Fife, Scotland, c.1855–1908.
Although Alloa Pottery's advertisements in the 1880s stated that they had been 'established over a century', it is generally agreed that James Anderson established Alloa Pottery in 1790 for the manufacture of coarse pottery. The works were afterwards carried on by William Gardner. Upon acquiring the works in 1855, the Baileys added majolica to the range of products. They registered seven designs between 1867 and 1878, mostly for rockingham glazed teapots. *Pottery and Glass Trades' Review* for October 1878 reported that the firm was

doing well and turning out some good useful work at a very low price. We have seen at their showrooms in Fore Street some goods that are well worth the note of our friends in the retail trade, particularly in brown and blue rockingham and jet, which cut a style somewhat novel for that class of ware.

They displayed majolica among their other wares at the Sydney International Exhibition in 1880. In *Pottery Gazette*, during 1881 through 1883, W. & J. A. Bailey advertised regularly. These full page advertisements offered

Majolica Ware in Flower pots, Dessert Ware, Teapots, Kettles, Jugs, Cheese Stands and Covers, Jug Stands, Match Strikes, Sugars, Creams, Tobacco Jars, Bread Trays, Cans, &c., &c. ... Metal Covered Goods in Teapots & Jugs made in Fine Rockingham, Ivory & Majolica Ware.

McVeigh describes Alloa's majolica as indistinguishable from that of Dunmore Pottery.[*] Godden has recorded a marked majolica leaf plate, and this author has seen a vine pattern comport painted rather sloppily with thick brown, green and cobalt glazes.

**Bailey, Murrels & Co.**, Elm Street Works, Market Street, Hanley, *c.*1864–6.
Lidstone's *Londoniad* (1866) lists this firm as manufacturers of Majolica, Parian, etc. They also traded as John Bailey & Co. The firm was succeeded by Bailey & Bovington *c.*1867–8. A name mark has been recorded on Parian wares.

**Alfred Ball**, Drury Works, Normacot Road, Longton, *c.*1883–6.
An advertisement in *Pottery Gazette*, 2 June 1884, announced: 'Majolica Superseded … Crates of Best Majolica Jugs, 120 sets £4 7 6.' Apparently their goods were not of the better quality. Alfred Ball was formerly a partner of E. Laurence & Co., whom he succeeded. A William Ball operated these works *c.*1889.

**Banks & Thorley**, Excelsior Works/New Street Pottery, Hanley, *c.*1873–5; Boston Works, High Street, Hanley, *c.*1875–87.
Banks & Thorley established the Excelsior Works in New Street in 1873. Mr. Banks was formerly a partner of Davenport & Banks.[*] In 1875, they moved to a newly erected premises, the Boston Works, High Street. In 1887, they became Banks & Co.; and Edward Banks from 1888 to 1889.

Jewitt describes their wares as 'cheese-stands, bread-trays, dessert services, jugs, egg-holders, jardinières, flower-pots, tea-pots, ladies' work baskets, water bottles and an infinitely wide variety of ornamental articles.' He goes on to say: 'Notable among the dessert services in majolica is one with a rich chocolate-coloured ground, which throws out, with a strikingly beautiful and rich effect, a naturally arranged group of ivy, ferns and anemones.'

In *Pottery Gazette*, February 1879, they advertised earthenware, porous goods, majolica, jet and stoneware. Majolica was included in their regular *Pottery Gazette* advertisements as late as 1886.

Banks & Thorley's most popular patterns were Basketweave & Bamboo and Fern & Bow. They registered three designs between 1876 and 1883. One of these was for the Basketweave & Bamboo pattern, and another, registered on 10 April 1883, was for the Fern & Bow pattern, which is a pastel design on an argenta ground. Marks (1983) illustrated eight pieces in these two patterns. They are well modelled, but the colours are weak.

The firm used no mark, but some pieces have been identified by their diamond registration marks.

**Bates, Read & Turner**, Wellington Works, Newport Street, Burslem, *c.*1881–2.
During 1882, this firm advertised stoneware, earthenware, ivory and jet, terracotta and majolica. No mark is recorded.

**Bayley, Murray & Co.**, Saracen Pottery, Possil Park, Glasgow, *c.*1875–1900.
This firm was known as Saracen Pottery after 1884. According to Fleming, while Murray was chief manager they made large quantities of majolica jam jugs, for preserve manufacturers. Their mark was impressed BM&CO/SARACEN POTTERY.

**Beech & Adams**, John Street, Stoke-on-Trent, *c.*1889–92.
Formerly Harvey Adams & Co., this firm advertised in *Pottery Gazette*, 1 January 1889: 'Art Majolique Ware/New Designs, Unique, Artistic, Grotesque/Shapes & Colours to suit all Buyers of Art Pottery/Specialities in/Flowerpots, Pedestals, Umbrella Stands, Dessert Ware/Tea & Coffee Pots, Jugs &c.

**Beech & Tellwright**, Lincoln Pottery, Hanley, *c.*1882–4.
Jewitt states that they made majolica for home and foreign markets. They registered one design in 1882. They illustrated the majolica 'Lily Cuspadore' and 'Chrysanthemum Jug' in an advertisement in *Pottery Gazette*, 1 February 1884. Subsequently Frederick Beech & Co., also known as the Lincoln Pottery Co., *c.*1885–90.

**Belfield & Co.**, Prestonpans Pottery, Prestonpans, Scotland, *c.*1837–1946.
Charles Belfield (b. 1788) was an employee of and, after 1812, owner of Barkfoot Pottery, known for its creamware. He later moved to Cuttle, to produce rockingham glazed sanitary and drainage wares. The Cuttle pottery made a speciality of tableware decorated with leaves, or sometimes in leaf shapes, in majolica glazes. On 30 November 1872, the firm registered a Bamboo & Ribbon Teapot; a sepia photograph in the Representations of Designs appears to illustrate a majolica example.

In 1836, Belfield's son, James, became his partner, and from 1840, they were known as Charles Belfield & Son. Their establishment at Prestonpans produced rockingham glazed ware, sanitary ware and majolica. Most marked pieces occur after 1879. The firm remained in the Belfield family until the 1930s.

**Benson & Bailey**, Sylvestor Works, Burslem, *c.*1882–92.
This firm advertised 'majolica, jet &c' in *Pottery Gazette* during 1885 and 1886.

**J. W. Beswick**, Baltimore Works, Albion Street, Longton, *c.*1894–9; Brittania Works, High Street, Longton, *c.*1896–1905; Gold Street Works, *c.*1898–present day.
James Wright Beswick and his son began potting in Longton in 1894. An advertisement in *Pottery Gazette*, 1 January 1895, lists 'Majolica and Earthenware Specialities' and 'Leading Lines in Majolica Jugs' prominently among the wide range of goods produced. In *Pottery Gazette Diary* for 1907, an entry lists them as earthenware and majolica manufacturers. In an advertisement in the same diary, the firm advertised 'majolica ware' and 'Flower Pots in Majolica Art Colours'.

Although Beswick's later wares have been well documented, nothing is known about the shapes or patterns of the majolica wares. As Beswick appears not to have marked their earlier wares, it is difficult, if not impossible, to attribute any pieces to the factory. For further information about the factory and its later productions, the reader is referred to Harvey May's *The Beswick Collectors' Handbook*.

**J(ames) & T(homas) Bevington**, Marsh Street, Hanley, *c*.1865–7; Burton Place Works, New Street, Hanley, *c*.1867–78.

Jewitt writes that this factory discontinued manufacture of Parian statuettes and majolica in 1870. This is the only mention of their having made majolica that this author has been able to discover. Although Jewitt states that the Bevington family held the Burton Place Works continually from 1862, *The Staffordshire Potters' Daily 1868* lists J. & T. Bevington, makers of china and Parian, at Marsh Street, Hanley. *Keates's Directory 1875–6* lists J. & T. Bevington as makers of china and earthenware at Burton Place. The firm registered four designs for Parian between 1878 and 1880.

**John Bevington & Co.**, Clarence Street Works, Hanley, *c*.1860–8; Great York Street, Hanley, *c*.1868–72; Kensington Works, St James Street, Hanley, *c*.1872–92.

John Bevington advertised in the *Staffordshire Potters' Directory for 1868* as a manufacturer of 'Majolica, Parian, Fancy China, Figures, Vases, Earthenware, &c.' According to Jervis, he was brother to James and Thomas Bevington,* and to Ambrose Bevington, also a potter. *Keates's Directory 1875–6* lists him as a Parian manufacturer. Likewise, advertisements in *Pottery and Glass Trades' Journal* in 1878 and *Pottery Gazette* in 1882–7 no longer mention majolica, although the firm still manufactured it. However, one advertisement in *Pottery Gazette*, June 1887, mentions 'Fine Art Majolica'.

John Bevington registered two designs: the first was in 1878, and the second on 21 November 1881. This latter is for a Swan Ewer which is illustrated in Marks (1983). Kathy Hughes reproduced a photo from the Representation of Designs which she describes as a stoneware jug. In *Staffordshire Porcelain*, Godden lists this as a porcelain piece, but the shape could well have been made in pottery and porcelain or Parian bodies. Several of Bevington's porcelains in the Dresden style are illustrated by Godden in that work.

**Thomas Booth & Sons**, New Hall Pottery, Hanley, *c*.1845–80; Church Bank Factory, Tunstall, *c*.1850–1948.

In *Pottery Gazette*, February, 1878, this firm advertised 'Brittania Metal Mounted Jugs and Tea Pots, in Jasper, Majolica, Stone, and Other Fancy Bodies'. On 1 April 1895, *Pottery Gazette* said of their tiles: 'Those in relief are extremely elegant in appearance, and the designs and colours with which they are ornamented are produced with charming effect. The majolica colours are among the best we have seen, and are carried out in a variety of ways.'

There is a great deal of confusion about the history of this firm, exacerbated by the several premises they occupied, sometimes simultaneously. The above-quoted advertisement states that the firm was established in 1845. In an article in *Pottery and Glass*, August 1951, R. H. Colls writes:

> [T]he present company was founded by Thomas Booth and William Evans in 1841. The first factory, of very modest proportions, was at Knowle Works, Burslem, but at the end of ten years the business had prospered so well that its founders were able to move to larger premises at Tunstall, the site in fact on which the present Church Bank factory, was later built.

None the less, some sources have the firm located at Knowle Works as late as 1868.

*141*

In a recent article on relief-moulded jugs, R. K. Henrywood has written of his discovery that Thomas Booth & Co. were Britannia metalsmiths listed in Staffordshire directories as early as 1850, at Vine Street, Shelton, and later at Lichfield Street, Hanley. Henrywood does not believe Booth to have begun potting until 1864. Thus, some of the later references to the firm's establishment in the 1840s may have been references to its beginnings as a metal foundry.

A partnership between Thomas Booth and William Hales Turner at Church Bank, under the style Thomas Booth & Co., was dissolved on 11 November 1872.

From 1872 to 1880, Thomas Booth & Sons occupied a part of the New Hall Works, Great York Street, Hanley. It is this address which is cited in the 1878 advertisement. A partnership between Thomas, Walter and Henry Booth, under the style Thomas Booth & Sons, was dissolved on 15 September 1874. The dissolution notice reads that the partnership 'All of Hanley and carrying on business there as earthenware manufacturers and metal mounters and also at Brownfields, near Longton as Collier Proprietors under the style of Thomas Booth & Sons is dissolved.' None the less, Thomas Booth & Sons did continue to operate; possibly one of the sons had dropped out or they had taken on an additional partner. We do know that by 1881, Henry and Walter were in New York, as partners in Odell & Booth Bros. (See Appendix B.)

Thomas Booth & Co. did register a design from a Burslem address as late as 1869. On the other hand, they registered a design from a Hanley address as early as 1867, but did not register a design from Tunstall until 1872.

To further confuse things, *Keates's Directory, 1875–6* lists Thomas Booth & Sons at Brook Street, Hanley; Thomas Booth & Son at High Street, Hanley. Possibly these may have been showroom addresses, as they are not mentioned elsewhere.

**John Boulton**, Cliff Bank Pottery, High Street, Stoke-on-Trent, *c*.1884–8.
Late Nixon & Boulton of Tunstall, John Boulton advertised 'White stone, majolica, jet and rockingham in teapots, jugs, &c.' in *Pottery Gazette*, 1 January 1884.

**Boulton & Floyd**, Cliff Bank Pottery, High Street, Stoke-on-Trent, *c*.1888–91; Lovatt & Hall Street Works, Stoke-on-Trent, *c*.1892–1901.
This firm advertised regularly in *Pottery Gazette* from 1889. There is no mention of majolica until 1891. They then offered 'Decorated Earthenware and Majolica in Tea Pots, Flower Pots, Cuspidores, &c.' They termed themselves 'Specialists in Brilliant Art Colours.' On 1 April 1895, *Pottery Gazette* recommended:

> Messrs. Boulton & Floyd have a nice selection of samples of enamel and majolica ware, some of which are decided novelties. … This firm also have four shapes of American ice jugs in majolica, which have only recently been added to their already large variety in the jug line, among which, too, we noticed the 'Kaiser' and 'Wilson' shapes in a number of decorative styles. The cuspadores and spittoons are of good design, both in the round and square shapes.

The firm was succeeded by R. Floyd & Co.* in 1901.

**James Bradbury**, Clayton Pottery, Edensor Road, Longton, *c*.1889–90.
James Bradbury advertised 'Earthenware, Jet, decorated Toilet Jugs, Majolica, &c.' in *Pottery Gazette*, 1 January 1890.

**F.D. Bradley**, Elkin Works, Edensor Road, Longton, c.1876–82; Clayton Street Works, Longton, c.1880–7; Normacot Road, Longton, c.1888; Flaxman Pottery, Sutherland Road, Longton, c.1887–96.

Bradley advertised 'Ornamental Goods in China and Majolica' in *Pottery and Glass Trades Journal* in November 1878. Porcelains rarely bear an impressed BRADLEY, but no marked majolica has been recorded.

**F(rancis) Brewer & Son**, St. Martin's Lane, Longton, c.1862–4; Stafford Street, Longton, c.1864–6.

Francis Brewer was born in Derby in 1814. He became a china and pottery manufacturer in Longton, employing 30 men and 10 boys in 1861. He registered a Pineapple in Basketweave Plate on 15 October 1863. Although the illustration in the Representation of Designs is in the biscuit state, Marks (1983) illustrates a crisply moulded example in brilliant green and yellow majolica glazes.

**Brough & Blackhurst**, Waterloo Works, Longton, c.1872–95.

In *Pottery Gazette* during 1884–8, this firm advertised 'Majolica & earthenware Suitable for Home, Australia and other Foreign Markets'.

**Alfred Bullock & Co.**, Pelham Street Works, Hanley, c.1880–6; Waterloo Pottery, Hanley, c.1896–1902; Kensington Pottery, Hanley, c.1903–15.

Jewitt said that the Pelham Street Works were 'built in 1881 by Alfred Bullock & Co. for the manufacture of majolica, and jet ware, both of which they produced in large quantities and of great excellence in body and decoration'. *Pottery Gazette*, February 1884, reported that the works had been destroyed by fire on 22 January 1884. The works were rebuilt and from 1887 to 1893 were operated by Bullock & Cornes, and from 1984 to 1902 by Bullock & Bennett.

**Alfred Capper & Co.**, Park Hall Street, Longton, c.1887–9; Bradwell Works, Longport, c.1890–3.

On 1 January 1891, Alfred Capper advertised 'jet, earthenware, majolica and terracotta ware' in *Pottery Gazette*.

**W(illiam) E(dward) Cartlidge**, Villa Pottery, Cobridge, c.1879–92; Bourne's Bank, Burslem Grange, c.1875–8.

The firm registered three designs in 1872 and one on 21 February 1878, for a Hunt Teapot. *Keates's Gazetteer 1875–6* lists the firm as at Bourne's Bank, Burslem Grange. A letterhead mounted in the Representations of Designs, along with the Hunt Teapot illustration reads 'Bourne's Bank Works, Bought of W. E. Cartlidge, Manufacturer of Earthenware, Stone, Majolica, Parian, etc.' This is confusing, as the design is registered to W. E. Cartlidge, while the letterhead implies he was no longer involved with the firm.

Jewitt records this firm as having made 'Britannia-metal-mounted goods, ordinary earthenware, jet figures, rockingham, and majolica' at the Villa Pottery.

**Colclough & Co.**, Anchor Works, Anchor Road, Longton, c.1890–5; Goddard Works, Goddard Street, East Vale, Longton, c.1896–1900.

The firm was established in 1890 by Herbert Joseph Colclough, later Lord Mayor of Stoke-on-

Trent. Colclough was known as a hard-working man; and a company history recalls that 'he used to fire two ovens himself, many times working all day and sitting beside one of his ovens all night.' The firm advertised majolica in *Pottery Gazette* during the early 1890s. *Pottery Gazette*, 1 January 1895, announced that Colcough & Co., until lately run by H. J. Colclough and T. H. Hawley, would now be run by Colclough alone, Hawley having left the partnership to form Hawley, Webberly & Co.*

The firm was forced to move to larger premises at Vale Works in 1896. In 1898, the size of the Vale Works doubled and the manufacture of bone china begun. In 1900, the factory was reorganized, and the manufacture of majolica and decorated earthenware discontinued.

On 2 September 1895, *Pottery Gazette* reported, 'Messrs. Coclough & Co., Anchor works, Longton, had a variety of new patterns in majolica and barlotine [sic] goods.' The firm advertised in *Pottery Gazette* extensively during 1895. They seem to have specialized in plant pots and jugs, but offered many other shapes.

The known pieces are as follows (names are as given in advertisements):

| | |
|---|---|
| Argus Flower Pot, 8 sizes | Saxon Flower Pot, 8 sizes |
| Bluebell Jug | Shannon Flower Pot, 8 sizes |
| Clematis Jug | Sunflower Jug |
| Clyde Flower Pot, 8 sizes | Titan Flower Pot, 9 sizes |
| Dahlia Jug | Waterlily Jug |
| Hybrid Jug | Wild Rose Jug |
| New Fern Jug | |

**J(ohn) T(homas) Cope**, Broad Street Works, Hanley, *c.*1885–9.
J. T. Cope, formerly of Grove & Cope,* advertised 'Ornamental China, Parian & Majolica' in *Pottery Gazette*, during 1885–6.

**Dale, Page & Goodwin**, New Town Works, Longton, *c.*1876–92.
Formerly Dale, Page & Co. at Church Street Works (*c.*1867–77). They registered one 'pattern' in 1881. They advertised majolica in *Pottery Gazette* from mid 1881 until 1887. In 1883, Jewitt announced that Page had lately died and the firm was carried on as Page & Goodwin.* 'Majolica was added to the other productions of the firm in the 1870s.'

**Davenport, Banks & Co.**, Castle Field Pottery, Hanley, *c.*1860–73.
Jewitt includes 'majolica in all its varieties' in his list of this firm's wares. They registered two designs in 1863 and 1867. On 9 April 1873, this partnership between John Davenport, Edward Banks and James Robert Machin was dissolved. Banks left to form Banks & Thorley,* and Davenport carried on the Castle Field Pottery as Davenport, Beck & Co. (1873–80).

**J. T. Dudson**, Hope & Hanover Streets, Hanley, *c.*1838–present day
In Audrey Dudson's definitive work *Dudson*, she reports that Dudson made some majolica between 1885 and 1910, using a stoneware body. Plain tankard jugs and spittoons in 'Begonia' and 'Rose' patterns being their most successful designs. She illustrates a tankard jug with a rope handle. However, Dudson advertised majolica, albeit in small print, in *Pottery Gazette* as early as 1881.

**Sir James Duke & Nephews**, Hill Pottery, Burslem, *c.*1860–4.
Although this firm was best known for its porcelains, they exhibited some majolica and Palissy wares at the London Exhibition of 1862. Waring said, 'Some of the Majolica Ware

contributed by this firm was remarkable for good taste and fine painting, executed principally by Mr. Eyre, by whom the elegant ewer in our illustration was designed, the painting being by Mr. J. Bennett.' Formerly Samuel Alcock's works, the Dukes sold to Thomas Ford in 1865. The firm's mark was an impressed hand.

**Dunmore Pottery**, Airth, Stirlingshire, Scotland, c.1860–1911.
The Airth Pottery was established in the early part of the nineteenth century to produce coarse domestic crockery and tiles from the nearby red clay. After Peter Gardner acquired the pottery in 1860, the pottery rapidly gained national recognition. Gardner brought clay from Cornwall and Devon, which improved the quality of his wares. The earlier productions of this firm were of fine quality, but declined somewhat in later years. His shapes have been described variously as unorthodox or exotic. They were, in fact, the sorts of leaves, fruit and animals typical of majolica. A teapot in the form of a tortoise with its head forming the spout described by Fleming sounds more interesting than the more usual forms, such as dolphin comports. An 1855 advertisement lists 'Vases, Afternoon Tea Sets, Garden Seats, Flower Pots, Dessert Plates, Leaves, Mantelpiece, Dining-room and Toilet Table Ornaments, Etc'. From a pottery family in Alloa, Gardner was an expert on glazes. These rockingham brown, cobalt blue, yellow, crimson and copper green glazes were and are universally admired for depth of colour and softness. The green is said to be as fine as that of Wedgwood or Minton.

The pottery was situated on the estate of the Earl of Dunmore. He and the Countess of Dunmore took an active interest in Gardner's work. Through their good offices, Dunmore found outlets for his work at the better china-dealers in London. After an 1871 visit to the factory by the Prince of Wales, the wares became popular among fashionable people. Dunmore exhibited at the Glasgow and Edinburgh Exhibitions, winning a medal at Edinburgh in 1886. Gardner retired in 1903, but the pottery continued in operation until 1911.

The Scottish Pottery Society's *Archivist's Newsletter*, No. 2, notes that Dunmore is always marked, although, apparently due to a faulty die stamp, some pieces are marked DUNMOR. Pieces are more usually impressed DUNMORE, or bear a circular mark: Peter Gardner. Dunmore Pottery. Dunmore pottery can be seen at the Glasgow Museum & Art Gallery, and at the People's Palace Museum, Glasgow.

**Edwards & Sons**, Trent Works, Joiners Square, Hanley, c.1887–1914.
This firm advertised Parian and majolica regularly in *Pottery Gazette* during 1887–95. Stanway, Horne & Adams had built the Trent Works in 1859, and Edward & Sons succeeded Thomas Adams, the sole surviving partner. As late as March 1914, the firm was mentioned in *Pottery and Glass Record* as having exhibited their wares at the Pottery and Glass Fair at Stafford; '... as regards price and quality combined, they have no equal. Certainly for middle-class goods they will take some beating ...' No mention is made of majolica among the wares displayed there.

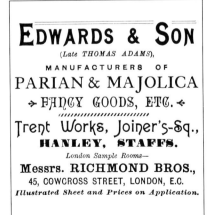

**James Ellis & Son**, Hanley, *c.*1869.

On 26 October 1869 James Ellis & Son registered a Corncob Jug, which was produced in Parian often with yellow and green majolica glazes and a pink lining. This relatively common piece is found with an applied diamond registration mark, but no other markings. The jugs are of good quality.

**John Fell & Co.**, Adelaide works, Heathcote Rd, Longton, *c.*1883–7; Union Place, Market
   Street, Longton, *c.*1887–8.

Fell advertised majolica in *Pottery Gazette* during 1884–6 as follows: 'Buyers requiring majolica not liable to craze, please call.' He registered three designs in 1884: a pattern for a dessert plate, and two jugs.

**William Fielding**, Cannon Street Works, Hanley, *c.*1891–1907.

Fielding advertised majolica in *Pottery Gazette* during 1891.

**R. Floyd & Co.**, Lovatt & Hall Street Works, Stoke-on-Trent, *c.*1907–30.

This firm, formerly Boulton & Floyd,* is listed as a manufacturer of earthenware and majolica in *Pottery Gazette Diary* for 1907. By 1914 the firm was R. Floyd & Sons, and majolica was no longer advertised. The firm's mark was a horizontal diamond enclosing the initials R F & S.

**R. H. Gibbons**, Great York Street, Hanley, *c.*1887–92.

This firm advertised in *Pottery Gazette*, during 1884–8, as follows:

R.H. Gibbons
(Late Neale, Harrison & Co.)
China, Earthenware & Majolica
of all descriptions
For Home & Export
The latest designs & shapes in Tea,
Breakfast & Toilet Sets. Assorted
Crates of Earth, China, Majolica &
Jet Ware packed to suit the
convenience of customers. Large
Stock of Seconds Crates ready packed.

**Grimwade Bros.**, Winton Pottery, Hanley, *c.*1886–1900; other addresses *c.*1886–1964.

This business was founded by Leonard, Edward and Sydney Grimwade. Beginning as factors, they soon developed the pottery side and later joined with James Plant's Stoke Pottery. Presumably the S. Grimwade mentioned in a Hackney & Co. advertisement in *Pottery & Glass Trades' Journal* during 1879 refers to Sydney. A full-page advertisement in *Pottery Gazette* during 1889–90 illustrated their 'Fern Majolica Jugs' at $9\frac{1}{2}$d per set. Another full-page advertisement there in June 1890 illustrated the 'Stratford' majolica jug (with roses on the top half and Japanese motifs on the lower) and the 'Buttercup' majolica jug.

**Grove & Cope**, Broad Street Works, Hanley, *c.*1884.

Frederick Wedgwood Cope and John Thompson Grove advertised 'ornamental china, parian and majolica' in *Pottery Gazette* during 1884.

**Guest Bros.**, Brettell Lane, Stourbridge, *c.*1880.
Guest Bros. were glass manufacturers who patented a process for acid etching designs on ceramics. An advertisement in *Pottery Gazette* during 1880 offers Nocturne Ware, 'An entirely new style of Decorating China, Earthenware, Majolica, Jet Ware, &c., &c., by Patent Process'. Pieces so decorated were engraved GUEST BROS.

**F. Hackney & Co.** Railway Pottery, Stoke-on-Trent, *c.*1878–9.
Although this is a relatively unknown factory whose products have not been identified, the thorough reporting in the trade journals makes fascinating reading. There is a Hackney and Co. listed at Daisy Bank, Longton, in *The Staffordshire Potters' Directory* for 1868. This was probably the venture of one of Frederick Hackney's relatives, as an account in *Pottery and Glass Trades' Review* for May 1878 states that Hackney and his partner Kirkham had worked in the fancy goods department at Wedgwood & Sons for over twenty years.
   In May 1878, *Pottery Gazette* described a visit to this firm. It is worth quoting in full as it gives an indication not only of the nature of the firm's wares, but of what qualities were admired in the trade at that time:

> We have much pleasure in recording a visit to the above manufactory, the proprietors of which we may state are young potters, having but recently entered into the business. The premises are large and roomy, giving plenty of scope for enterprise and energy. An additional oven is being erected, new machinery put down and extensive rearrangements made. Altogether the outlook is very promising.
>    The class of manufacture aimed at is general ware, at the same time special care will be taken of the art department. This branch of the manufacuture is under the management of Mr. Hackney, he is a gentleman of experienced ability. Judging of the ware so far produced, we may say that the majority is assuming a style which is sure to meet with success and if only proper attention be given will acquire a name in the best markets. Of course a large part of study and patience will be necessary, for new firms cannot rush to the front at one bound.
>    It is impossible in so short a notice to give a complete review of the productions of the works; we will, however, select one or two articles. Amongst the most conspicuous is the Trentham garden pot, which looks well in a dark brown background of rustic work. These garden pots are produced in several sizes and various styles of decoration. The sunflower vase is a handsome piece of work; so named from the principal feature of decoration, having a sunflower in high relief coloured naturally, the whole fairly set off by a deep Mazarine blue. Attention may be drawn to the dessert ware, which has many points of excellence in both form and style. The green glazed ware, although capable of improvement (the green being at present not sufficiently decided) – will compare well with that of most other firms. But it is in the brighter colours that a greater excellence is attained, and articles sustaining these we hold in preference. The leading colour is plum, which is well developed and has a good effect. Ample use is made of this, as also of the olive, brown and turquoise, and all are very becoming in dessert ware decoration. Another colour used in good style is the Japanese blue on a white ground. These, again, are called into requisition in their bread trays, butter-pats, pickle-trays, trinket trays, card trays and numerous other articles.
>    In jugs, the firm are laying themselves open to do a good trade, and a large assortment is being made. These will be produced in majolica and white with blue Japanese decoration. The Whieldon jug is the finest in shape, and is decorated in the old cloudy style so famous in the last century. Special mention may also be made of their beer sets, consisting of a jug, two tankards and a tray.

Again, in August 1878, *Pottery and Glass Trades' Review* wrote admiringly of the Hackney majolica. This time they describe a new article with such precision that perhaps some reader may be able to identify the piece in his or her collection. This is an oyster tray with five cups and a centre hole for the lemon. The cups are painted mazarine blue, light blue, plum, pea green and olive; the centre is lemon yellow. *Crockery Journal*, 18 August 1878, describes the firm's cloudy ware in imitation of beryl, amethyst and other stones, 'which are really very happy'. On 21 November 1878, *Crockery and Glass Journal* commends the fox fruit dish: 'The surface of the dish has a fine grouping of ferns and foliage, and the handle or knob is formed by a well-molded fox that is intently watching a rabbit peeping from beneath a burrow.'

Apparently, the firm did not quite fulfil the rosy forecasts. A year later, in April 1879, *Pottery and Glass Trades' Journal* reported:

> Messrs. Hackney & Co., of Stoke, have made wonderful strides during the past few months. Their majolica is equal to any we have seen. ... The new members who joined this firm a few months since have done much to improve its production.

But this improvement was apparently insufficient, for the firm disappears from sight after the middle of 1879, although Hackney himself turned up in Baltimore, where he worked for D. F. Haynes & Co. (see Chapter Five). Hackney & Co. advertised regularly during 1878 and 1879 in *Pottery Gazette*.

**F. Hackney, J. Kirkham & Co.**, Railway Pottery, Sutherland Street, Stoke-on-Trent, c.1878-9.

This firm is the same as F. Hackney & Co.,* above. It is perplexing, but the same firm definitely traded under two styles simultaneously.

**Hall & Miller**, Marlborough Works, Union Street, off Hope Street, Hanley, c.1880.

This firm advertised 'Majolica, Earthenware, Green Glaze, Rockingham, Terra Cotta, Jet &c. of the best quality at low prices' in *Pottery Gazette*, 1 January 1881. The partnership was dissolved 12 October 1880, and the works were operated by Hall, Miller and Mountford, which partnership was dissolved on 8 March 1881. The works were then operated by Hall, Mountford & Thomas* until that partnership was dissolved on 29 July 1881.

**Hall, Mountford & Thomas**, Marlborough Works, Union Street off Hope Street, Hanley, c.1881.

This very short-lived firm advertised 'Majolica, Earthenware, Green Glaze, Rockingham, Terra Cotta, Jet &c. of best quality at low prices' in *Pottery Gazette*, June 1881. In September 1881, *Pottery Gazette* announced that Mr. Hall had retired and that the firm would now be known as Mountford & Thomas.*

**Hawley, Webberley & Co.**, Garfield Works, High Street, Opposite the church, Longton, c.1895-9.

Formerly a partner of Colclough & Co.,* T. H. Hawley joined the above in 1895. *Pottery Gazette* on 1 January 1895 announced in 'American Buyers' Notes', 'Messrs. Hawley, Webberley, & Co. start a new business today ... They will manufacture majolica. It being an entirely new concern, the moulds and patterns are specially designed, and as most new brooms sweep clean, they will no doubt strive to give every attention and satisfaction to buyers visiting their works.' None the less, the wares of the new firm bear a very close resemblance to those of Colclough & Co. Even the advertisements are nearly identical. The firm seem to have specialized in plant pots and jugs, but also advertised toddies, bread trays, spittoons and tobacco boxes. Simon Fielding unsuccessfully brought suit against the firm for infringement of his registered Fan argenta design, but the press seemed to have thought that he had the rights of it (see Chapter Four). They advertised extensively in *Pottery Gazette* during 1895.

The following are the known patterns and shapes (names as in advertisements):

| | |
|---|---|
| Cecilia Shape Flower Pot, 7 sizes | Shell Shape Flower Pot, 9 sizes |
| Blackberry Jug | Star Shape Flower Pot |
| Garfield Shape Flower Pot | Troy Shape Flower Pot, 9 sizes |
| Passion Flower Jug | Waterlily Jug |
| Primrose Jug | Wild Rose Jug |
| Raleigh Spittoon | York Shape Flower Pot |

**Thomas Heath**, Park Hall Street Works, Longton, *c.*1882–9; Baltimore Works and Albion Works, High Street, Longton, *c.*1887–1913.

Heath was a regular majolica advertiser in *Pottery Gazette* during 1881–95. He was listed in *Pottery Gazette Diary* as late as 1907.

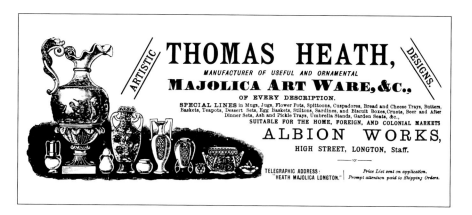

**T. & W. Heath**, Park Hall Street Works, Longton, *c.*1882.

Majolica was previously made at these works by Daniel Sutherland & Sons* and by Hugh Sutherland.* T. & W. Heath advertised in *Pottery Gazette*, 2 January 1882: 'Majolica in Jugs, Flowerpots, Spittoons, Cuspadores, Bread and Cheese Trays, Butters, Baskets, Teapots, Dessert Wares, Egg Baskets, Sardines, Tête à Tête sets, Vases, &c., &c., Good Value for Money.' On 4 October 1882, *Crockery and Glass Journal* reported that, 'Mr. T. Heath, Park Hall Street Works, Longton has some new designs in majolica articles that are bound to increase business.' So apparently W. Heath had withdrawn from the business during the year.

**Heath, Blackhurst & Co.**, Hadderidge Potteries, Bath Street, Burslem, *c.*1860–77.

Lidstone's *Londoniad* (1866) praised this firm:

> The Majolica pattern is a Work of Art,
> Here from the brake I see a pheasant start!

Thousands of forms in Beauty me engage,
While their Bacchic Jugs revive a classic age;
Fruits and Flowers Hesperian, crown field
And arbour! Mr. Heath was once with Brownfield.

An informative, if not inspirational, verse! Little else is known of the firm, which was succeeded by Blackhurst & Tunniscliffe. The firm's mark was H & B or H B & Co.

**William Hines**, Wharf Street; High Street, Longton, *c.*1882–6.
William Hines advertised Opaque Porcelaine, majolica and green glazed wares in *Pottery Gazette*, January 1883. There are no marks recorded.

**Jones & Co.**, New Street, Longton, *c.*1889–99.
Jones & Co. regularly advertised in *Pottery Gazette* during 1889–95 as follows: 'Jones & Co.,/ Manufacturers of Majolica/ New Street, Longton, Staffordshire./ CHEAP LINES IN JUGS.'

**E. W. Jones & Co.**, 9 St. Andrew Street, Holborn Circus, London, EC, *c.*1886.
This firm advertised in *Pottery Gazette*, January 1886, as a manufacturer of 'Majolica Ware, Flower Pots, Pedestals, Jugs, Bread Trays, Teapots, Cheese Stands, etc.'

**Jones & Bromley**, Lockett's Lane, Longton, *c.*1881–97.
This firm of china and earthenware manufacturers and merchants advertised majolica in the *Pottery Gazette* during 1881 and 1882. It is not known whether they actually manufactured majolica or just sold it.

**Jones & Howson**, Ebenezer Works, Market Street, Longton, *c.*1882–91.
This firm advised that 'Crates of assorted China, Earthenware & Majolica, &c. can be had' in *Pottery Gazette*, during 1884. Jewitt said that they made 'usual classes of china goods in tea, breakfast and dessert services for the home and foreign markets. Many of their shapes and patterns were of great beauty and the quality of the body was good.' William Jones and George Howson dissolved their partnership in 1891, and William Jones continued the works on his own until *c.*1905.

**John Kent & Sons**, Market Place, Longton, *c.*1851–83+.
This firm advertised as china and earthenware manufacturers and merchants in *Pottery Gazette* during 1880–4. They offered a 'large assortment' of majolica, but it is not made clear whether or not this was of their own manufacture. Another advertisement in 1883 describes them as merchants only.

**Kessell & Son**, 11 Southwark Street, Bow, London, *c.*1880.
This firm offered 'Patent Crystal & Majolica Fountains' in *Pottery Gazette* advertisements during 1880. It is unlikely that they actually manufactured the majolica themselves. More probably they assembled the fountains from pieces provided by another firm.

**William Kirkby & Co.**, Sutherland Pottery, Fenton, *c.*1879–85.
This firm advertised in the *Crockery and Glass Journal*, 24 November 1881, as manufacturers of china, earthenware and majolica, 'Patronized by His Grace the Duke of Sutherland, K. G.' They also advertised majolica in the *Pottery Gazette* during 1880–3. Their marks were K & Co. or W. K. & Co.

*72. Samuel Lear 'sunflower and classical urn' teapot. Impressed diamond registration mark for 27 August 1887. Height 15 cm.* Author's collection

**Samuel Lear**, Mayer Street Works, Hanley, *c.*1877–86; High Street, Hanley *c.*1882–6.
Samuel Lear built a small works in 1877, on Mayer Street. In 1882, he expanded into new premises in the High Street. At this second location, Lear produced majolica, ivory and jasper. Advertisements in *Pottery Gazette* during 1882–6 note, 'Buyers' attention is particularly called to the Superior Quality Majolica'. A waterlily jug is one of the pieces illustrated in these advertisements. Creditors closed the works in 1886 and it was purchased by Thomas Forester (see Chapter Four). In January 1887, *Pottery Gazette* announced, 'Considerable surprise has been excited over this bankrupt and his sudden disappearance has, to say the least of it, been a matter of much trade gossip.'

Lear is best known for the Sunflower and Classical Urn pattern, registered 27 August 1887. This was made as teapots, jugs, moustache cups and probably other shapes. The jugs and teapots sometimes have Britannia metal lids. Lear registered six other designs between 1878 and 1882.

**Lincoln Pottery Co.** (Frederick Beech & Co.), Lincoln, Pottery, Hanley, *c.*1885–90.
This firm, late Beech & Tellwright,* advertised 'every description of majolica' in *Pottery Gazette* during 1885.

**Malkin, Edge & Co.**, (Edge, Malkin & Co.), Newport and Middleport Potteries, Burslem, *c.*1870–1902.
This firm which is best known for their wide range of earthenwares, did advertise majolica

in 1891. Some of their green glazed wares are marked with an impressed EDGE, MALKIN & CO., and it is likely that majolica would also have been so marked. There are no recorded pieces of majolica, however.

**Mrs. Mary Massey**, Havelock Works, Broad Street, Hanley, c.1882.
According to Jewitt, Mrs. Massey, formerly of Mayer Street, made earthenware jugs, teapots and general majolica. These may have been the works formerly operated by George Ash.*

**Maw & Co. (Ltd)**, Worcester, c.1850–2; Benthall Works, Broseley, Salop, c.1852–83; Jackfield, Salop, c.1883–1969.
Primarily a tile manufacturer (see Chapter Seven), Maw also made mass-produced 'art pottery', including some majolica pieces. In their Catalogues for 1888 and 1893, at the Irongorge Museum Trust Library they listed, 'Majolica Vases, flower pots, jardiniers, etc., etc., Made in a variety of artistic forms and sizes and richly glazed in enamels of different colours.'

*73. Maw & Co. hanging basket. Impressed marks.*
*Diameter 36 cm. c.1870.* Sotheby's

*74. Maw & Co. jardinière. Impressed mark and 'No. 8'. Length 61 cm. c.1880.* Sotheby's

Godden's *Jewitt* says that the majolicas were 'more or less decorated with raised or surface ornamentation. They were of excellent design – the body light but compact and the decorations of remarkably good and artistic character.'

**Meigh & Forester**, Melbourne Works, Longton, *c.*1883-6.
This firm, late Ridge, Meigh & Co., advertised majolica in *Pottery Gazette* during 1884. They registered four designs in 1885, all specified as shapes for 'Majolica, China or earthenware'. The partners, Clement Meigh and Thomas Forester (see Chapter Four), dissolved their partnership in 1886, after which Forester continued the works alone.

**J. Dunlop Mitchell & Co.**, Montrose Street, Glasgow, *c.*1872-84.
This merchant advertised 'Majolica Ware comprising Jugs, teapots, cups & saucers, plates, comports, vases, &c., &c.' in *Pottery Gazette* during 1884.

**Moore & Co.**, Old Foley Pottery, Longton, *c.*1872-92.
Moore & Co. specialized in white granite and majolica for the American market. The firm's partners were Thomas C. Moore, Thomas Bickly, Robert Leason and Rosella Taylor. During 1882 and 1883, they advertised majolica in *Crockery and Glass Journal* and during 1882-7 in *Pottery Gazette. Crockery and Glass Journal* commended their 'Cairo' jug as 'extremely novel'. They registered three designs for salad bowls in 1885, which were probably made in majolica: 'salad bowl with crabs', 'embossed seaweed, coral & shells with embossed coral handle' and 'fluted salad bowl with lobster handles'.

**Moore (Bros.)**, St. Mary's Works, Longton, c.1872–1905.

Moore Brothers produced some high-quality majolica. Some of this was heavily gilded, and the oriental influence was strong – a finely modelled Camel Teapot being one of their more sought-after pieces (registered 11 May 1874). Other teapots made in majolica include the Dragon Teapot (registered 1 January 1872) and the Squirrel Teapot (registered 11 May 1874). The Stork Teapot, registered on 13 January 1883, is one of their more commonly found pieces. The design of this piece is very ordinary, and examples are poorly painted with overly thick glazes. Pieces may be impressed MOORE or, after 1880, MOORE BROS., but the majolica appears to have been often left unmarked. A large number of designs were registered by the firm and the diamond registration marks will identify some of them. The firm did not mention majolica in its advertisements.

Bernard Moore worked for his family's firm 1878–1905, when he left to form his own workshop. No doubt the knowledge he acquired during his long years of manufacturing majolica was vital to the marvellous glazes, such as the sang-de-boeuf, which his workshop later produced.

**Morris & Co.**, Joiners Square, Hanley, c.1887–1912.

This firm advertised majolica in *Pottery Gazette* during 1887.

**Mountford & Thomas**, Marlborough Works, Union Street, Hanley, c.1881–8.

John Mountford claimed to have invented Parian while working for Copeland & Garrett (c.1833–47). He worked for Ridgway during the 1840s. He was in partnership with Samuel Keys, Keys & Mountford, 1850–7. They exhibited Parian and received an honourable mention from the Great Exhibition in 1851. Mountford continued that business alone, 1857–9. In 1864, Mountford operated the Dresden Pottery, Stoke. Mountford & Thomas took over the Marlborough works from Hall & Miller* in 1881.

Jewitt said that this firm made 'good quality majolica dessert sets, baskets, tea-sets, garden seats, etc.' Its colours were said to be especially good. In its early years the firm seems to have concentrated on majolica production. *Crockery and Glass Journal*, 29 June 1882, reported: 'Their showrooms overflow with articles of domestic utility and ornament in majolica.' Their advertisements in that journal during 1882 offer:

> Dessert Sets, Jugs, Teapots, Butters, Ice Creams, Tea Sets, Fruit Baskets, Sardines, Oyster Plates, Mugs, Cuspadores, Spittoons, Déjeuner Sets, Bread Trays, Marmalades, Cruets, Vases, Match Pots, Honey Pots, Bedroom Candlesticks, Jewel Trays, Salad Bowls, Pickles, Fish Dishes, Spills, Tobacco Jars, Salts, Garden Seats, Centre Pieces, Ice Trays, Milk Sets, Teas, Breakfast-Moustache Cups, etc., etc.

An advertisement in the same journal on 19 December 1882, adds the following to the above list: Toy Tea Sets, Brackets, Cheese Stands, Individual Butters, Tapers, Fruit Sets, Egg Frames, Match Boxes, Baskets, Smoking Sets, Punch Bowls, Flower Pots, Jardiniers, Umbrella Stands, and Shrimp Trays. They still advertised majolica in *Pottery Gazette* as late as 1888. The firm registered two designs in 1883. The firm was subsequently operated by Uriah Thomas.* Below is a list of known Mountford & Thomas majolica patterns (the names are the manufacturer's own):

| | |
|---|---|
| Wild Rose | Melon |
| Flowery Vine | Chrysanthemum |
| Japanese | Sunflower |

| | |
|---|---|
| Lily | Hop |
| Acorn | Raspberry |
| Begonia Leaf | Pansy |
| Bramble | Bird |
| Basket | Ivy Leaf |

**B. Nield**, Edensor Road, Longton, *c.*1889–92.

In June 1890, this firm advertised as a 'Manufacturer of cheap decorated toilets, jugs, jet, majolica &c.' in *Pottery Gazette*.

**Oakes, Clare & Chadwick**, Sneyd Pottery, Albert Street, Burslem, *c.*1876–95.

Formerly Williams, Oakes, & Co.* *Pottery and Glass Trades' Journal*, June 1878, reported:

> The firm are now introducing a new flower-pot of octagon form, of rather elegant shape and which has the character of being chaste. The panels divided have grape decoration with foliage and butterfly just alight in the fruit. Several grounds are adapted for the panels, and the design has the quality of looking well in all. The grapes are colored naturally, and the inside was lined with pink. Two designs in jugs were also shown, which seem to be a new adaptation of the tankard jug, that in itself admits of so many styles. In the present design, the article is divided into panels with the pea flower in relief with foliage colored naturally. The jug is registered. The second design of this character is a 'rustic' jug with animals in panel. Both forms are well adapted to majolica decoration.... Our attention was also called to a dessert service in 'shell' design, in which the mottling was excellent – a style of decoration which prevails here.

It is to be hoped that with the assistance of the above detailed description, one or more of these pieces will turn up to be attributed. The Pea Flower Jug was registered 1 December 1877. The firm advertised majolica in *Pottery Gazette* as late as 1880.

**Page & Goodwin**, New Town Works, Longton, *c.*1883–92.

Formerly Dale, Page & Goodwin,* Jewitt reported that 'Majolica has of late been added to the productions of the firm.'

**Phillips & Pearce**, London, *c.*1869–72.

This London retailer registered nine designs between 1869 and 1872. At least one, for a trough form vase, was majolica.

**Pollitzer, Dixon & Co.**, 11 Bartell's Buildings, Holborn Circus, London, *c.*1895.

They advertised in *Pottery Gazette* for 1 January 1895 as 'Retailers of glass, china, majolica etc.'

**Thomas Poole**, Cobden Works, Edensor Road, Longton, *c.*1880–1924.

This firm advertised majolica in *Pottery Gazette*, 1883–91. *Pottery Gazette*, June 1889, reported that their Chrysanthemum majolica jugs were 'having a good run'. Although their advertisement in *Pottery Gazette* for January 1895 does not mention majolica, this firm was listed in the index to advertisers as manufacturers of 'China, Majolica etc.' The firm was formerly Johnson and Poole.

The first Thomas Poole was originally a potters' printer. His first venture was at the Bridge Pottery, Heathcote Road, Longton, under the style of Poole & Sutherland, in 1846. He later established his own pottery at the back of Longton market. In 1860 he went into partnership with a L. Johnson at Park Works, Longton, formerly James Warren & Thomas, where they made china. In 1870, he moved to Edensor Road where he and Johnson took over the Cobden works. In 1883, some years after the partnership with Johnson had been dissolved, his sons, the second Thomas Poole and Albert James Poole, took over the business. After Albert's death in 1896, the second Thomas continued the business alone. He is credited with such revolutionary inventions as the installation of steam-heated mangle dryers for flat ware, and the 21-piece teaset (as opposed to the 40 or 44 pieces standard at the time). The second Thomas Poole ran the business until his death in 1938, at the age of 83.

**J. Poole & Son**, John Street, Stoke-on-Trent, *c.*1878–86.
Advertisements in *Pottery Gazette* for this firm between their inception in 1878 and 1883 read, 'Manufacturers of Parian Statuary, Terra-Cotta, Ornamental China, Tea and Dessertware, majolica, &c.' J. Poole was formerly of Poole, Stanway & Wood.* No marked specimens are recorded.

**Poole, Stanway & Wood**, Copeland Street Works, Stoke-on-Trent, *c.*1875–8.
This firm was formerly Turner, Hassall & Bromley.* It produced vast quantities of unmarked Parian, some of which was decorated with majolica glazes. In 1878, J. Poole* left to form his own firm, and the firm was known as Stanway & Son* until 1880, when it became Turner & Wood.*

**Poole & Unwin**, Cornhill Works, Longton, *c.*1871–7.
They were formerly Poole, Sutherland & Hallam; subsequently Joseph Unwin & Co. Jewitt records, 'The productions are middle-class earthenware, stoneware jugs, &c., chiefly intended for the home market. Gold and silver lustres of the ordinary kind and rustic majolica were also at one time made.'

**Pugh & Glover**, Pelham Street Works, Hanley, 1875–87.
Pugh & Glover, formerly Pugh, Glover & Davies of the Waterloo Works, Hanley, built the Pelham Street Pottery in 1877. The firm advertised majolica in *Pottery Gazette* during 1883–5. Pugh & Hackney succeeded Pugh & Glover at the Pelham Street Works, 1887–92.

**Charles Purves**, Goven Pottery, Glasgow, *c.*1869–90s.
According to Jewitt, Purves produced rockingham and majolica glazed earthenware and jet.

**Ridgways**, Bedford Works, Stoke-on-Trent, *c.*1879–1920.
The firm was founded by Edward John Ridgway (1814–96), son of William Ridgway. He was in partnership with L. J. Abington at Church Works in Hanley, and then continued alone. He built the Bedford Works in 1866. In 1870, he took his sons, John Ridgway (1843–1916) and Edward Ackroyd Ridgway (b. 1846), into partnership. In 1872, Edward John Ridgway retired. During the period 1873–9, his sons carried on the works with Joseph Sparks, who was their London agent, under the style Ridgway, Sparks & Ridgway. Upon Sparks's death in 1878, they carried on as Ridgways.

This firm advertised majolica in *Pottery Gazette* during 1880, but their advertisements after that year no longer mention majolica. Ridgways registered their well-known 'Bow' trademark in 1880, but no majolica is known with this or any other Ridgway mark has been recorded.

**Elijah Rigby, Jr**, Providence Pottery, Chell Street, Hanley, c.1882–9.
Rigby advertised majolica in *Pottery Gazette*, June 1884.

**G. A. Robinson**, Church Street, Longton, c.1870–6.
According to Jewitt, Robinson made Parian, jasper and majolica at these works, until their demolition in 1876. Robinson then moved to Sutherland Road, using the style Robinson until 1886.

**Robinson & Chapman**, Royal Porcelain Works, Anchor Road, Longton, c.1875–82.
These works were built as a model factory in 1872. David Chapman continued the works alone from 1882 to 1889; and with his sons, under the style David Chapman & Sons, 1889–95. The firm moved to the Atlas Works in 1895.
*Crockery and Glass Journal*, 15 December 1881, announced: 'Messrs. Robinson & Chapman had added the manufacture of jet ware, stone jugs, and majolica to their other goods, …' This firm advertised as a 'Manufacturer of every description of China, Majolica, Jet and Stone Ware' in *Pottery Gazette* during 1882. No mark has been recorded.

**Robinson, Leadbetter & Leason**, Victoria Pottery Co., Lonsdale Street, Stoke-on-Trent, c.1882–?
*Crockery and Glass Journal*, 10 August 1882, contained the following article about this firm. It is reproduced in full in the hopes that some of the many pieces described in detail may now be identified by collectors.

The Victoria Pottery Co., Stoke-on-Trent (Messrs. Robinson & Leadbetter, with Mr. Robert Leason), have been for some time preparing their new works, where they intend to manufacture not only high class majolica, but also ornamental and useful articles in ivory and colored earthenware. Their first selection of majolica fancy goods and ornaments are now ready, and if they continue to produce articles of the same excellence as the specimens we had the pleasure of inspecting, their position as manufacturers of high class majolica is assured. 'The Victoria design (registered) [it was not registered by Robinson, Leadbetter & Leason or by Robinson & Leadbetter] is a combination of bamboo canes and foliage, with a groundwork of rushes skillfully interlaced. This novel design is carried out in a most thorough manner. The umbrella stand, garden seat and Stilton cheese stands (three sizes) are remarkable for their extreme elegance in form and the harmony of their bright colors. The background of rushes in dull brown throws up in relief the cane color of the bamboo and foliage, the rushes being treated in a most natural manner, showing the joining where new rushes have been inserted, or where the rushes have split under the weaver's fingers. The same design is carried out in jugs, bread trays, sardine and sugar boxes, butters, kettles, tea-pots, teas, and many other articles in various styles of coloring, all equally effective. Three new sardine boxes (in fact all the designs are new) attracted our attention – the 'Lotus', having a flower springing from the very centre of a group of leaves in a rush basket; the 'Sardine', with four or five specimens of the finny tribe lying on a bed of rushes; and more particularly the 'Kingfisher'. This box has a kingfisher with open wings just alighting on a bed of lotus leaves with a fish in its bill. The plumage of the bird is skillfully modelled and brightly colored. A desert [sic] set [the 'Alexandria'] consisting of six fruit subjects, the 'Vine', 'Filberts', 'Orange', 'Apple', 'Strawberry', and 'Fig Leaves' is very pleasing, the comports and centre pieces, all varied, being an additional attraction. Some charming ornaments formed by a lotus leaf, brightly colored, with flowers and basket handles are very quaint. The same style of decoration is carried out in single, double, and triple baskets with equal success. The 'Sunflower' cuspadore is a very clever adaptation of this fashionable flower in conjunction with drapery, tassels and cords. The colors are so rich that it seems a pity to hide it. A strawberry and cream set, formed by a rush basket held in the centre by handles from which panier-like loops hold the sugar amd cream, suggesting the appropriate name of 'The Panier' strawberry set. The same idea is carried out in single and double baskets. An oyster set is a charming combination of oyster shells, seaweed and coral. The 'Marigold' tête-à-tête set, consisting of teapot, sugar and cream bowls, sexagon in form with rustic handles, having the marigold flower modelled in high relief on the side is an elegant set when painted with flowers on an ivory ground with rich green handles. The effect is very pleasing. The cups and saucers in the same form and decoration are quite unique, being remarkably light and graceful. We must not omit to mention the blackberry Stilton cheese and umbrella stands, the bold foliage and delicate flower being shown up to advantage by the blue ground. The 'Lemon' trinket tray and 'Bird' ash tray are good; and last but not least in merit the 'Darwin' jewel tray formed by a monkey seated on a cushion, is very quaint in design and brightly colored.

*Crockery and Glass Journal,* 21 December 1882, described a few more of the firm's articles:

The 'Boar's head' game pie dish (in three sizes) is quite an acquisition. The conventional flower decoration, having a rich blue ground, is very striking, and the boar-head reversed makes an appropriate handle. The 'Diamond' jug – quite a new departure – is well adapted for decoration and useful. The maroon, ivory and turquoise colors on it are nicely balanced. ... A pair of umbrella stands with raised apples, plums, and blossoms are beautifully modelled after nature. Their single, double and triple baskets, with raised flowers, chrysanthemums, roses and pansies are feelingly treated. The 'Bird' ash tray has fulfilled our prediction by becoming a general favorite; they can scarcely produce them quick enough. We can recommend their 'Buttercup' ice cream tray, butter and salad bowl of shells and seaweeds. Good potting, new ideas, and good coloring are the special features of the Victoria Pottery Co.

Jewitt records that the firm was of very short duration, and indeed they do not seem to have advertised after January 1883. This firm should not be confused with Robinson & Leadbetter, who produced only Parian.

**Rosslyn Pottery**, Fifeshire, Scotland, *c.*1883–1930.
This pottery was established in the 1850s by Morrison & Crawford. In 1883 the pottery was enlarged, and production of majolica begun, although the works principally produced domestic crockery.

**Joseph Roth**, London, *c.*1877–82.
A retailer, he registered seven designs between 1880 and 1882. The only recorded pieces of majolica with his mark are a wall pocket and a jug. He specialized in importing continental majolica, so it is likely that these pieces are not English.

**Royal Art Pottery Co.**, St. Louis Pottery, Longton, *c.*1906–61.
*Pottery and Glass Record,* 1913–1915, lists this firm as a producer of majolica, although their advertisements do not mention it specifically. The advertisements offer 'flower pots, vases, pots and pedestals, clock sets, etc., in endless variety.' The firm was established in 1906 by Alfred Clough in a small Longton pottery. They later took over the Aynsley factory, where they made earthenware dinner and tea services, as well as fancies.

**Salopian Art Pottery**, Broseley, Shropshire, *c.*1880–1912.
An advertisement in *Pottery Gazette,* January 1884, declared, 'National Gold Medal for majolica Vase, awarded last year to our designer Mr. F. Gibbons.' The manager in 1882 was William Allen. A fine collection of Salopian Art Pottery can be seen at the Clive House Museum, Shrewsbury. The firm's mark was SALOPIAN.

**R. G. Scrivener & Co.**, Norfolk Street Works, Hanley, *c.*1870–80.
*Pottery and Glass Trades' Review* for November 1877 reported that this firm had added majolica to their china business 'this year'. Jewitt opined that their products had a 'more than average degree of artistic decoration'. Very little is known about their majolica, but they registered a floral cup and saucer and the Holly Bird Tray on 3 November 1871.
   The firm was established in 1870, at Cauldon Place between Stoke and Hanley, by R. G. Scrivener and Thomas Bourne. They were succeeded in 1883 by Pointon & Co.

**Shorter & Boulton**, Copeland Street Works, Stoke-on-Trent, 1878–1905.
The firm was founded by Arthur Shorter, who was meant to follow his father's footsteps as a railway station master. The railway did not suit Arthur, so he signed on as an apprentice china painter with Minton. He then went on to work as a journeyman painter for Bodleys China Works, Burslem. In the late 1860s, Shorter established his own premises as a decorator in Hanley. In 1872, he sold these premises to A. Wenger,* and acquired the Copeland Street Works. Soon afterwards he was joined by James Boulton, a biscuit fireman, who had been working for Wedgwood for many years. In 1891, Shorter left the works in Boulton's charge, while he took over the works of his late uncle, A. J. Wilkinson. Boulton was succeeded by his son William in 1897; and in 1900 John Guy Shorter, Arthur's youngest son, took over management of the works. The firm was succeeded by Shorter & Sons* in 1905.
   This firm produced enormous quantities of mediocre majolica mostly for the American and Australian markets. They regularly advertised majolica in *Pottery Gazette,* 1879–80. One of their most popular designs was the Bird & Fan, registered 17 March 1881.

**Shorter & Sons**, Copeland Street, Stoke-on-Trent, *c.*1905–62+.
In 1905, John Guy Shorter left this firm to assist his father and elder brother, Arthur and Colley Shorter, at A. J. Wilkinson Ltd. Shorter & Sons was managed by Arthur Holdcroft, then Mr. Lovatt, and in 1932 by Harry Steele. In 1933 the firm was converted into a private limited company.
   According to *Pottery and Glass Record,* April 1914, this firm '… make a speciality of flower pots and bulb bowls in different coloured majolica glazes'. Production of these items continued into the 1930s. They also made corncob jugs. Pieces may be marked with an impressed SHORTER ENGLAND.

**J. & J. Snow**, Albert Works, Stoke-on-Trent, *c.*1882–95; Pyenest Street Works, Hanley *c.*1896–1907.
These works were previously operated by Snow & Littler.* Messrs. Snow manufactured terracotta, jet, majolica, etc. They advertised majolica in *Pottery Gazette,* 1886–91.

**Snow & Littler**, Albert Works, Liverpool Road, Stoke-on-Trent, *c.*1879–81.
This pottery was formerly operated by Turner & Wood,* and subsequently operated by J. & J. Snow.* In 1879, they advertised 'a great variety of useful goods in jet and majolica' in

*Pottery and Glass Trades' Journal.* They continued to advertise majolica in *Pottery Gazette* during 1880, but in 1881 their advertisements, under the style Snow & Co., no longer mention majolica.

**Stanway & Son**, Copeland Street Works, Stoke-on-Trent, *c.*1878–80.
J. Stanway, formerly of Poole, Stanway & Wood,* and his son operated here briefly. *Crockery and Glass Journal*, 18 August 1878, announced: 'Messrs, Stanway & Son, of Stoke, have brought out some very chaste designs in stone, Parian, majolica, and china.' After Stanway's death, the following year, the firm was sold to Turner & Wood.*

**Edward Steele**, Cannon Street, Hanley, *c.*1875–1900.
According to Jewitt, Steele produced earthenware, stoneware, majolica and Parian. According to Bernard Hughes, Steele manufactured elaborate majolica figural centrepieces, comports, vases, teapots, jugs and dessert services. These had body and colours of 'unusual excellence'. Steele registered two designs in 1882. An advertisement in *Pottery Gazette* in 1879 reads: 'Manufacturer of every description of earthenware, Parian and majolica, suitable for the home, foreign and colonial markets.'

**Daniel Sutherland & Sons**, Park Hall Street, Longton, *c.*1863–77.
Jewitt listed Sutherland's wares as 'majolica jugs, vases, tripods, flower-holders; bread, cheese and fruit dishes; water-bottles, tea and coffee pots, kettles and other articles'. They also made Parian, terracotta and stoneware. They advertised Parian, ivory and majolica in *Keates's Directory 1875–6.* Hugh Sutherland* succeeded in 1877.

**H(ugh) Sutherland**, Park Hall Street, Longton, *c.*1877–82.
The successor to Daniel Sutherland & Sons,* this firm advertised in *Pottery and Glass Trades' Review* for August 1877 as follows:

**HUGH SUTHERLAND,**
MANUFACTURER OF
MAJOLICA, GREEN GLAZE, FLOWER POTS, VASES, &c.
LOW PRICES AND GOOD QUALITY.
Works:—PARKHALL STREET, ANCHOR ROAD, LONGTON, STAFFS.
WRITE FOR LIST OF PRICES.

They continued to advertise majolica in *Pottery Gazette* as late as 1881.

**Thomas Sutherland**, Market Lane Works, Longton, *c.*1888–97.
Thomas Sutherland advertised 'China, earthenware, majolica, Jet and general useful and fancy goods' in *Pottery Gazette* during 1888–90.

**Taylor & Kent**, Florence Works, Longton, *c.*1867–present day.
Mostly known for their bone china, they also made a wide range of majolica ware. *Pottery Gazette*, January 1884, announced that they had recently begun majolica production. They advertised majolica there during 1884–5, particularly 'cheap lines in majolica jugs'.

**Uriah Thomas & Co.**, Marlborough Works, Hanley, *c.*1888–1905.
Formerly Mountford & Thomas,* this firm carried on majolica production.

**Toft & Cope**, Swan Works, Cliff Bank, Stoke-on-Trent, *c.*1884–6.
This firm advertised majolica in *Pottery Gazette*, June 1884.

**Turner, Hassall & Bromley**, Albert Works, Liverpool Road, Stoke, *c.*1859–1862.
This firm was established by George Turner, Joseph Hassall and William Bromley for the .
manufacture of Parian. William Bromley died in 1862; in 1863 a larger works was built at
Copeland Street, under the style Turner, Hassall & Peake. The new partner, Thomas Peake
retired in 1871, and the firm became Turner, Hassall & Poole. In 1873, Hassall retired, and
the style became Turner, Poole & Stanway. In 1875, Turner retired and the firm became
Poole, Stanway & Wood.*
   Jewitt wrote: 'A speciality of the works introduced by Mr. [George] Turner, was the novelty
of decorating the Parian body with majolica colours, by which means a clearness and
brilliancy as well as softness of colour is attained and a pleasing effect gained.'

**Turner & Wood**, Copeland Street Works, Stoke-on-Trent, *c.*1878–88.
George Turner and Josiah Wood succeeded Stanway & Son,* formerly Poole, Stanway &
Wood.* They advertised 'superior majolica' alongside their principal product, Parian, in
*Pottery Gazette*, 1880–7. They also made Parian majolica. This journal, in January 1881,
described some of their majolica:

> They have a set of jugs in majolica especially suitable for the American market with wide
> mouths. It is called the 'pebble jug'. The surface is roughened or covered with raised stones
> to represent pebbles. It has a blue background relieved with floral patterns. Another
> feature is 'shell ware', which they have in various goods such as salads, creams, dessert
> plates, &c. Oyster plates with side dishes are well done, as this perhaps gives more scope
> for imitating the different tints shown in the pearly appearance of a shell. We noticed a very
> unique breakfast cruet set made up of a water lily leaf and flower. The leaf forms the shell,
> holding an opening lily for the mustard, the cover is supposed to be the top of the flower
> with a butterfly resting upon it for a handle; a closed bud is the pepper caster.

*Crockery and Glass Journal*, October 1881, commented: 'The "Leafage" dessert, in majolica,
is a very charming service, the autumnal tints of the vine foliage, rich orange, browns, olive-
greens, and maroon are blended in harmony and sweet confusion.'

**Wagstaff & Brunt**, Off Stafford Street, Longton, *c.*1879–1927.
This firm advertised majolica in *Pottery Gazette* during 1884, but it is not certain whether
they were manufacturers or dealers.

**Wardle & Ash**, James Street, Shelton, Hanley, *c.*1859–65.
James Wardle, later of Wardle & Co. (see Chapter Four), and George Ash* made Parian,
majolica and figures at this address. Pieces may be marked with the firm's name or intitials.

**Warrilow & Cope**, Wellington Works, Longton, *c.*1880–7.
On 21 April 1881, *Crockery and Glass Journal* announced that this firm had 'added the
manufacture of majolica to that of china. Being new in the trade, they have a great variety of
designs, but they have naturally followed in the footsteps of the old-established firms, and
produced many of the "good" things already in the market.' Jewitt reported: 'Majolica was
introduced by Warrilow & Cope with good artistic and commercial results.' During the early
1880s, this firm advertised 'every description of majolica for home and export' in *Pottery
Gazette*. The firm was subsequently George Warrilow. There are no recorded marks.

**A. Wenger**, Parker Street Works, Hanley, *c.*1870s–1960s.

Albert Francis Wenger was born in 1837 in Lausanne, Switzerland. After serving an apprenticeship at Nyon, he became head of the technical department of Richard & Co., Milan. He emigrated to England to manufacture feldspathic porcelain. In time, the firm became known as a supplier to the other potteries, specializing in colours. This firm advertised majolica in *Pottery Gazette* during 1878 and 1879.

**Wilkinson's Pottery Co.**, Whitehaven, Cumberland, *c.*1815–85.

This firm advertised majolica in *Pottery Gazette*, January 1885.

**Williams, Oakes & Co.**, Sneyd Pottery, Albert Street, Burslem, *c.*1867–76.

Among other goods, Jewitt records the production of rockingham, jet and majolica here. In 1876 the firm became Oakes, Clare & Chadwick.*

# MINOR AMERICAN MAJOLICA MANUFACTURERS

**A. M. Beck**, Evansville, Indiana, *c.*1882–4.

An Englishman who established a pottery of three kilns for the manufacture of majolica in 1882. Mr. Beck died in 1884, whereupon Bennighof, Uhl & Co. acquired the premises for the manufacture of whiteware. By 1891, the pottery had been acquired by the Flentke family and operated under the style of the Crown Pottery and Crown Potteries Company. No mark is recorded.

**Cartwright Bros.**, East Liverpool, Ohio *c.*1880–1924+.

According to John Ramsay (*Hobbies*, May 1945), they made majolica about 1880. This has often been repeated, but the author has been unable to locate any primary sources which confirm it. The firm's advertisements only mention white-lined, rockingham and yellow ware.

**William Colclough**, East Liverpool, Ohio, *c.*1850–81.

In May 1881, *Crockery and Glass Journal* reported that 'Mr. Wm. Colclough continues his experiments in majolica.' On 11 August of the same year, they announced 'Mr. Wm. Colcough, manufacturer of majolica ware, has sold out his stock, and intends quitting the business. He is an old and experienced potter, and his goods were unequaled by any in the market.' There is no other evidence of William Colclough's brief career as a majolica producer.

**Croxall & Cartwright**, Union & Mansion Potteries, East Liverpool, *c.*1856–87.

Thomas Croxall, with his father and brothers, purchased the former Bennett pottery soon after their arrival in East Liverpool in 1844. This small pottery producing rockingham and yellow ware was destroyed by a flood in 1852.

In 1856, Thomas and John Croxall, Joseph Cartwright and Jonathan Kinsey purchased the Union Pottery (formerly Ball & Morris). Two and a half years later Thomas Croxall and Jonathan Kinsey withdrew, the firm then operating under the style Croxall & Cartwright.

In 1863, they acquired the Mansion Pottery, and added two storeys to the Union Pottery. By 1876 they employed 100 hands, being one of the largest potteries in the district.

Croxall & Cartwright in 1878 were manufacturing rockingham, yellow and white-lined wares. They still operated the two potteries, one on either side of Second Street. Each pottery boasted two kilns, which were converted from coal to steam power in that year. Having been established in 1845, by Ball & Morris, this site was considered one of the oldest in the country.

*Crockery and Glass Journal,* 8 January 1880 reported:

> For some time past Messrs. Croxall & Cartwright, of the Union and Mansion Potteries, have been experimenting in colored glazes and majolica, with a few [sic] to the manufacture of fancy ware of this character in a commercial way. Some very neat specimens have come out of their kilns, and as soon as they have satisfied themselves with the quality and finish of the ware we may look for a large production. Several shapes have already been modeled in striking and beautiful designs.

On 29 July 1880, the same publication announced: 'Messrs. Croxall & Cartwright's experiments in odd shapes, designs and colors have proved eminently satisfactory; and they are so much encouraged over their success that an effort will be made to supply the market.' The author has been unable to determine whether or not this promised majolica was actually put on the market. The firm marked some of their wares: CROXALL & CARTWRIGHT/ EAST/ LIVERPOOL/ OHIO.

In 1887, Cartwright died and Croxall bought out his interest. The firm operated as J. W. Croxall and Sons, until Croxall's death in 1905.

**Eureka Pottery**, Trenton, New Jersey, *c.*1883–7.

The Eureka Pottery first appears in the Trenton directories in 1883 under the proprietorship of either R. or Leon Weil. *Crockery and Glass Journal,* 10 May 1883, reported: 'Majolica and Limoges ware is getting a foothold here, and the Eureka Pottery – a small but busy establishment – turns out some nice goods.' On 17 May, they announced:

> The new majolica works, known as the Eureka Pottery, has about twenty paintresses at work, and they are now beginning to turn out a class of goods that will bear comparison with anything that is now in the market. They are just now fairly underway and ready for the market.

On 11 October of the same year:

> The Eureka Pottery manufacturing majolica have recently produced some pieces of goods that I consider a very creditable departure for a modest concern that was predicted to fail for want of greater capacity and better luck. These latter efforts, however, have changed opinions somewhat, and those who were the first to utter predictions are now making such remarks as 'good enough', 'a step in the right direction', and the like. I have not seen the proprietor for some weeks because he and I differed slightly as to my want of enthusiasm for the ordinary shapes and styles of majolica, but having seen his latest work outside of the factory, I enthuse thus spontaneously without solicitation.

The quality of the pieces is certainly better than much American majolica. The colours are bright and true and the modelling crisp, if the potting is rather heavy. The best-known patterns of this factory are Bird and Fan (several variations have been noted), and the 'Trenton-Type Bird' which is a stork wading in a marsh. Pieces are clearly marked EUREKA POTTERY/TRENTON.

The enterprise was short-lived, however, for on 14 February 1884, *Crockery and Glass Journal* reported: 'The Eureka has been closed after a brief career, and the shops are to be used for some other branch of the pottery art.' According to the Trenton directories, in 1884 Noah and Charles Boch took over the pottery and it became the Eureka Porcelain Manufactory. It is not likely that this latter concern made majolica.

**Faience Manufacturing Company**, Greenpoint, Long Island, New York, *c.*1880–92.

Established in 1880, in the pottery district of Greenpoint, in the eastern part of Brooklyn, this firm also maintained a showroom in Manhattan. They first made pottery encrusted with hand modelled flowers, which they incorrectly called 'barbotine'. Their majolica consisted of plain shapes dipped in various coloured glazes, and in some cases marbled. An incised mark FMCo was used on these early productions.

# FMC̦

The firm is better known for its art china, produced under the directorship of Edward Lycett. Although Lycett was director of the firm from 1884 to 1890, it seems unlikely that he would have closely concerned himself with the more mundane majolica. Lycett is best known as a china painter, and for his experiments with porcelaneous bodies and glazes. It is not certain whether majolica was still made during his tenure.

**Richard Harrison**, Peekskill Pottery Co., Peekskill, New York, *c*.1882–92.
According to Ketchum (1987), Richard Harrison, formerly a crockery and glass merchant, had become a manufacturer by 1882. The pottery made majolica Toby jugs, pitchers and breadtrays. At least some majolica items were marked either PEEKSKILL POTTERY CO. or HARRISON'S POTTERY WORKS.

**J. E. Jeffords**, Philadelphia City Pottery, Philadelphia, *c*.1868–1901.
This firm was established in 1868 as the Port Richmond Pottery Co. by J. E. Jeffords, formerly of Morrison and Carr (see Chapter Five). At the United States Potters' Association Exhibition at the Philadelphia Centennial in 1876, his medal-winning display included yellow, rockingham, majolica and lava wares. The majolica included large jardinières with stands and a 26-gallon teapot on a four-foot majolica pedestal. Jeffords left a case of rockingham, white-lined, buff-stone, lava and majolica ware on display at the Permanent Exhibition.

Jeffords was a major advertiser in *Crockery and Glass Journal*, but none of his many, elaborately illustrated advertisements so much as mentions majolica. Nor do the many articles about the firm, which appear in that same publication, although they go into great detail about all of their other lines. It thus seems unlikely that Jeffords produced very much majolica.

**Kirkham Art Tile & Pottery Co.**, Barberton, Summit County, Ohio, *c*.1891–3.
This firm's letterhead advertised Palissy, Roubelle [sic], and Vergonia [sic], among other wares. Joseph Kirkham, the pottery 'superintendent and ceramacist', went on to start Kirkham Tile and Pottery Co., in Tropico, California. He also worked, at one time, for the Providential Tile Works in Trenton.

**Holland Manley**, East Liverpool, Ohio, *c*.1881.
*Crockery and Glass Journal*, 10 December 1880, reported: 'The new factory in course of erection by Holland Manley is nearly completed. Special attention will be given to majolica and other fancy wares.' Yet just a few weeks later on 27 January 1881, the same publication announced: 'The novelty works of Manley, Surles [sic] and Gamble are now nearly ready to commence operation in the manufacture of many popular and handsome designs.' It can be reasonably conjectured that Holland Manley, lacking funds to continue, had acquired partners. On 17 March 1881, *Crockery and Glass Journal* announced the start up of the

works. On 27 July 1881, they reported that the firm had placed their goods on the market – 'Fruit jars and stewpans are their specialities'. Then, on 8 September, they announced that Holland Manley had disposed of his interest in the firm, which became Fleutke, Harrison & Co. It is not certain, then, that the factory ever actually produced any majolica, although it is quite possible.

**Mayer Brothers**, Arsenal Pottery, Trenton, New Jersey, c.1877–1900.
Joseph S. Mayer exhibited a selection of finely modelled majolica Toby jugs at the Philadelphia Centennial in 1876, although the Arsenal Pottery does not appear in the Trenton directories until 1877. In 1880, Joseph was joined by his brother James, and the style became Mayer Bros. Sometime in the 1880s Joseph S. Mayer acquired the Beaver Falls Pottery in Pennsylvania. He maintained his interest in, and remained active in, the Trenton operation as well. It seems that James left Trenton to supervise the Beaver Falls operation in 1885.

On 14 February 1884, *Crockery and Glass Journal* mourned: 'Majolica is no more in Trenton excepting that made at Mayer's Pottery.' So it seems that his goods were successful enough to sell despite the waning popularity of majolica at this time. In 1885, *The Pottery and Glassware Reporter* stated: 'The colors are much superior to the general run in this class of goods, and Mr. Mayer has a good reputation among the handlers of majolica wares.' *The Pottery and Glassware Reporter*, 17 November 1887, reported:

> Joseph S. Mayer, Arsenal Pottery, is one of the most reliable manufacturers of majolica and barbotine ware in the country. His make is known everywhere for its reliability and attractive appearance and his products are in steady and extensive demand throughout the entire land.

In 1893, Barber called Arsenal 'probably, the only concern in the United States which manufactures the so-called majolica ware.' Lehner's *Encyclopedia* lists 85 marks used by the Beaver Falls concern, but it appears that the products of the Arsenal Pottery may not have been marked.

**McDevitt & Moore**, California Pottery, East Liverpool, Ohio, 1871–1900.
The California Pottery was built by Edward McDevitt, Stephen Moore, Ferdinand Kepper and others in 1868. McDevitt and Moore took over in 1871. An advertisement in *Crockery Journal*, 3 June 1875, offers rockingham and yellow wares. A reporter for *Crockery and Glass Journal*, 15 February 1877, waxed quite poetic about the pottery, although giving the modern reader an idea of the difficulties of transport during that era:

> This lies about a mile and a half over the hills back of East Liverpool. I am afraid to say how deep the mud was on the road, or how steep the hills were; but at all events I reached there in safety, passing loaded teams on the road, which seemed to get along much better than I did. The pottery is located in a most romantic valley, and a beautiful mountainstream dashes along before its doors. The spot must be, as one of the proprietors styled it, 'a paradise in summer when the mountains put on their green dress.' A new kiln has been erected here during the fall, adding greatly to the capacity of the works. This is a yellow and rockingham ware pottery. They are doing a fair opening business and look for a good season.

In 1878, the firm still had two kilns and employed twenty hands. Apparently the firm did not mark their wares. A majolica cake stand attributed to this firm is displayed at the East Liverpool Museum of Ceramics. The firm closed in 1900, to reopen as the Trentvale Pottery.

**Morley & Company**, Pioneer Pottery Works, Wellsville, Ohio, *c.*1878–84; Lincoln Pottery, East Liverpool, Ohio, *c.*1884–90.

George Morley, a Staffordshire potter, settled in East Liverpool in 1852. He worked for several potteries, including Woodward, Blakely and Company. In 1870, he formed a partnership with James Godwin and William Flentke, to operate the Salamander Pottery Works. In 1878, Morley moved to Wellsville, where he founded the Pioneer Pottery Company at the southwest corner of Commerce and Ninth Streets, with Isaac B. Clark and Harmer Michaels. They must have had considerable financial resources, because the pottery began operations with sixty hands – a very large establishment for that time. It was initially a whiteware manufactory. On 17 March 1881, *Crockery and Glass Journal* announced: 'The experiments in majolica at Morley & Co.'s pottery, Wellsville, are proving uniformly successful.' An advertisement in the same publication on 10 January 1884 includes 'American Majolica'. Later in 1884, George Morley sold his interest in Pioneer, which discontinued majolica production.

Morley and his two sons returned to East Liverpool and purchased the Lincoln Pottery from Messrs. West & Hardwick. Here they continued to make white granite and majolica, somtimes employing the same moulds for both bodies. On 23 October 1884, *The Pottery and Glassware Reporter* noted: 'George Morley is running his pottery (formerly West, Hardwick & Co.'s) on full-time, and making a lot of handsome novelties as well as staple wares. His specialties are white ware and majolica.'

Among their known wares are leaf dishes, bamboo and basketweave teasets and napkin plates (featuring a neatly folded napkin in the middle of the plate). 'Rustic' jugs and mugs, with tree bark grounds, came uncovered or with pewter tops, with thumb lift and hinge built into the handle. Spittoons were octagonal or rounded with 'rope' rims. Many collectors seek his figural owl and parrot pitchers. The fish-shape bouquet holders (known as 'Gurgle Jugs', because of the sound they made when poured from) are quite commonly found. Plaques included a pair of trout in high relief. Most sought after is the bivalve-shaped bowl on shell-shaped feet, which seems to be a copy of a design by Joseph Holdcroft.

In 1890, George Morley retired from the pottery business, and became mayor of East Liverpool until 1896. The firm went into receivership in 1891, and all assets were sold in order to pay debts.

**John Moses & Co. (Sons)**, Glasgow Pottery, Trenton, New Jersey, *c.*1863–1905.
Founded in 1863, this firm traded as John Moses and Co. until 1895. Between 1895 and closure in 1905, they traded as John Moses & Sons. Besides majolica, they made hand-painted and transfer-printed ironstone, white granite ware and cream-coloured ware. They made institutional china, commemorative wares, tea and table wares, and toilet sets.

John Moses was born in Ireland in 1832. He is known to have been working in the United States from the early 1850s. With his brother James and two silent partners, he established the Glasgow Pottery in 1863, it being one of the first ten potteries in Trenton. In 1873, the Moses brothers bought the interests of their partners. This two-kiln pottery grew prodigiously. *Crockery Journal*, 23 January 1875, stated that they had 200 hands. An illustration reveals an enormous factory with six kilns visible.

Charles Rebert contends that Glasgow majolica was left unmarked, so that dealers could apply their own labels, making it thus almost impossible to identify. Lehner's *Encyclopedia*, however, gives 27 different marks used by the firm on various wares. While none of these is specified as a majolica mark, it seems probable that one or more of the marks might have been used on the majolica.

**New Milford Pottery Co.**, New Milford, Connecticut, *c.*1887–1908.
Charles Reynolds joined the newly established New Milford Pottery Company in 1887. He had previously worked as a designer for a pottery in Cleveland, Ohio. Initially the firm produced whitewares, cream-coloured wares and semi-opaque china (a poor sort of Parian ware). Reynolds soon introduced the 'Duchess' ware line of majolica, with mottled glazes. They produced many large items, such as umbrella stands, cuspadores and jardinières on pedestals. A three-armed rustic candelabra had to be discontinued because it was so badly designed that the wax poured all over the base. The Top Hat Planter was a design unique to the firm. The pieces were generally decorated with streaky green, blue and mauve glazes.

The firm was reorganized in 1892 as the Wannopee Pottery Co. as the result of financial difficulties. In 1896, Reynolds patented a 'McKinley' pitcher, commemorating McKinley's election to the presidency in that year. Barber complains of these very poor-quality Parian type jugs which the firm began to produce in 1895: other subjects were Napoleon, Beethoven and Mozart. Around 1901, they produced 'Scarabronze' artwares, which had a glaze resembling copper. Also in 1901, they introduced the 'Lettuce Leaf' pattern. The moulds for this were actually made from cabbage leaves. 'Lettuce Leaf' is lightweight and glazed in pink or pale green. Some twenty-five sizes and shapes were produced in dinner and tea services, as well as a series of jugs.

The firm closed in 1903, and when its assets were liquidated the following year, Reynolds,

*75. Wannopee Pottery 'Lettuce Leaf' Jug. Impressed marks, 'W' in sunburst; '217'. Height 17.5 cm. Collection of Don Kelly and Warren Fitzsimmons*

who was credited with the creation of 'Lettuce Leaf', purchased the moulds. He continued, for a short time, to make 'Lettuce Leaf' at a Trenton pottery, in association with George H. Bowman Company of Cleveland, Ohio, a distributor.

A manuscript concerning the factory by Howard Peck was not available to this author as it is being edited for future publication. The New Milford Historical Society displays a collection of New Milford majolica.

**Odell & Booth Brothers**, Tarrytown Pottery, Tarrytown, New York, *c.*1881–5.
Charles Mortimer Odell leased a building for his new pottery on Main Street, Tarrytown, in 1880. He had the financial backing of his financier father, but lacking practical experience in the business sought partnership with Henry and Walter Booth. The Booth

brothers were newly arrived from Staffordshire where they had been in business with their father as Booth & Sons (see Appendix A). The factory began production in January 1881.

The decorating department was headed by Joseph Bishop Evans, formerly a painter and designer for Minton, Hollins & Co., Minton and Wedgwood. Godden (*Minton*) lists Evans as a land and seascape painter *c.*1860–85. Batkin says that he joined Wedgwood in December 1874, designing tiles and table wares, as well as painting art tiles.

Previous writers have been astonished at the quality of Odell & Booth Brothers' early work, but this initial success is not really surprising, considering the talented veterans who were at the helm. The Booth brothers had been making majolica in Staffordshire and Evans had worked for the two greatest majolica producers. Evans left Tarrytown at the beginning of 1882 to head the decorating department of the Mercer pottery in Trenton. He was replaced by Edward E. Blackmore, a South Kensington trained artist.

The pottery's wares included majolica and underglaze decorated faience. They won a silver medal at the Mechanics' Fair in Boston. *Crockery and Glass Journal*, 12 January 1882, described them as 'large producers of majolica'. On 15 June 1882, they reported:

> In the production of majolica Messrs. Odell & Booth Bros. have had long experience and painstaking familiarity, the best evidence of which is the display they are able to make in this line. Their factory is running with full orders, a number of which are in special designs furnished with the orders when they were handed in.

An advertisement in the same journal on 20 September 1883 offered, 'Limoges, Barbotine, Faience, and Majolica. In Ornamental Vases for Lamps, Gas Fixtures, Silverware, etc.' In 1884, Walter Booth returned to England, and the firm became Odell & Booth. They now made only utilitarian majolica and ivory ware, as well as some industrial ceramics. After disagreements between the partners in 1885, the factory shut down. It reopened as the Tarrytown Pottery Company, run by Henry Booth and Warren C. Brown, but this venture was short-lived and closed within months. Many unmarked pieces, particularly Toby mugs, jugs and bread trays, have been attributed to this firm.

The Historical Society of the Tarrytowns has a display of unmarked but attributed pieces.

**J. L. Rue Pottery Co.**, Matawan, New Jersey, *c.*1875–95.
Having been at Swan Hill Pottery of South Amboy, New Jersey, since 1860, J. L. Rue moved to Matawan in 1875, where he still operated under the style Swan Hill Pottery. In 1880, he changed the style to J. L. Rue Pottery Co. *Crockery and Glass Journal*, 17 January 1895, reported that Isaac T. Rue, secretary and treasurer of the concern, had asked the Vice Chancellor in Newark to appoint a receiver, as the firm was insolvent.

Two pieces of majolica from this factory were displayed at the exhibition titled 'Pottery and Porcelain of New Jersey' staged at the Newark Museum in 1947. The first was a 'Majolica basket, openwork border in the form of intertwining stems, crossed bail handle. Relief designs of leaves and flowers growing out of border, in greens, blues and browns on yellow ground.' The second was a 'Majolica pitcher, pale green, blue and brown glaze, pink lining. Pear shape, scroll handle; relief design of anchor and chain either side of body, palmette rising from base back and front.'

**Tenuous Majolica.**
Good-quality pieces of majolica with this mark have been recorded, but their origins are unknown.

**United States Pottery Company**, Bennington, Vermont, *c.*1849–58.
This well-documented firm, usually known as Bennington, primarily made flint enamel, porcelain, rockingham ware, scroddled ware, whiteware and yellow ware. However, Richard Barrett in *Bennington Pottery & Porcelain* illustrates an 'extremely rare majolica type pineapple jug and grapevine pattern vases'. A Bennington catalogue includes 'hanging vases and ampler vases in majolica'.

**Willets Manufacturing Co.**, Excelsior Pottery Works, Trenton, New Jersey, *c.*1879–1909.
Joseph, Daniel and Edmund R. Willets purchased the Excelsior Pottery Works from William Young & Sons in 1879. Originally manufacturers of semi-porcelain wares, they were particularly known for their porcelain table wares and Belleek wares in later years. An article in the *Trenton Times*, 6 November 1883, stated that they were the largest pottery in Trenton, both in terms of production and number of employees. During their four-year tenure the Willets brothers had increased the factory from five kilns to eleven, 'including two of the largest decorating kilns in Trenton'. The site was six acres and included twenty-two buildings, some of four storeys in height.

*Crockery and Glass Journal*, December 1881, remarked '... what is more gratifying, perhaps, than any other move that they have made this season, is the beginning of a remarkably good line of majolica, which is quite as attractive as some of the better class of goods from Europe.' The same journal noted on 2 February 1882 that they were 'pushing their majolica department forward as rapidly as possible, and they are now bringing out goods for which they find a ready sale.' Their first advertisement for majolica appeared on 6 April 1882: 'Majolica goods of brilliant color, equal to the finest imported.' On 25 May 1882 it was noted that: 'Marked improvements in coloring have been made by burning this ware in a separate kiln by itself.'

An advertisement in December 1882 also included Lily Jugs, Nos. 1, 2, 3, 4, 5, Round Fan Teasets, Lily-Covered Butters and Drainers, Rose and Lily Cuspadores, Leaf and Colored Border and Green Leaf 5-inch plates, Fan-Handled Coffees, Small Jugs, Comports, Salads, Nappies, etc. According to Barber, Willetts did not mark their majolica ware.

**William Young & Sons**, Excelsior Pottery Works, Trenton, New Jersey, *c.*1853–79.
*Trenton Times*, 6 November 1883, reported that William Young 'did more to develop and advance the pottery industry in this country than any other individual'. Young and others rented the Hattersley Pottery in 1853, making rockingham, yellow-ware, common white ware and, later, cream-coloured ware. Having outgrown the Hattersley Pottery, Young built the Excelsior Pottery Works in 1857. His three sons, William, Edward and John, carried on as William Young's Sons after William Young retired in 1870. The firm won a bronze medal for their display of porcelain hardware trimmings, white granite and cream-colour wares at the United States Potters' Association Exhibit at the Philadelphia Centennial in 1876. They later manufactured domestic earthenware, white granite, semi-porcelain, ornamental porcelain and sanitary ware. Dinnerwares and toilet sets with underglaze decoration were a speciality. It can only be assumed that they made majolica. Kovel & Kovel state that Charles Bailey, later of Stockton Terra Cotta Company, was manager of their Majolica Department. The works were bought by Willets Manufacturing Co.* in 1879.

# Designers, Modellers and Decorators of British Majolica

The designers, modellers and decorators were crucial to the majolica manufacturers. For as a genre, majolica probably taxed the imaginations of the decorators, and the skills of the modellers, more than any other type of ware. They are not relegated to an appendix as an indication of unimportance, but because most of them worked for several of the major majolica manufacturers, often on a contract or freelance basis, and it would be inappropriate to include them elsewhere. The decorators included here worked on exhibition pieces for the most part, and they are often best known for their work on porcelains of the period.

The importance accorded to these artists can be seen by these descriptions of the ideal persons for these tasks printed in *Pottery and Glassware Reporter*, 7 May 1885:

> The designer must be a well educated man, must have a good knowledge of the various historic styles of art not to commit anachronisms. He must have judgement to see what was the point of any work of art or ornament that he saw, capability to seize it and duplicate to other uses, handicraft to apply it, and a knowledge of his materials and methods of manufacture, in order to produce his idea in the cheapest way consistent with quality.
>
> The modeller must be very intelligent. In the same role, he must carry out his designs with taste and knowledge, he must have facility in making rapid sketches of clay, suggestions for selection and approval. ... The painter must be able to decorate a given space at a given price, surely in harmony with the shape and decoration of the piece.

The names of modellers may sometimes be found incised on pieces. Painters sometimes signed or initialled their work.

### Lady Marian Alford
Designed a fountain, pattern no. 705, exhibited by Minton at the London Exhibition in 1862.

### Thomas Allen
Born in 1831, Allen began to work at Minton in 1845. He is known to have decorated porcelains for the 1851 exhibition. He studied at the Stoke School of Art and won the first National Scholarship to the South Kensington School in 1852. He also studied at Somerset House during this period. Returning to Minton in 1854, he painted on majolica and tiles, as well as porcelains. Part of the tiling in the Victoria & Albert Museum was painted by Allen. He also painted a majolica ewer and plateau, from engravings by Raffaelo Guidi after Polidoro de Carvaggio, exhibited by Minton at the London Exhibition of 1862. He left Minton in 1875 to join Wedgwood, where he decorated bone china. His first major exhibition of

Wedgwood wares was at the Paris Exhibition of 1878. In March of that year he became Wedgwood's Art Director, a post which he retained until his partial retirement in 1898. He retired completely in 1904, but lived on until 1915. Allen did not sign Minton's pieces, but those made on his own time or for Wedgwood bear a monogram of his initials, A.T.

### William Beattie

Beattie exhibited his sculptures at the Royal Academy frequently c.1829–64, and at the British Institute c.1834–48. Best known for his sculptures, some of which were reduced and published as bronzes, he also modelled Parian and majolica wares. He is known to have worked freelance for Bates, Brown-Westhead, Moore & Co., W. Adams & Sons, Sir James Duke & Nephews, W. T. Copeland, Minton and Wedgwood (c.1856–63). He specialized in biblical and allegorical figues and groups in a neo-classical style.

### John B. Bebbington

Modelled majolica tablewares (including a Japanese dessert service) and Parian for Wedgwood during the early 1860s.

### John Bell

Born in Hopton, Suffolk, in 1812, Bell was an important sculptor, as well as a ceramic modeller. He trained at the Royal Academy in 1829, and first exhibited there in 1832. He worked in many mediums, including marble, terracotta and cast iron. His best-known statues are Queen Victoria (1841) and his America group for the Albert Memorial, among his many Royal and Official commissions. He designed many Parian figures and groups c.1847–55, many for Summerly's Art Manufactures. The most notable of these was his Dorothea, which was produced between 1848 and 1890.

For Minton, Bell designed 'Bell's Bread Tray', registered 4 March 1848, and subsequently made in majolica. His Parian figure group of Una and the Lion produced by Minton was adapted for a majolica plaque. Summerly commissioned two of his designs, the Bonfire Spill and the Dolphin Spill, from Wedgwood. His style, described as romantic, sentimental and full of bathos, went out of fashion in the 1870s, although he continued to design public monuments. He died in Kensington in 1895.

### J. Bennett

Bennett painted a majolica ewer exhibited by Sir James Duke & Nephews at the London Exhibition of 1862.

### Simon Birks

Simon Birks was probably responsible for a great many more majolica designs than we are now able to attribute to him. While an apprentice at Minton, he studied at the Stoke School of Design. He won a prize offered by Smith Child for a wine cooler in the majolica style during this period. This was later exhibited by Minton at the London Exhibition in 1862. He worked at Wedgwood c.1867–75.

### Hamlet Bourne

A pupil of Protât, Bourne modelled the Tremblay centre dessert wares made by Wedgwood for Thomas Goode c.1861. For Minton he modelled the Soulage Ewer and Stand, after a Palissy ewer in the Soulages Collection at the South Kensington Museum.

*Joseph Brown*
Brown was the Head Designer at Brown-Westhead, Moore & Co. He designed the nine-foot majolica candlesticks and the majolica tiger group exhibited in Paris in 1878 (see Chapter Four).

*Henry Brownsword*
Born in 1825, this modeller, painter and designer was apprenticed to Wedgwood in 1838. He studied under Protât at the Stoke School of Art, and became a modeller for Wedgwood in 1852. From the 1860s, he worked closely with Emile Lessore. After Lessore's return to France, he made frequent visits to him there. It was Brownsword who negotiated the purchase of the Tremblay moulds and glaze formulae from the Rubelles factory (see Chapter Three). He died in 1892.

*Albert Carrier de Belleuse* ( *c.*1824–87), known as Carrier de Belleuse, was a talented and internationally celebrated French sculptor. He studied at the Ecole des Beaux Arts, Paris in the 1840s, before working for Sèvres. He also modelled free lance for leading English manufacturers: Minton, Wedgwood, Brownfield, and T. J. & J. Mayer, among others. He became Minton's Chief Designer for about five years after Jeannest's death in 1857. A pair of figures introduced in 1850, Boy and Girl with Baskets, was made in majolica glazes. He modelled the great vases (more than six feet in circumference) exhibited by Minton at the London Exhibition, 1862. The support was formed of a group of four cupids; the central part decorated with a wreath of roses. The vase was surmounted and surrounded by an enormous snake. There is also a contract to provide models for Minton dated 1881 in the Minton Archives. He also modelled for Coalbrookdale.
Upon his return to France, he became the Art Director at Sèvres, and modelled for Hautin, Boulenger et Cie, Choisy-le-Roi.
Some models bear his signature.

*Paul Comolera*
This sculptor and *animalier* was born in Paris in 1818. He studied under the neo-classical sculptor François Rude, and made his debut at the Paris Salon in 1847. His speciality was birds, and many of his designs were published as bronzes. His model of a cock was produced in faience by Hautin, Boulenger et Cie, Choisy-le-Roi. He worked for Minton in the mid 1870s, his most famous pieces being the life-size majolica Peacock and the Fawn garden ornaments. His figure of an organ grinder was produced in both Parian and majolica.

*Theodore Deck*
Theodore Deck was one of the most influential ceramic designers and modellers of the nineteenth century, both in Britain and on the Continent. Born in Alsace in 1823, he was unable to fulfil his childhood dream of becoming a sculptor, and began working as a ceramic stovemaker in France, Germany and Austria. He finally settled in France, where he rose to the position of foreman. In 1859, he and his brother opened their own studio, where he produced ceramics influenced by the Middle East, and later, Japan. They also made Henri Deux ware (also known as St. Porchaire), and reproductions of Italian maiolica. The Decks gathered a band of notable ceramic artists at their studio. An article on the opulent Deck establishment in Paris by Margaret Bertha Wright, printed in *Crockery and Glass Journal*, 13 October 1881, quotes Deck as saying 'with exultant pride':

I am the greatest inventor of color in the world. Not the Japanese, not the Indians of the Orient, not Bernard Palissy himself, or any of the ceramic colorers of the Italian Renaissance, or of modern times, have succeeded so well in color as I have

Yet it is as a designer that Deck is best remembered in England, most particularly for his majolica designs made for Wedgwood. In 1887, he became the Art Director of the Sèvres factory. On his death, an obituary in *Pottery Gazette*, 1 June 1891, lamented:

In him France has lost the chief living authority on china, ancient and modern. His face was that of a prophet, or even of a Messiah. His disposition was that of an angel. Ever ready to talk of his art and to do a service, Deck will be remembered as a bright vision by French literary men.

### Dr. Christopher Dresser

Dresser, a botanist, designer and writer on design, worked freelance for Minton, Wedgwood and other majolica makers. Born in Glasgow in 1834, he studied at the Government School of Design at Somerset House and at South Kensington. Having secured a doctorate in botany, he was professor of that subject at several institutions, including South Kensington. At the same time he became Britain's leading industrial designer, working in many media including textiles, metalwork, silver, glass and ceramics.

### Bernard Edwards

Edwards painted some of the majolica plaques which decorated Brown-Westhead, Moore & Co.'s showrooms.

### James Evans

Evans was Brown-Westhead, Moore & Co.'s head modeller *c.*1878. His work included the nine-foot majolica candlesticks exhibited by the firm at Paris in 1878.

### George Eyre

Eyre (*c.*1815–87) trained at Stoke School of Art and Somerset House in London (*c.*1843–7). On his return to Stoke, he designed tiles for Minton Hollins. Around 1854, he moved to Samuel Alcock and Co., remaining at the works after its bankruptcy and takeover by Sir James Duke. Waring wrote that Eyre designed the majolica which Sir James Duke & Nephews displayed at the London Exhibition in 1862. He also worked for Cockson & Harding and painted for Wedgwood in the Lessore style *c.*1863. Eyre eventually became Art Director at W. T. Copeland *c.*1864–5.

### T. Fay

Marks (1986) illustrates a Holdcroft umbrella stand marked 'T. Fay Sculptor'.

### F. Gibbons

This designer for Salopian Art Pottery won a National Gold Medal for majolica in 1883.

### William James Goode

The son of Thomas Goode the London retailer, William (*c.*1831–92) was a painter and designer. His designs, usually of figures or animals, were sold to both Minton and Wedgwood *c.*1865–90. William Goode may have been responsible for some of these Wedgwood shapes (nos. 308, 765, 1037, 1641, 1861, 2095–).

*A. Gravier*

Gravier painted some dishes displayed by George Jones at the Paris Exhibition in 1878.

*Thomas Greatbach*

Greatbach modelled the Tremblay centres for Wedgwood's Limoges dessert service commissioned by Thomas Goode *c.*1861. He was later a partner in Collingwood and Greatbach (*c.*1870–87), who made porcelains, including Derby-style Japan patterns.

*James Hadley*

Hadley is best known for his many splendid models for Royal Worcester porcelain. Geoffrey Godden has called him 'the most talented British ceramic modeller of the nineteenth century'. However, as is discussed in Chapter Four, many if not most of these models were also made in majolica. In particular, Hadley was responsible for many of the candle extinguishers, which were made in majolica as well as porcelain. Hadley worked for Kerr & Binns, and subsequently Royal Worcester until 1876. Thereafter, he set up his own studio, but Royal Worcester bought nearly all his production. In 1896, he set up his own factory with his three sons, which was eventually purchased by Royal Worcester.

*John Henk*

The son of a German painter, Christian Henk, who also worked at Minton, John was apprenticed in 1859, and remained with Minton all his life. He eventually became Chief Staff Modeller, specializing in animals, especially in majolica.

*76. Pair of Minton Hen and Cockerel Flower Holders, after a model by John Henk. Impressed mark, date code, and shape numbers 1982 and 1983. Heights 35 cm and 31 cm. c.1876. Sotheby's*

## Louis M. Jahn

Born in 1839 in Thuringia, Jahn worked in Vienna before coming to England in 1862. He worked as a painter for Minton (c.1862 72), before becoming Brownfield's Art Director (c.1872–95). Jahn is often credited with the great success of Brownfield during this period. Although the fine porcelains are most often mentioned, some very good-quality majolica was made as well. In 1895, he returned to Minton as Art Director. In 1900 he became the Curator at Hanley Museum, where he remained until his death in 1911.

## Pierre Emile Jeannest

Jeannest (c.1813–57) became Minton's Chief Designer in 1846, on the death of Samuel Bourne. He also designed silver for Elkington's in Birmingham during this period (c.1848–54); and he may have worked for Brownfield as well. He modelled a majolica ewer and plateau shown by Minton at the London Exhibition of 1862. He was also master of the Model Class at the Stoke School of Design.

## Thomas Kirkby

Born in nearby Trentham in 1824, Kirkby painted for Minton from c.1841–87. His speciality was figure subjects on majolica in imitation of maiolica. At the London Exhibition of 1862, Minton displayed some plates painted by Kirkby with copies of Mantegna's 'Triumphs of Caesar'. These were among a great many fine exhibition pieces which he painted.

## Emile Lessore

Lessore (c.1805–76) was a French painter who studied at Ingres's studio; he was also a ceramic decorator, trained at Sèvres (c.1852–8). He worked at Minton (c.1858–62) and, subsequently, for Wedgwood. During the Minton period he painted majolica in the Italian style, such as a plaque with a detail of 'Battle of Milvian Bridge' by Raphael. In 1867 he returned to Paris due to ill health, but continued to work on contract for Wedgwood for the rest of his life.

## Sir Coutts Lindsay, Bart.

Lindsay designed a plate decorated with sea nymphs for Minton, which was shown at the London Exhibition of 1862.

## Léone Mallet

Best known for his paintings of fruit, Mallet painted some majolica plaques which decorated the showroom of Brown-Westhead, Moore & Co.

## William Calder Marshall

Marshall was born in Edinburgh in 1813 and studied at the Edinburgh Academy and the Royal Academy. He studied for two years in Rome, before settling in London. An eminent and prolific classical sculptor, he modelled Brown-Westhead, Moore and Co.'s Tiger Group shown at the Paris Exhibition of 1878. He also modelled a Parian figure for Sir James Duke & Nephews. Grant in his *Dictionary of British Sculptors* commented: 'But excellent as he was in portraiture, Marshall's reputation will always depend on the works of imagination which he designed and carved with such fancy and consummate craftsmanship ... Perhaps of all our Sculptors Marshall is the most poetical and imaginative, whilst in sheer workmanship he may rank with the highest.'

*Francis Wollaston Moody*
Moody (*c.*1824–86) was a designer and painter of majolica. He was an instructor in decorative art at South Kensington. He was involved in designing Minton's tiling schemes for the South Kensington Museum.

*Rowland James Morris*
Born in 1847, Morris studied at the Hanley School of Art under Protât. He then went on to study at South Kensington *c.*1863. He worked as a modeller, chiefly of majolica, for Wedgwood in the early 1870s, before going to work for Moore Bros. among others. He modelled the façade of the Wedgwood Institute at Burslem.

*M. William Mussill*
A Bohemian-born painter, Mussill worked at Sèvres before coming to England. He worked for Minton from *c.*1872–1906, specializing in bird, fish and flower painting. There are also some Wedgwood wares painted and signed by Mussill. Mussill and his assistant Pilsbury spent many hours in the conservatory making gouache studies which were later translated into paintings on ceramics, mostly earthenware. *Pottery and Glass Trades' Review*, April 1878, described one of his pieces at the Paris Exhibition: 'A pair of large majolica vases with red ground, ornamented with a broad black band, and painted with tropical plants, and standing about forty inches high, are also good specimens of his work.'

*77. Minton ewer and stand, after a design by Hughues Protât, shape number 787. c.1859.* Sotheby's

## Eugene Phoenix

He modelled the 'Greek style' 'Palissy' candelabra exhibited by Minton at the London Exhibition in 1862.

## Hughues Protât

A French sculptor who exhibited at the Paris Salon c.1843–50. Protât worked for Minton c.1845–58. He was a modelling instructor at the Stoke School of Design c.1850–64. He also worked for Wedgwood c.1858–64, as well as for Royal Worcester, Brownfield, Copeland, Sir James Duke & Nephews and Samuel Alcock as a freelance. Subsequently, he founded a thriving design studio in London. He specialized in Parian figures, but also designed many ornaments in majolica and porcelain. Some of his models have an impressed HP monogram.

## Augustus Welby Pugin

Pugin (c.1812–52) was an architect (responsible for the Houses of Parliament), designer and writer, as well as a close friend of Herbert Minton. He designed encaustic tiles for Minton from 1842, and designed tableware, tiles and garden seats c.1849–52. His majolica tile stove was exhibited by Minton in the Medieval Court at the Great Exhibition. Pugin's Bread Plate was one of Minton's very successful early majolica designs (see Chapter Two).

## Edouard Rischgitz

A French painter, Rischgitz (c.1828–1909) worked for Minton c.1864–70. He painted landscapes and figures in a style similar to Lessore's, sometimes on majolica.

## Frederick Bart Russel

Russel designed majolica for Wedgwood in the late 1860s. His designs include the Caterer's Jug and the Flowering Rush Jug, both very successful. Some of his designs have an impressed monogram on the base.

## Alfred Stevens

A painter, sculptor and designer, Stevens (c.1817–75) was best known for his monument to the Duke of Wellington in St. Paul's Cathedral. Grant described him as 'perhaps the most naturally gifted of all our Sculptors … Stevens's most outstanding characteristic, his mastery of composition and of pure line.' He also designed for Minton (c.1859–61), and his 'Italian Majolica' vase was displayed by the firm at the London Exhibition of 1862.

## John Thomas

Thomas (c.1813–62) is best known for his public commissions, including the sculptural decoration of the Houses of Parliament, and the fountain of the Horticultural Society's Garden. He was so much in demand that overwork brought him to a premature end. One of his last commissions was the Saint George's Fountain for Minton at the London Exhibition of 1862 (see Chapter Two).

## J. Thorley

Thorley painted majolica for Minton. One of his pieces was displayed at the Paris Exhibition of 1867 (see Plate 30).

## Charles Toft

Toft is best known for his work on pâte-sur-pâte and Henri Deux ware for Minton (c.1872–7).

However, during his period as Chief Modeller for Wedgwood (c.1877–83?) he modelled the famous Athletic Jug, which was subsequently copied by Griffin, Smith & Hill. In all probability, he was responsible for many other majolica models during that period. He is also known to have worked for Kerr & Binns, Royal Worcester and Elkington, Birmingham. He was subsequently a partner in Toft & Cope (see Appendix A).

*Henry J. Townsend (c.1810–90)* was a designer and modeller who exhibited at the Royal Academy c.1839–66. He designed tablewares and figures for Summerly's Art Manufactures, including Minton's famous Hop Pickers Jug (1847).

*William Wise*
Wise (c.1847–89) designed printed tiles and painted majolica for Minton c.1870–85. He exhibited at the Royal Academy in 1876. At the Paris Exhibition of 1878, Minton displayed a majolica vase painted by Wise after an Urbino model.

# LISTS OF SHAPE AND PATTERN NUMBERS

## MINTON MAJOLICA SHAPE NUMBERS

The following list is compiled from the 1884 Shape Book and various recorded pieces. Names in quote marks are factory shape names, other names are either those in common usage or the author's own descriptive inventions. Sizes, where indicated, are as given in the Shape Book. This is a very small sample of the Minton majolica shapes, and it is to be hoped that collectors with marked pieces bearing shape numbers will contribute this information to future listings.

128 Cherry Blossom Jardinière, 4, 5, 6, 7, 8, 9, 10, 11, 12 in.
178 'Flower Bracket'
189 'Infant Neptune'
198 Peony Jardinière, 4, 5, 6, 7, 8, 9, 10, 11, 13, 15, 18 in.
256 Marine Vase
257 'Children & Goat'
258 'Children & Goat'
268 Leaf Border Jug
286 French Horse
288 Waterlily Covered 'Sugar' & Butter
293 'Hogarth Match Boy'
294 'Hogarth Match Girl'
296 Basketwork Dish
312 'Ink'
318 'Double Cupid Salt'
326 'Seahorse with Shell'
342 'Ivy Jardinière', 4, 5, 6, 7, 8, 10, 12, 14, 15, 18 in.
346 'Pompeian Cup, Eagle'
358 'Loving Cup'
367 'Bell's Bread Tray'
368 'Pugin's Bread Tray'
376 'Vintager with Basket'
402 Primrose Covered Butter
405 'The Vintagers'
406 Matches 405
413 'Man with Wheelbarrow'
421 'Boy Resting on Basket'
423 'Bark Suspension Basket'

427 Wheat Sheaf Bread Tray
431 'Girl Resting on Basket'
437 'Nautilus Shell'
451 'Perforated Garden Pedestal'
464 'Dolphin Tazza'
466 Cherub & Cart Centrepiece
480 'Bamboo' Jardinière, 4, 5, 6, 7, 8, 9, 10, 12 in.
481 'Bamboo Garden Seat', 19 in.
487 Peasant Dancers Jug
489 Peony Vase
497 'Shrewsbury Vase'
513 Floral Jug
526 'Marine Vase'
529 Column Candlestick, 6 in.
531 Narcissus Vase
532 'Plain Semper Flower Vase'
534 Sea Nymph Jardinière, 10 in.
537 'Palissy Tray'
538 Pineapple Jug
545 Candleholder
546 Ivy 'Cheese Stand'
547 Oak Bread Tray
549 Wrapped Leaf Jug
553 Oak Leaves Jug
555 Broad Jug
560 'Dolphin Wafer Cup'
578 'Suspension Basket'

580 'Christmas Jug'
586 'Garden Pot – Passion Flower'
586[sic] Lily Jug
588 'Indian Garden Seat', 20 in.
589· Monkey Garden Seat
594 Chestnut Dish
596 'Verulam Jug'
600 Vase
605 Geometric Jug or Cream Stand
607 Japanese Floral Jug
613 'Salt Boy with Girl'
614 'Oval Cistern, supported by two cupids' (Baptismal Font)
616 Ewer & Stand
617 Chinese Floral Jardinière, 9, 10, 12 in.
618 Bamboo Jug
620 Mouse Cheese Dish
624 'Alhambra Bottle'
625 'Tall Bottle'
630 'Vases Snake Handle Italian'
631 Victoria Wine Cooler
636 Oyster Stand
640 Baroque Vase
642 'Déjeuner Service Leafage'
644 Triple Gourd Shaped Vase, 5¾ in.
649 'Queen's Vase'

650 'Oak Garden Pot' & Stand
654 'Jug & Stand'
658 'Vase Snake handles'
668 Game Pie Dish
678 Moorish Tray
680 'Daisy Basket, Cupid Support'
696 Double Flower Pot, 4 in.
697 Triple Flower Pot, 3 ½ in.
705 'Fountain'
709 'Cream Bowl & Stand, Palissy'
713 'Garden Pot & Stand'
714 Greek Key Vase, 9½ in.
718 'Tripod Jardinière'
720 'Oriental Flower Pot & Pedestal'
726 Holly Dish
727 'Garden Pot – Ramshead & Festoon'
732 Soulage Ewer & Stand
734 'Pierced Basket, supported by a Bacchante'
735 'Pierced Basket, supported by a Satyr'
736 'Mussel Dish & Stand'
742 'Low Comport, pierced'
743 Floral Vase
762 'Wine Cooler'
763 Wicker Cheese Stand
765 'Candlestick in Palissy Ware'
766 'Vase'
767 'Cupid Bracket'
768 'Vase'
771 'Dish Henry IVth'
772 'Garden Seat'
773 'Comport Palissy'
777 'Pigeon Pie'
778 'Triple Horn Flower Holder'
782 'Tazza'
783 'Luncheon Tray, 3 Compartments'
786 'Garden Seat'
787 'Ewer & Stand'
788 'Vase & Pedestal'
799 'Luncheon Tray Embossed'
802 Lazy Susan
804 'Vase'
806 'Wine Cooler'
808 'Triton Cornucopia'
809 Foliage Cheese Stand
811 Bramble Jardinière, 7, 8, 9 in.
813 Una & the Lion Plaque
814 Shell Jug
815 Diamond Cut Vase

816 Seaweed Bread Tray
827 'Vase, Renaissance'
830 'Candlesticks-3 Lights-Boy Support'
836 Cherub Tazza
837 'Inkstand'
838 'Garden Seat'
839 Waterlily Candleholder
842 'Italian Cistern'
846 'Cornucopia Flower Vase'
847 'Table, cupid supports'
852 'Shell Comport, merman support'
853 'Shell Comport, mermaid support'
864 'Christmas Dish – Art Union'
871 'Tall Candelabra, 10 lights, supported by a group of figures representing Love, Peace & Abundance
875 Lattice Work Jardinière, 7, 8, 10, 12, 16 in.
886 Two Compartment Dish
891 'Garden Pedestal'
895 'Vase'
900 'Barrel Jug with Cupids'
901 'Vase'
902 'Cream Bowl-Shell, Dolphin Support'
906 'Bonbonnière'
911 'Amorini Fountain'
922 'Flower Stand'
930 'Oval Comport, supported by 2 cupids'
935 Quintuple Vase with Ribbons, 7 in.
937 'Oval Perforated Basket, supported by 2 mermaids'
940 Renaissance Garden Seat, 18 in.
942 'Oval Victoria Basket, perforated, with 2 oriental figures reclining at foot'
944 'Vase'
948 'Large Centre Basket, supported by figures representing the Seasons'
949 'Large Basket supported by 3 cupids' or 'garden seat'
964 Sleeping Hound Game Pie Dish
966 'Large Shell, supported by Red Coral'
969 'Beehive & Blackberry Stilton Cheese Stand'
972 Ivy Bread Tray
973 Stag salt
980 'Maskhead Vase'
981 'Triangular Basket'

982 Architectural 'Garden Seat', 18 in. or 'Fish Dish, bulrush embossed'
990 'Vase, Ramshead handles, supported by a group of 4 cupids'
991 'Flower Holder, Chinese Leaf in Palissy' on black stand'
921 'Nautilus Shell, supported by 2 mermen'
1010 Waterlily 'Tray 3 Compartments'
1023 'Jardinière'
1037 Classical Vase
1040 Lattice Work Jardinière, 8½ in.
1056 Lily of the Valley Jardinière, 14, 16 in.
1070 Ship Vase
1073 Dragon Jardinière, 13½ in.
1076 Tripod Floral Jardinière, 14 in.
1081 Japanese Floral Jardinière, 6, 7, 8, 9, 10, 11, 12 in.
1086 Waterlily Pickle Dish
1101 Vase & Cover
1102 'Ink'
1107 Quintuple Cactus Flower Vase, 8 in.
1136 Protât Jug
1140 Toby Jug
1141 Tripod Jardinière, 12 in.
1147 'Pine Tray'
1151 Bamboo Spittoon
1152 Sea Urchin Spittoon
1157 Negro Male
1158 Negro Female
1171 Alhambra Jardinière, 11 in.
1172 'Basket'
1182 'Shell/Flower Bearers'
1185 Waterlily Candleholder
1187 Floral Jardinière, 10, 12, 14 in.
1219 Japanese 'Garden Seat', 18 in.
1223 Fern Basket, 6 in.
1228 Water Lily Jug
1231 Tower Jug
1241 Heron Ewer
1256 Jardinière & Stand
1296 'Shell Carriers'
1323 'Oyster Plate'
1324 'Oyster Plate'
1328 Prometheus Vase
1330 'Strawberry Plate'
1331 'Wilbraham Tray'

1359 Classical Vase
1361 Tree Trunk Garden Pot
1362 Baroque Vase
1383 'Sardine Box'
1390 Owl vase
1417 Fish Pickle Tray
1420 Pompeian Jug
1457 Canoe Sauceboat
1499 Hive 'Honey Pot'
1517 'Lamp Stand'
1524 Trefoil Dish
1525 Pine Cone Inkstand
1531 Rabbit & Leaf Dish
1545 'Butterfly Plate'
1554 Vase
1560 Shell 'Flower Holder', 6½ in.
1565 'Persian Bottles'
1572 Leaf 'Cucumber Tray'
1577 Seasons Flower Holders
1590 Chinese Jardinière, 8 in.
1604 Log 'Box'
1620 Ring Handled Jardinière
1625 'Chinese Ornament'
1628 Rope Jardinière, 15 in.
1655 Chinese Vase
1662 'Ink'
1679 Partridge Jardinière, 12½ in.
1685 Oriental 'Jardinière', 14 in.
1691 Sunflower Ice Tray
1692 Monkey Match Pot
1694 Diamond Panel Jardinière, 7½ in.
1720 Vase
1797 Oriental Jardinière
1807 'Jardinière Tripod'
1837 Helmet 'Shell Spoon Warmers'
1838 Chinaman Teapot
1844 Monkey 'Teapot'
1849 Waterlily Cup & Saucer
1862 Scallop Shell Jardinière
1870 'Shell'

1881 Bird & Oak Leaf Sweetmeat Dish
1884 Teapot & Cover
1909 Cockerel Teapot
1916 Heron Umbrella Stand
1917 Heron Umbrella Stand
1924 'Cat Milk Jug'
1926 Japanese Boat
1960 Napkin 'Strawberry Plate'
1982 Cockerel Spill Vase
1983 Hen Spill Vase
1984 Serpentine Spittoon
1990 Hare Game Pie Dish
1993 Wicker Bread Tray
2012 'Cat Cream Jug'
2045 Peacock
2062 Mushroom Game Pie Dish
2079 Oak Leaf Dish
2081 Chinese pedestal
2137 Leaf Tray
2196 Wide Lattice Work Jardinière, 6 in.
2212 Floral Garden Seat, 18 in.
2239 'Oyster Plate'
2255 Chrysanthemum Jardinière, 12½ in.
2266 Draped Umbrella Stand
2267 Bamboo & Bow Umbrella Stand
2279 'Strawberry Plate'
2281 Basket with Bow, 10½ in.
2315 Waterlily Tray
2335 Woven 'Asparagus Plate'
2358 Lattice Garden Seat, 18½ in.
2364 Basket Ground 'Oyster Plate'
2365 Fish & Scallop 'Oyster Plate'
2366 Fish & Seaweed 'Oyster Plate'
2370 Basketweave Dish
2602 Quadrefoil Tray
2608 Holly Spittoon

2618 'Serpentine Handled Urn', 15 in.
2665 'Greek Key Border Jardinière', 9½ in.
2666 'Flower Banded Jardinière, 8½ in.
2667 'Floral Jardinière', 10¾ in.
2669 Nautilus 'Spoon Warmer'
2679 Snail 'Spoon Warmer'
2719 Mosaic Fountain, 4 ft.
2720 Cupid & Shell Fountain, 27 in.
2721 'Wicker and Ribbon Jardinière', 4, 6, 7, 8, 14 in.
2722 'Chrysanthemum Jardinière', 6½ in.
2723 Chrysanthemum, Butterfly & Dragonfly Garden Seat, 19 in.
2730 Woman in Niche Fountain, 3 ft 1 in.
2731 Draped Woman Fountain, 40 in.
2755 Floral Panel Jardinière, 6, 8, 10, 12 in.
2761 Woven Umbrella Stand
2907 Goode's Elephants
2985 Ribbon Waisted Garden Urn, 17½ in.
3013 Fish Scale Border Jardinière, 6, 10, 14 in.
3049 Claw Foot Jardinière, 15 in.
3051 Swirl Jardinière, 7½, 10, 13 in
3053 Medallion Pedestal, 11 in
3061 Medallion Column, 20 in.
3063 Swirl Jug
3068 Umbrella Stand, 21 in.
3075 Swirl Garden Urn, 17, 20½ in.
3076 Leaf Border Jardinière, 10, 12, 15 in.

## WEDGWOOD MAJOLICA PATTERN NUMBERS

The following list has been compiled from the Wedgwood Majolica Pattern Books. As will be noticed some numbers are skipped or duplicated. All shapes are described as in the books themselves, although it has been necessary to standardize the spellings, which are sometimes quite exotic. The entries were made in many hands over the years, and in some cases it has been impossible to read them or to decipher them with certainty. In some cases the listings are very detailed, in others cryptic. To describe the decoration used on each piece would require a full length book by itself. Shape numbers and sizes are indicated when given. The list is published by kind permission of the trustees of the Wedgwood Museum.

**M Series (Nos. 30-3348)**
30 Cambridge Ale Jug
31 Water Bottle & Stand
32 Gipsy Teapot
33 Twig Basket & Stand
34 Twig Basket Plate
35 Strawberry Basket, Shape 863
36 Vase, Shape 6
37 Ristoricus Déjeuner Set
38 Persian Style Urn, Shape 352,
39 Persian Style Vase
40 Déjeuner Set
41 Vase, Shape 941
104 Vase
125 Pie with Cauliflower Nob & Rim
126 Flowerpot & Stand, Shape 1031
127-8 Round Twig Basket & Stand
129 Howard Teapot
130 Teapot Stand
131 Barrel Shape Tobacco Jar
132 Black Teapot
134 Creaux, Shape 317
135 Creaux, Shape 1061
136-7 Cambridge Ale Jug
139 Water Bottle & Stand, Shape 988, 10 in.
140 Déjeuner Set for Two Persons
141 Jardinière or Urn
146 Water Bottle & Stand
155-8 Doric Jug
159 Nelson Dessert
160-1 Dublin Toilet
163 Doric Jug
164 Vase, Shape 489
165 Vase, Shape 950
166 Teapot & Butterfly Cover
167 Persian Style Candlestick
168 Vase, Shape 941
169 Embossed Traced Vase
170 Wine Cooler
171 Four Handled Vase
173 Vase, Shape 93
174 Plymouth Vase
175 Cigar Vase
176-7 Wine Cooler, Shape 317
178 Wine Cooler, Shape 1061
179 Wine Cooler, Shape 1090
180 Wine & Water Vase, Shape 23
181 Vase, Shape 262
182-3 Ring Stand
184 Large Vase
185 Wine Cooler, Shape 317

186 Creaux, Shape 1061
187 Creaux
188 Wine Cooler, Shape 317
189-90 Alhambra Style Water Bottle, No Stand
191 Vase, Shape 278
192 Vase, Shape 1009
193 Water Bottle & Stand
194 Dorset Butter
195 Shape 29
196 Shape 57
197 Vase, Shape 941
198 Pillar Candlestick, Corinth Style
199 Alhambra Water Bottle & Stand, Shape 988
200-3 Howard Teapot
204/19 As 198 (mistakenly entered as new pattern)
205/198 Spill Vase
206 Square Match Box
207-8 Pearl Jug Stand
209 Doric Jug
210 Flower Pot & Stand
211 Beattie's Vase
212 Vase, Shape 43
213 Cambridge Ale Jug
214 Doric Jug
215-16 Howard Teapot
217-18 Doric Jug
219 Jug Stand
220 Creaux, Shape 317
221-2 Doric Jug
223 Jug Stand
224 Howard Teapot
225 Palissy Candles
226 Ring Stand
227 Alhambra Style Pillar Candlestick
228 Embossed Shape Ink
229 Embossed Shape Candlestick
230 Cambridge Jug
231 Embossed Shape, Pillar Candlestick
232 Creaux
233 Jug Stand with Bead Edge
234 Jug Stand
235 Jug Stand
236-8 Doric Jug
239-40 Howard Teapot
241 Vase, Shape 174
242-3 Howard Teapot
244 Teapot, Shape 146
245 Lamp Body, Globular Shape 43
246 Lamp Body, Tall Shape 30
247 Lamp Body, Globular Shape 43
248 Oblong Match Box

249 Square Match Box
250 Tooth Powder Box
251 Oblong Match Box
252 Pillar Candlestick
253 Covered Paste Box
254 Pillar Candlestick
255 Howard Teapot
256 Doric Jug
257 Round Ink
258-64 Jug Stand
265 Howard Teapot
266 Maltese Jug
267 Spill Vase
268 Jug Stand
308 New Club Jug, Mr. Goode's Shape
309-10 Jug Stand
311 Howard Teapot
312 Doric Jug
313 Howard Teapot
314-15 Dolphin Comport
317-18 Griffin Flower Stand
319-20 Doric Jug
321-3 Jug Stand
324-5 Tooth Powder
326-7 Red Arabesque Teapot, Shape 159
328 Teapot
329 Jug Stand
330 Antique Salt
331 Arabesque Ewer & Basin
332 Fawn Scroll Ewer & Basin
333-6 Arabesque Ewer & Basin
337 Laurel Flower Pot & Stand
338 Flower Pot & Stand, Shape 317
339 Laurel Flower Pot & Stand
340 Tulip Shape Flower Pot & Stand
341 Flower Pot & Stand, Shape 317
342 Flower Pot & Stand, Shape 1061
343 Flower Pot & Stand, Beattle's Wine Coolers
344-7 Jug Stand
348 Dolphin Shell Dessert
349 Key Edge Plate
354-5 Beattie's New Dessert – Limoges
356 Beattie's New Creaux
357 Vase, Shape 1102
358 Bracket
359 Beattie's Creaux
360-1 Griffin Flower Stand
362 Flower Pot & Stand, Shape 317
363 Flower Pot & Stand, Shape 1060

364 Flower Pot & Stand,
   Shape 1061
365 Basket
366 Basket
367 Vase, Shape 1102
368 Antique Salt
369 New Flower Sprite Stand
370 Ewer & Basin
371 Wine Cooler, Shape 1058
372 Wine Cooler, Shape 978
373 Wine Cooler, Shape 990
374 Antique Salt
375 Jug Stand
378 Osbourne Ewer & Basin
379 Vase, Shape 1099
380-1 New Rope Handle Jug
382-3 Osbourne Ewer &
   Basin
384-5 Jug Stand
386-7 Vase for Pujol
390-1 Limoge Dessert Plate,
   Same as 355
392 Limoges
393 Limoges Dessert
394 Limoges
395 Jug Stand, Lace Pattern
396-7 Teapot
398 Jug Stand, Cord Edge
399 Jug Stand
401 Maltese Jug
402 Florence Jug
403 Vase, Shape 1087
404 Doric Jug
405 Maltese Jug
406 Florence Jug
407 Flower Vase, Shape 1107
409 Garden Pot, Shape 317
410-12 Jug Stand
413 Garden Pot & Stand
414 Garden Pot & Stand,
   Shape 317
415 Garden Pot, Shape 1060
416 Garden Pot, Shape 317
468 Elizabethan Flower Vase
469 Passion Flower Tree Pot
470 Imperial Flower Tree Pot
471 Limoges Dessert Plate
476 Teapot, Globe Shape
478 Cambridge Ale Jug
479 Limoges Dessert
480 Bonbonnière no. 3
481 Teapot
482-4 Round Ink
485 Imperial Spill
486 Reed Spill
487 Cup
488 Dolphin Spill
489 Imperial Spill
490-2 Reed Spill
493 Bonfrise (?) Spill

494 Bonbonnière no. 3
495 Oval Ink with Twisted
   Handles
496 Trophies Square
   Jardinière
497 Reed Spill
498 Dolphin Salt
499 Tea Set
500-1 Teapot
502 Cigar Vase, Shape 1127
503 Barrel Cigar Holder,
   Shape 1132
504-5 Ione Spill
506 Spill Case, Shape 1131
507 Spill Case
508 Jewel Stand, Shape 1133
509 Jewel Stand
510 Spill Case
511 Imperial Spill
512 Key Plates
513 Shell Plate
514-17 Jug Stand
518-19 Goblet Vase, No. 8
520 New Rope Candlesticks
521 Teapot, Shape 159
522 New Rope Jug Stand
523 Teapot, Shape 159
524 Teapot, Shape 146
525 Toilet Boxes
526 Limoges Salt
527 Shell Dessert
528 Key Dessert
529 Imperial Flower Pot,
   Dresden Style
530-6 Imperial Flower Pot
537 Square Jug
538-9 Elephant Vase
540-1 Reed Spill
542 Tooth Powder Box
543 Jug Stand
544 Beattie's Candlestick
   Figure with Draperies
545 Reed Spill
546 Imperial Creaux
547 Imperial Flower Pot, 8 in.
548 Jug Stand
549-52 Cambridge Ale Jug
553 Jug Stand
554 Doric Jug Stand
557 Teapot, Shape 159
558-9 Doric Jug
560 Cable Jugs
561 Imperial Flower Pot
562 Reed Spill
563 Imperial Flower Pot
564 Cambridge Ale Jug
565 Shell Dessert
566-7 Round Tobacco Jar
568-9 Round Ink
570-1 Small Toothpaste Box

572 Round Salts
573 Spills Case
574 Round Cigar Ashtrays
575 Teapot, Shape 146
576-8 Teapot
579-80 Teapot, Shape 159
581-2 Shell Dessert
583 Tooth Powder
584 Cambridge Ale Jug
585 Déjeuner Service, 2
   Persons
586 Rope Pattern
588 Jug Stand
589 Cambridge Ale Jug
590 Flower Spill by Dresser
591 Jardinière by Dresser
592-3 Dresser Flower Spills
594 Sickle Bread Tray
595 Dresser Flower Spills
596 Rope Jug Stand
597 Lamp Base
598 Imperial Spill
599-600 Imperial Flower Pot
601 Imperial Spill
602 Round Tray, 8 in No. 8
   Class
603-4 Sicilian Dessert
605 Laurel Jug
606-9 Disraeli Flower Pot
610-11 Dolphin Flower Pot
612 Dresser's Sceaux
   Ornament
613 Sickle Bread Tray
614-15 Danish Vase
616-17 Cupid Ring Stand
618 Egyptian Candlestick
619 Nautilus Centre
620 Dolphin Flower Pot
621-2 Bismark Sceaux
623-4 Cambridge Ale Jug,
   Dresser's Border
625 Doric Jug
626 Teapot, Shape 159
627 Brussels Tankard
628 Globe Teapot
629-32 Trophy Tiles
633 Déjeuner Set
634 Teapot, Shape 159,
   Dresser's Border
635 Teapot, Shape 159, Ivy
   Border
636-7 Dresser's Jardinière
   Ornaments
638 Caterer Tankard
639 Nautilus Centre
640 Elizabethan Vase
641 Disraeli Flower Pot
642 Neptune Centre
643 Philia Candle
644 Stanley Butter & Stand

645–6 New Flemish Jug
647 Leafage Tray on Rustic
 Foot
648 Flower Vase, Shape 1100
649 Ewer Vase, Shape 1101
650 Market Woman
651 Vase, Shape 496
652 Vase, Shape 1099
653 Sickle Bread Tray
654 Egyptian Vase, Shape 796
655 Cambridge Jug
666 Cambridge Jug
667–8 Dolphin Flower Pot
669 Reed Spills
670 Clarendon Shape
 Tobacco Jar
671–3 Egyptian Candle
674 Caterer Jug
675 Imperial Flower Spill
676 Teapot, Shape 159
677 Coral Salt
678 Trentham Vase
679 Disraeli Flower Pot
680 Vine Yard Flower
681 Vase, Shape 1102
682 Palissy Dish, No. 20
683 Limoges Tazza
684 Sleeping Child
685 Stanley Plate
686 Dresser's Jug
687 Oyster Tray, Small Size
688 Limoge Flower Pot
689–90 Dolphin Sceaux
691–2 Cylinder Tobacco Jar
693 Beattie's Cupid Bracket
694 Sickle Bread Tray
695–7 Imperial Flower Pot
698–700 Nile Shape Flower
 Pot
701 Imperial Flower Pot
702 Nile Flower Pot
703 Teas
704–7 Nile Flower Pot
708–10 Imperial Flower Pot
711–15 Cambridge Ale Jug
716 Imperial Flower Pot
717–18 Cambridge Ale Jug
719 Howard Teapot
720–1 Tooth Paste
722 Caterer Jug
723–4 New Reed Jug
725 Cambridge Ale Jug
726 Small Toilet Ware
727–8 Flora Flower Pot
729 Elizabethan Jug
730–2 New Reed Jug
733 Dutch Shaving Mug
734 Nile Flower Pot
735–7 Imperial Flower Pot
738 Caterer Jug

739 Ewer & Basin
740 Shell Cigar Ash Tray
741 Nile Flower Pot
742 Sickle Bread Tray
743 Elizabethan Vase
744 Cottage Ewer & Basin
745 Elizabethan Jug
746 Eugenia Centre
747 Shell Dessert Service
748 Howard Teapot
749 Flower Pot
750–1 New Flowering Reed
 Jug
752–4 Doric Jug
756 Déjeuner Set
757 Jug Stand
758 Rope Jug Stand
759 Doric Jug
760 Jug Stand
761–3 Tobacco Jar
764 Teapot
765 Bamboo Sceaux (T.
 Goode Shape)
766 Déjeuner Tray
767 Tobacco Jar
768 Sir Walter Raleigh
 Tobacco Jar
769–73 Crown Prince Tobacco
 Jar
774 Teapot
775 Cambridge Ale Jug
776 Imperial Cup & Saucer
777–9 Belgian Shape Cup &
 Saucer
780 Teapot, Shape 159
781–4 Teapot, Shape 146
785 Carrier Vase
786–9 Ramshead Incense Vase
790 Alexander Centre
791–3 Square Hyacinth Pots
794–6 Cobalt Shell, Nymph
 Pink
797 Niad Shape Centre
798–9 Vesper Jewel Tray
800–1 Lotus Pickle with Bird
802 Flower Holder, Volute
 Shape No. 8
803 Bamboo Kettle (Sent to
 Messrs. Goode Nov. 15,
 1869)
804 Volute Shape Flower
 Holder
805–7 Shell Salt, Tridacna
 Shape No. 8
808 Raleigh Biscuit Jar
809 Brocolia Round Bread
 Tray, 12 in.
810–15 Brocolia Oval Bread
 Tray
816 Small Kneeling Figure

 Centre, Key Top
817–22 Shell Jug
823 Plain Vase
824 Siesta Flower Stand
825–6 Onion Flower Holder
827 Cupid Jewel Tray
828 Flora Flower Pot
829–30 Wine Cooler, Shape
 1058
831 Trentham Vase
832 Centre-3 Figure
833 Sickle Bread Tray
834 Reed Jug
835 Stanley Butter Tub
836 Basket Shape Oval Box
837–8 Basket Shape Pickle
839 Corn Shape Butter
840 Wine Cooler, Shape 1090
841–2 Stanley Butter
843–6 Treble (?) Vase, Shape
 266
847–8 Tortoiseshell Vases
849 Biscuit Jar
850 Disraeli Flower Pot
851 Bramble Flower Pot
852 Fern Stand
853 Alexander Centre
854 Raleigh Tobacco Jar
855 Strawberry Trefoil Dish
856 Bamboo Pot & Stand
857 Cupid Jewel Tray
858 Raleigh Jar
859 Basket, Oval 6 in.
860 New Pope Jug
861–2 Boucher Dessert
863 Elizabethan Teapot
864–5 Partridge Pie
866 Raleigh Biscuit Box
867 Boucher Plates
868 Deck Flower Pot
869 Round Tray
870 Vesper Jewel Tray
871–2 Flemish Jug
873 Swan Vase, Shape 35
874 Vase, Shape 271
875 St. Vincent Centre
876 Wine & Water Vase
877 St. Vincent
878 Boucher Double Flower
 Stand
879 Raleigh Flower Pot
880–1 Elizabethan Flower Pot
882 Satyr Flower Holder
883–4 Vase, Shape 10,
885 Cauldron Flower Pot
886 Old Wedgwood Shape
 Fluted Vase
887 Old Wedgwood Shape
 Tobacco Jar, Festoon &
 Trophies

888 Lobster Pot or Box
889 Bird & Nest Salt
890 Thistle Spill
891 Elizabethan Flower Pot
892 Ewer Shape Vase, No. 8, 18 in.
893–4 Satyr Dessert
895 Bulbous Root Pot
897–8 Cauldron Flower Pot, No. 22
899 Elizabethan Flower Pot
900 Lizard Tray
901 Puck Tray
902–3 Vase, 6 in., Made for 1871 Exhibition, Dragonfly on Black Ground
904 Square Jug 8
905 Lizard Vase, No. 8
906 China Vase
907 Bachelor's Dessert
908 Large Fern Stand
909–10 Clock Vase
911 China Vase
912 Wine & Water Vase
913 Eugenia Centre
914 Flora Flower Pot
915 Trentham Centre
916 Birch Tray
917 Raleigh Flower Pot
918 Partridge Pie
919–20 Pigeon Tray
921 Detogen Strawberry Dish, 10 in.
922 Leaf & Berries Comport
923 Bird & Berries Comport
924 Louis XVI Vase
925 Oriental Bamboo Kettle
926 Swan Vase as 873
927–8 Vase, No. 80
929 Puck Candlestick
930 Philia Candlestick
931 Ursule's Basket Jug
932 Raleigh Flower Pot
933 Leo Card Tray
934 Dolphin Candlestick
935–6 Caterer Jug
937 Dutch Shaving Mug
938 Fish Vase
939 Eastern Water Bottle
940 Jug Stand
941 Fontainebleu Vase
942–3 Fluted Vase
944 Mermaid Vase
945 Old Wedgwood Snake Handle Vase
946 Old Wedgwood Vase, Shape 1033
947 Old Wedgwood Snake Handle Vase
948 Old Wedgwood Vase,

Shape 80
949–52 Strawberry Plate, J. Mortlock's
953–4 Indian Vase
955 Vase 950
956–8 Vase 381
959–60 Beattie Vase
961 St. Vincent Centre
962–3 Sardine Box
964 Caterer Jug
965 Palissy Dish
966 Jewel Casket
967 Satyr Dessert
968–9 New Rustic Bird Nest & Basket Centre
970–1 Satyr Dessert
972 Flemish Tankard
973 Fish Vase
974 Nanquin Vase, Dresser
975 Caterer Jug
976 Reed Jug
977 Jug Stand

*July 1871*

978 Soap & Tray with Figures
979 CC, Shape 496
980 Celery Vase, Done for Briggs
981 Indian Vase
982–3 Elephant Vase
984–5 Indian Vase
986 Jug Stand
987 Bulbous Root Pot
988 Beattie Bracket
989 Louis XVI Vase
990–1 Elizabethan Flower Pot
992 Vine Flower Stand
993–4 Sea Horse Jug
995–6 Stanley Bread Tray
997 Chiswick Flower Pot
998–9 Wicker Plate
1000–1 Vine & Strawberry Plate
1002 Strawberry Bread Tray
1003–4 Trophies Tobacco Jar
1005 Celery Jar
1006 Oval Game Pie Dish
1007 Boucher Flower Pot
1008 Rustic Vine Centre
1009 Bacchus Tobacco Jar
1010–11 Satyr Tobacco Jar
1012 Satyr Dessert
1013–14 Oak Shape Cheese Cover & Stand
1015–16 New Rope Tobacco Jar
1017 Leda Tray
1018 Pekin Kettle
1019 Pekin Teapot
1020–4 Strawberry Dish

1025 Satyr Bread Basket with Ivy Border
1026–7 Vase with Satyrs
1028 Mermaid Vase
1029 Sandwich Tray
1030 Flower Pot
1031 Globe Kettle, No. 6
1032–3 Indian Vase
1034 Art Journal Vase
1035–6 Egyptian Ink
1037 T. Goode's Vase
1038 Spoon Rest 23
1039 Spoon Rest 6
1040–1 Stanley Flower Pot
1042 Cauldron Flower Pot
1043–4 Part Pot
1045 Bread Basket
1046 Stanley Dessert Set
1047–8 Reed Jug
1049–50 Small Indian Vase
1051 Limoges Candlestick
1052 Lessore Tankard, no. 8
1053 Satyr Bread Tray
1054–5 Sea Horse Jug
1056 Cat's Head Vase, no. 8
1057 Cat's Head Vase, No. 23
1058 Art Journal Vase, no. 23
1059 Indian Vase
1060 Art Journal Vase
1061 Caterer Jug
1077–80 Oyster Trays for 4
1081 [Illegible]
1082 Leopard Card Tray
1083 Mermaid Vase
1084–5 Delhi Vase
1086 Mermaid Vase
1087 Delhi Vase
1088 Wright Jug
1089–90 Dragon Flower Pot
1091–8 Louis XV Jug
1099–103 Leopard Flower Pot
1104–11 Aquarium Flower Pot
1195 [sic] Proteus Ewer & Stand with Lessore Panels
1112–13 Duck Flower Vase
1114 Leopard Flower Holder
1115–18 Dragon Flower Holder
1119–21 Amphora Flower Holder
1123 Mask Match Pot
1124–7 Mayo Strawberry Basket
1128 Mayo Flower Basket
1129 Mayo Strawberry Basket
1131–2 Violet Holder
1133 Volute Flower Holder, Large Size no. 8
1134–5 Griffin Vase
1137–8 Cauldron Flower

Holder
1139-40 Hanging Match Pot
1141 Grape Gatherers, Female & Male
1143 Wicker Butter
1144 Dolphin Vase
1145-6 Valoria Jardinière
1147-8 Watteau Dessert Plate
1149-52 Dolphin Card Tray
1153 Mayo Strawberry Basket
1154 Wicker Butter
1155 Fly Match Holder
1158 Amphora Flower Holder
1159 Cauldron Flower Holder
1160 Griffin Flower Holder
1161 Lily Flower Holder
1162 Griffin Flower Holder
1163 Leopard Flower Holder
1164 Sleepy Boy Match Box
1165 Basket Flower Holder
1166 Moresque Vase
1167 Dolphin Vase
1168-9 Wicker Dessert Service
1170 Wicker Cheese Dish & Cover
1171 Delhi Vase
1172 Fluted Column with Sutherland Centre
1175-7 Bamboo Flower Tray
1179-81 Bamboo Bread Tray
1182 Bamboo Card Tray
1183 Watteau Dessert Service
1184-5 Column Paperweight
1186 Dresser Flower Pot
1187-8 Wedgwood Vase
1190 Raleigh Flower Pot
1191 Net Cigar Tray
1192-3 Valoria Jardinière
1195 Proteus Ewer & Stand
1196 St. Vincent Candelabra
1197-8 Round Satyr Basket
1199 Cheswick Flower Pot
1200 Cheese Dish, Oak Borders
1201 Elizabethan Flower Pot
1202 Horse Vase
1203 Vesper Ink
1204 Chest Ink
1205 Lotus Ink
1206 Mayo Strawberry Basket
1208 Pekin Ink
1209-10 Fish Woman
1211 Key Handle Pekin Vase
1212 Flora Centre
1213 Dragon Kettle
1214-15 Dragon Oyster Tray
1216 Dragon Kettle
1218-19 Déjeuner Set
1220-1 Dragon Flower Pot
1222-3 Round Trays

1225 Oriental Kettle
1226 Raleigh Flower Pot
1227-8 Wicker Bread Tray
1229-30 Leopard Flower Holder
1231 Dante Vase
1232 Jug
1233-4 Dome Shape Fluted Match Box
1235 Wicker Dessert
1236 Strawberry Dish
1237 Leopard Flower Pot
1238-9 Strawberry Dish
1240-1 Stanley Plate
1242-3 Aquarium Flower Pot
1244 Dresser Flower Holder
1246-7 Dresser Flower Pot
1248 Oval Pierced Basket
1250-1 Dragon Kettle
1252-4 Round Bow Handle Basket
1255 Nautilus Centre
1256-7 Wicker Plate
1258 Reed Spill
1259 Oriental Déjeuner
1260 Flute Tobacco Jar, Dome Shape
1261 Raleigh Tobacco Jar
1262 Round Bamboo Tray
1263 Round Basket Bamboo
1264 Trentham Vase
1265 Flower Stand with Boy & Fish
1266 Sea God Jardinière
1267 Crane Jardinière
1268 Flower Stand with Boy & Fish
1269 Helmet Ewer
1270 Flora Figure
1272 Leopard Flower Holder
1274-6 See C Book
1277 Vesper Jewel Tray
1278-9 Lamp Base 12 in.
1280 Lorne Tazza
1281 Helmet Ewer
1282-5 Dragon Déjeuner Set
1286-7 Dresser Jardinière
1288 Spoon Rest
1289 Fish Boy Flower Stand
1290 Key Dessert
1291 [Illegible] Dessert
1292 Moresque Desert
1293 Aquarium Flower Pot
1294 Nautilus Crocus Pot
1295 Bismark Flower Pot
1296 Fish Man to match Fish Wife 1210
1297-8 Elf Flower Holder
1299 Reed Spill
1301 Match Holder

1302 Match Holder, Rustic with Figure
1303 Valoria Round Fruit Bowl
1304 Oval Bow Handle Basket
1305 Hare Flower Holder
1306 Sleepy Boy Paperweight
1307 Cigar Ash Tray
1309 Italian Cigar Tray
1311-12 Italian Cigar Tray
1313-14 Nautilus Shell Bracket
1315 Nautilus Shell
1316 Cambridge Ale Jug
1317-8 Oak Jug
1319-21 Vine Border Butter & Stand
1322 Shell Salt
1324 Diaper Teapot
1325 Low Round Ivy Flower Stand
1326 Fly Vase
1327 Harp Vase
1328 Boy & Shell Flower Holder
1329 Bamboo Flower Holder
1330 Watteau Dessert
1331-2 Dresser Tray
1333 Dresser Jug
1334 Volute Flower Holder
1335 Bismark Flower Pot
1336-7 Wicker Dessert
1338-9 Triaquelia? Vase
1340 Streatham Vase
1341-2 Roman Lamp
1343 Convulvus Vase
1344 Bismark Flower Pot
1345 Double Ring Flower Holder
1346 Griffin Flower Holder
1348 Double Ring Flower Holder
1349 Sea God Jug
1350-1 Protât Jug
1352 Lorne Tazza
1353 Low Round Ivy Flower Stand
1355 Oval Bow Handled Basket
1356 Dresser Flower Pot
1359 Cressa Jug
1360 Caterer Jug
1361-2 Net Cigar Tray
1363-4 Oval Pierced Basket
1365-6 Butter Plate
1367-9 Louis XV Dessert
1370 Helmet Ewer
1371-2 Basket Work Dessert
1373 Moresque Desert
1374 Alhambra Card Tray
1375 Corinthian Candlestick

*187*

1376 Fluted Tobacco Jar
1377-8 Square Bulbous Pot
1379 J. Mortlock Tapioca
  Teapot
1380 Leopard Flower Pot
1381 Match Holder
1382 Versailles Basket
1383 Lorne Tazza
1384 Cheese Dish & Stand
1385-89 Tremblay Dessert,
  Embossed Shape
1390-1 Lorne Dessert
1392-3 Dalton Jug
1394-7 Basket Spills
1398-9 Protât Jug
1400-1 Garden Seat
1402 Versailles Basket
1403-8 Lion Head Flower Pot
1409-10 Primrose Flower Pot
1411 Bramble Jug
1412 Crane Jug
1413 Tremblay Dessert
1414-15 Helmet Ewer
1416-18 Rosette Jug, Dalton
  Shape
1419 Primrose Flower Pot
1420 Tremblay Dessert
1421 Blackberry Jug
1422 Fish Boy Flower Vase
1423 Dresser Candlestick
1424 Spitting Pot
1425 Trentham Centre
1426-9 Tremblay Dessert
1430-5 Tremblay Tile
1436-8 Tremblay Octagon Jug
  Stand
1439-42 Tremblay
  Paperweight
1443 Tremblay Triangular Tile
1444-5 Tremblay Oblong
  Scallop Pen Tray
1446 Tremblay Square Box
1447-8 Tremblay Snuff Box
1449 Tremblay Square Box
1450-1 Tremblay Pin Tray
1452-7 Tremblay Cigar Ash
  Tray
1458-9 Tremblay Pen Tray
1460 Tremblay Long Square
  tile
1461 Tremblay Tile
1462-3 Tremblay Jardinière
  Tile
1464-7 Tremblay Kite Shape
  Tile
1468-9 Tremblay Angular
  Scalloped Tile
1470 Tremblay Oblong
  Scalloped Tile
1471 Tremblay Ink Stand

1472 Tremblay Kite Shape Tile
1473 Tremblay Flat Taper Stick
1474-8 Tremblay Octagon
  Spill
1479 Tremblay Candlestick
1480-1 Tremblay Bread Dish
1482-3 Tremblay Knife
  Handle
1484 Tremblay Door Plate
1485-6 Tremblay Elephant
  Bowl
1487 Leopard Flower Pot
1488-9 Tremblay Déjeuner
  Set
1490 Burgundy Jug
1491-2 Tremblay Plates
1493 Bonbonnière

*Persian Colour (Nos.
1494-1519)*

1494 Scallop Pickle
1495 Bonbonnière
1496 Dove & Lotus Tray
1497 Japanese Vase
1498 Leopard Flower Holder
1499 Delhi Vase
1500 Vase 1203
1501 Dragon Flower Holder
1502 Dragon Lamp Base
1503 Dragon Flower Pot
1504-5 Ivy Flower Holder
1506 Hyacinth Vase
1507 Indian Vase
1508-9 Reed Spill
1510-12 Birds Nest Salt
1513-14 [Illegible] Salt
1515 Basket Salt
1516 Fish Baskets
1517 Scalloped Pickle
1518 French Vase
1519 Lamp Vase
1520-1 Lamp Vase
1522-27 Rosette Jug
1528 Tremblay Pierced
  Desert, Fruit Centres
1530-1 Garden Seat
1532 Rosette Jug
1533 Tremblay Round Tray
1534 Leopard Flower Pot
1535 Lorne Dessert
1536 Swan Handle Vase
1537-8 Tremblay Dessert,
  Landscape Centres
1539-40 Round Chinese
  Flower Pot
1541 Primrose Jug
1542-3 [Illegible] Jug
1544 Bramble Jug
1545 Rebert Vase, Banded
1546 Tankard Jug

1547-8 Rope Tobacco Jar
1549-51 Strawberry Dish
1552 Rosette Ewer & Basin
1553-4 Easel [Illegible] Stand
1555 Rosette Ewer & Basin
1556-7 Cigar Tray or Round
  Dish – Landscape Centres
1558 Oak Covered Cheese
  Dish
1559 Rustic Watchholders
1560 [Illegible] Watchholders
1561 Fern Pen Tray
1562 Helmet Ewer
1563 Primrose Jug
1564 Tankard Jug
1565-6 Watcholders
1567-8 Rosette Mug
1569 Rosette Ewer & Basin
1570 Helmet Ewer
1571 Primrose Jug
1572 Tremblay Dessert Ware
  – Fruit Centres
1573 Double Dolphin Pickle
1574-5 Watteau Ribbon Vase
1576-7 Griffin Ribbon Vase
1578-9 Fish Basket Ribbon
  Vase
1580-1 Fish Barrel Ribbon
  Vase
1582-3 Rosette Ribbon Vase
1584 Lorne Dessert
1585 Trentham Centre
1586-7 Tremblay Dessert
  Plate
1588-90 Temblay Dessert
  Plate Landscapes
1591-4 Butterfly Tremblay
1595 Griffin Dessert Ware
1596 Eugénie Centre
1597 Cupid Bracket
1598-9 Raleigh Flower Pot
1600 Raleigh Tobacco Jar
1601 Stein's Maria Figure
1602a Lorne Dessert
1602b Low Comport Tiger's
  Head
1602c Plate, Faun's Head
1602d Plate, Ox's Head
1602e Plate, Pointer's Head
1602f Plate, Ram's Head
1603a Lorne Dessert, Ferns
1603b Lorne Dessert, Spanish
  Chestnut
1603c Lornd Dessert, Waterlily
1603d- Lorne Dessert, Tulip
1603e- Lorne Dessert, Funghi
  & Fern
1603f Low Comport, Vine
1607 Raleigh Tobacco Jar
1608 Oval Shell Pickle

1609 Lotus Pin Tray
1610 Key Dessert
1611 Bull
1612 Cristofel Centre
1613–14 Cushion Garden Seat
1615 Eugénie Centre
1616 Cupid Bracket
1617 Plate
1618–20 Ribbon Oval
  Shellfish
1621 Key Dessert Ware
1622 Rosette Jug
1623–5 Dolphin Bonbonnière
1626 Hanging Masks
1627–8 Rosette Strawberry Set
1629–2 Rosette Ewer & Basin
1631–2 London Mug
1633 Griffin Dessert Ware
1636–7 Rosette Ewer
1638 London Mug
1639 Cigar Tray
1640 Assortment Vases no. 6
  for Harwood & Sons
1641 Goode's Embossed
  Kettle
1642–3 Tankard Beer Set
1644–5 Berlin Match Holder
1646 Reed Jug
1647–8 Albert & Queen Ash
  Trays
1649 Wicker Dessert Plate
1650–2 Wicker Plate
1653 Lotus Candlestick
1654 Leafage Pickle
1655 Shell Plate
1656 Fish Dish
1657 Tremblay Dessert Plate
1658 Tremblay Plate
1659 Hop Beer Set
1660 Acorn Egg Stand
1661 Chaffinch's Nest Flower
  Basket
1662–3 Primrose Jug
1664–5 Vine & Strawberry
  Bread Tray
1666 Dolphin Cigar Tray
1667 Thistle Ribbon Vase
1668 Vine & Strawberry
  Dessert Plate
1669–73 Lacquer Plate
1674–5 Tremblay [Illegible]
  & Cigar Tray
1676 Tremblay Tile, Man at
  Dinner
1677 Tremblay Tile, Woman
  at Dinner
1678 Flower Pendant
1679 Tremblay Round Tray
1680–1 Tremblay Knife
  Handle

1682 Wolsey Vase
1683 Tremblay Butterfly Plate
1684–5 Protât Jardinière,
  Cupids
1686 Protât Ewer & Stand,
  Cupids
1687 Raleigh Water Bottle
1688 Versailles Basket
1689 Flora Flower Pot &
  Column
1690–1 Brewster Custard Cup
1692–3 Tremblay Tile, Deer
  Hound
1694 Flower Table
1695 Bramble Jug
1696a Tremblay Tile, Deer
  Hound
1696b Temblay Tile, Boar
  Head
1696c Tremblay Tile, Fox
  Hound
1696d Tremblay Tile, Fox
  Head
1697a Tremblay Tile, Deer
  Hound
1697b Tremblay Tile, Boar
  Head
1697c Tremblay Tile, Fox
  Hound
1697d Tremblay Tile, Fox
  Head
1698 Leo Pot
1699 Bird Nest Salt
1700–1 [Illegible] Leaf
  Individual Butter
1702 Round Tremblay Tray
1703–4 Hop Beer Set
1705 Crocus Flower Holder
1706 Rustic Kettle
1707–11 Chapman & Hall
  Vase
1712 Passion Flower Tile
1713 Narcissus Tile
1714 Anemone Tile
1715–17 Square Tile
1718 Bird's Nest Salt
1719 Mermaid Clock Vase
1720 Dog's Head Vase
1721 Imperial Pot & Stand
1722 Tremblay Card Tray
1723 Japanese Spill, Lessore
  Panel
1724–5 Oak Cheese Bell &
  Stand
1726 Dragon Lamp Vase
1727 Hanging Vase
1728 Dragon Déjeuner Set
1729–30 Rosette Cruet Set
1731–3 Octagon Dessert Plate,
  Derby in Centre

1734 Tremblay Dessert,
  Pierced, Landscapes
1734[sic] Griffin Dessert,
  Lessore Panel Landscapes
1735 Vine Biscuit Box
1736 Mango Flower Basket
1737 Bow Handled Flower
  Basket
1738 Orange Front Bowl
1739–40 Cushion Garden Seat
1741–2 Foxglove & Fern
  Garden Pot & Stand
1743–4 Primrose Cheese Bell
1745–6 Vine Wine Stand
1747 Vine Biscuit Box
1748–9 Bramble Jug
1750 Rosette Smoking Set
1751–3 Passion Flower Pot &
  Stand
1754 Elephant Punch Bowl
1755 Lily Ash Tray
1756 Rosette Smoking Set
1757 Bramble Jug
1758 Tremblay Dish Card Tray
1759 Hooped & Lagged Jugs
1760–1 Cambridge Ale Jug
1762 Tremblay Card Tray,
  Snake Handles
1763–4 Crocus Flower Holder
1765 Poppy Ink Stand
1766 Gothic Sardine Box
1767–9 Shell Wine Tray
1770 Louis XVth Card Tray
1771 Curnan Leaf Pickle
1772 Tookan [sic] Pickle
1773 Vine & Strawberry Bread
  Tray
1774 Trentham Flower Basket
1775 Dresden Sandwich Tray
1776 Fern Pen Tray
1777 Basket Butter
1778 Sunflower Butter
1779–80 Nautilus Shell
  Bracket
1781 Etruscan Flower Stand
1782–3 Moresque Flower Vase
1784–5 Amphora Flower
  Holder
1786 Brewster Jug
1787 Gadroon Plain Salt
1788 Dolphin Card Tray
1789 Tremblay Saucer Card
  Tray
1790 Tremblay Twig Tall
  Comport
1791 Hope Tobacco Jar
1792 New Basket Tobacco Jar
  & Smoking Tray
1793 Fluted Tobacco Jar
1794 Square Raleigh Jardinière

1795-6 Tremblay Square Ash Tray
1797-9 Rosette Ribbon Burner
1800 Comport, Dolphin with Lizard
1801 Palissy Tray
1802 Dessert Plate, No. 7 Shape
1803 Tremblay Snake Handle Cigar Tray
1804 Alexandra Centre
1805 Tulip Teapot
1806 Sea God Jardinière
1807 Acanthus Dessert Plate
1808 Leo Flower Pot
1809-10 Spittoon – Printed Marble
1811-12 Tremblay Saucer Cigar Tray
1813 Sturcheon Individual Leaf Butter
1814 Tremblay Triangular Ash Tray
1815 Mrs Pollock Flower Basket
1816 Dolphin Oyster Centre
1817 Rustic Flower Stand
1818 'By Your Leave' Trinket Set
1819 Périssoire Stand, Male & Female
1820 Cushion Garden Seat
1821 Basket Butter Stand
1822 Vineyard Flower Holder
1823 Bramble Flower Pot
1824 Harp Vase
1825 Tremblay Cigar Tray
1826-7 Toast Rack & Egg Stand, No. 6
1828 Leafage Pickle
1829a Tremblay Tile, Ass & Fowl Centre
1829b Tremblay Tile, Rabbit Centre
1829c Tremblay Tile, Deer Centre
1830 Bramble Jug
1831 Round Leafage Bread Tray
1832 Doric Jug
1833 Vineyard Flower Holder
1834 Mrs. Pollock Centres
1835 Bramble Jug
1836 Basket Flower Pot & Stand
1837 Narcissus Tile
1838 Harp Vase
1839-41 Drinking Horns
1842 Leafage Broth Set
1843 Périssoire Canoe Stands

1844 Convolvus Flower Holder
1845 Paraquet Square Tile
1846 Vineyard Flower Pot & Stand
1847 Tremblay Comport
1848 Chiffonier Flower Holder
1849-50 Mrs. Pollock's Centre
1851 Flora Pot Column
1852a Griffin Dessert
1852b-f Boucher Dessert (White Peacock)
1854 Sultan Garden Seat
1855 Cabinet tile with Ribbons
1856-8 Cabinet Tile, Ivy Leaf
1859-60 Tremblay Square Tile
1861 Goode's Wicker Sceaux
1862-3 Tremblay Round Plaque
1864-5 R. Brigg's Dessert
1866-7 Square Parrot Tile
1868 Large Vase & Plinth
1869 Shell Wine Tray
1870 Lily Leaf Tray
1871 Vine Wine Tray
1872-3 Passion Flower Tile
1874 Sultan Garden Seat
1875 Leaf Pen Tray
1876-8 Strauss Jug
1879 Fern Pen Tray
1880 Leafage Plate; Low & Tall Comports
1881 Cylindrical Vase
1882 Shah Vase
1883-4 Primrose Cheese Bell & Stand
1885-6 Mrs. Pollock's Flower Basket
1887 Wicker Plate
1888 Sickle Bread Tray
1889 Caterer Jug
1890-1 Griffin Dessert Plate
1892 Low Comportier, Green Leaf Centre
1893 Griffin Dessert
1894 King William Jug
1895 Ranier Carrier Garment
1896-7 Leafage Butter
1898-9 Hooped & Lagged Cruet
1900 Rustic Flower Basket
1901 Trentham Vase
1902 Triton Candlestick
1903 Oak & Vine Candlestick
1904 Grape Gatherer
1905 Japanese Elephant Vase
1906 Season Spill
1907 Lorne Dessert Plate,

Birds Centre
1907b Lorne Dessert Plate, Dog & Partridge
1907c Lorne Dessert Plate, Dog & Gun
1907d Lorne Dessert Plate, Pheasant
1907e Lorne Dessert Plate, Partridge
1907f Lorne Dessert Plate, Hare
1908 Oak Garden Seat
1909 Caterer Jug
2000 Ivy Jug
2001 Vine Wine Tray
2002 Dragon Kettle
2003 Strawberry Plate
2004 Tremblay Round Tray
2005 Rosette Jug
2006 Bird Nest Bracket
2007 Hunting Jug
2008 Bird Nest Bracket
2009 Latch Butter
2010 J M Candlesticks
2011 Shell Wine Tray
2012 Boucher Centre
2013 Column for Tiffany Reed
2014 Boucher Dessert
2015 Raleigh Pot
2016 Elizabethan Jug
2017-18 Crane Tile
2019-21 Wheat Jug
2022 Tremblay Plate, Butterfly, Green Glaze
2023 Pierced Tremblay Plate, Landscapes, Green Glaze
2024 Alhambra Cigar Tray
2025-6 Orchids Tile
2027 Ellis's Vase
2028-9 French Fontainebleu Vase
2030-1 Covered Basket
2032 Plain Basket
2033 Basket
2034 Round Basket
2035 Round Basket
2036 Round Basket
2037 Basket Flower Holder
2038 Basket
2040 Hunt Tobacco Jar
2041 By Your Leave Figure
2042 Narcissus Tiles
2043 Goat's Head Vase
2044 Cupids & Easel
2045-6 Rosette Kettles
2047 Hyacinth Flower Holder
2048 Bamboo Bread Tray
2049 Ansty? Cheese Bell & Stand
2050 Herring Dish, No. 6

2051 Salmon Dish
2052 Grape Gatherer Boy
2053 Grape Gatherer Girl
2054 Cupid Jewel Stand
2055 Rustic Tray Salt
2056 Chiffonier Flower
  Holder
2057 Fern Tile
2058 Four Tiles, Early English
  Subjects
a. Boy & Girl, top
b. Boy & Girl, bottom
c. Two Girls
d. Girl Feeding Fowls
2059 Narcissus Tile
2060 Tremblay Diaper Tile
2061 Tremblay Tile
2062 Passion Flower Tile
2063 Crane Tile
2064-5 Lamp Vase, 381 Shape
2066-7 Lamp Vase, 372 Shape
2069 Louis XV Lamp Vae
2070 Vase Lamp Shape 381
2071-2 Louis XV Lamp Vase
2073 Tremblay Tile
2074 Narcissus Tile
2075 Basket
2076-7 Plaques
2078 Lorne Plate
2079-80 Tremblay Tile
2081 Cupid Tile
2082 Tremblay Diaper Tile
2083-4 Matt Bread Tray
2085 Dragon Kettle
2086 Rabbit Head Flower
  Holder
2087 Bow Handled Fluted
  Basket
2088 Caterer Jug
2089 Narcissus Vase
2090 Ovid Vase
2091 Primrose Flower Pot
2092 Bramble Jug
2093 Passion Flower Tile
2094 Tremblay Tile
2095-8 Goode's Bamboo
  Kettle
2099 Primrose Cheese Bell &
  Stand
2100-1 Basket Flower Pot
2102 Rosette Ewer
2103-5 Tremblay Tile
2106 Mermaid Clock Case
2107 Helmet Ewer
2108 Cupid Figure
2109 Satsuma Teapot & Kettle
2110 Large Column
2111 Oak Garden Seat
2112 Siesta Flower Vase
2113 Satyr Candlestick

2114 Bulbous Root Pot
2115 Ivy Jug
2116 Hooped & Lagged Jug
2117 Tankard Jug, No. 19
2118 Joiner's Bass
2119-20 Tremblay Tile,
  Rubelles Green Centre
2121 Alexandra Cigar Tray
2122 Trefoil Tray
2123 Mayo Flower Basket
2124 Double-handled &
  Double Spouted Kettle
2125 Crown Jug
2126 Bramble Flower Pot
2127 Fern Flower Pot
2128 Exhibition Tankard
2129 Triton Candlestick
2130 God's Head Candlestick
2131 Trentham Vase
2132 Cobalt Flower Holder
2133 Printed Japanese
  Jardinière
2134 Joiner's Bass
2135 Dolphin Vase
2136 Elf Flower Holder
2137 Corinthian Spill
2138 Watchholder Figure
2139 Scotch Fisherwoman &
  Man
2140 Primrose Pot
2141 Fluted Vase
2142 Rosette Tobacco Jar
2143 Rosette Kettle
2144 Stanley Butter & Stand
2145 Crane Tile
2146 Elizabethan Jug
2147 Joiner's Bass
2148 Primrose Flower Pot
2149 Dessert Plate, Tremblay
  Centre
2150 Griffin Dessert Plate
2151 Tremblay Tile
2152 Caterer Jug
2153 Bamboo Spittoon
2154 Tremblay Tile
2155-6 Diaper Tile
2157-8 O G Tile
2159-60 Tremblay Tile
2161 Tremblay Tile
2162-3 Clodian Tile
2164 Salmon Dish
2165 Round Tremblay Pen
  Tray
2166 Cupid Jardinière
2167-8 Vine Bread Tray
2169-70 Grape Bread Tray
2171 Matt Bread Tray
2172 Flowering Reed Jug
2173 Hooped & Lagged Jug
2174 Vine & Strawberry Tall

Comport
2175 Bramble Jug
2176 Lacquer Plate
2177 Basket, Oval & Stand
2178 Egyptian Candlestick
2179 Matt Bread Tray
2180 Leafage Pickle
2181 Lizard Tray
2182 Rosette Smoking Set
2183 Plain Stanley Plates
2184 Lacquer Plate
2185 Mayo Flower Basket
2186 Mermaid Clock
2188 Narcissus Tile
2189 Caterer Jug
2190 Primrose Garden Pot
2191 Primrose Jug
2192 Globe Clock Case
2193 Mermaid Jardinière
2194 Primrose Jug & Pot
2195 Tremblay Tile
2196 Oak Cheese Bell &
  Stand
2197 Bramble Jug
2198 Crown Jug
2199 Shell Jug
2200 Tankard Jug
2201 Flowering Reed Jug
2202 Stag Head
2203 Barrel Spill
2204 Jewel Tray, Dolphin &
  Shell
2205 Caterer Jug
2206 Stanley Bread Tray
2207 Wicker Cheese Bell &
  Stand
2208 Oak Cheese Bell &
  Stand
2209 Bramble Garden Pot
2210 Aquarium Garden Pot
2211 Dolphin Cigar Tray
2212 Bamboo Kettle
2213 Poppy Ink Stand
2214 Vineyard Flower Holder
2215 Watercress Basket, 665
  Shape
2216 Satyr Bread Tray
2217 Basket Dessert Plate
2218 Vine & Strawberry
  Dessert Tray
2219 Vine & Strawberry Bread
  Tray
2220 Hop Beer Set
2221 Diamond Jug
2222 Oak Spill
2223 Basket Tobacco Jar
2224 Kidney Smoking Set &
  Tray
2225-6 Vineyard Hanging
  Brackets

2227 Hanging Basket
2228 Globe Kettle
2229 Shell Plate
2230 Double Dolphin Centre
2231 Sprite Flower Holder
2232-3 Bow Handled Basket
2234 Rosette Basket & Stand
2235 Vine & Strawberry Bread Tray
2236 Pigeon Tray
2237 Pineapple Bread Tray
2238 Caterer Jug
2239 Rustic Hanging Basket
2240-1 Narcissus Vase
2242 Deck Flower Holder
2243 Elizabethan Vase
2244 Tycoon Vase
2245 Stag Pen-holder
2246 Dolphin Vase
2247 Hedge Hog Flower Holder
2248 Elephant Punch Bowl
2249 Disraeli Pot
2250 Oak Column
2251 Cupid Jardinière
2252 Tremblay Tile, Animal Centre
2253 Tremblay Tile, Cupid Centre
2254 Tremblay Tile, Female Centre
2255 Diaper Tile
2256 Stanley Butter
2257 Pigeon Tray
2258 Dresden Sandwich Tray
2259 Trefoil Strawberry Dish
2260 Goode & Co. Cable Jug
2261 Rush Jug
2262 Rosette Butter
2263 Leopard Flower Pot
2264 Bow Handled Basket
2265 Rosette Butter
2266 Elizabethan Vase
2267 Lorne Tazza
2268 Tremblay Tile
2269 Rosette Cruet Set
2270 Oyster Individual Butter
2271 Raleigh Tobacco Jar
2272 Hooped & Lagged Jug
2273 Joiners Bass
2274 Orchard Basket
2275 Barley Jug
2276 Raleigh Tobacco Jar
2277 Vase, 1218 Shape
2278 Delphi Vase
2279 Dante Vase
2280 Candlestick
2281 Satyr Double Figured Centre
2282 Trentham Flower Basket

2283 Satyr Flower Basket
2284 Musical Jardinière
2285 Mask Head Vase
2286 Mrs. Pollock's Centre
2287 Bird Nest Basket
2288 Wine Cooler, 990 Shape
2289 Dragon Lamp Vase
2290 Hedgehog & Stand
2291 Dragon Flower Pot
2292 Rabbit Lid Game Pie Dish
2293 Partridge Pie
2294 Vine Biscuit Box
2295 Rosette Mouth Ewer
2296 Beehive Crocus Pot
2297 Goode & Co. Kettle
2298 St. Vincent Centre
2299 Argentre Centre
2300 Vine Wine Tray
2301 Vine Biscuit Box
2302 Narcissus Vase
2303 Hunt Beer Set
2304 Cinquecento Candlestick
2302[sic] Rosette Kettle
2303[sic] Bacchus Tobacco Jar
2304[sic] Bacchanalia Jug
2305 Dove
2306 J M Dolphin Handle & Dolphin Spout Teapot
2307 Vineyard Flower Holder
2308 Double Dolphin Lamp
2309 Strauss Jug
2310 Elizabethan Sceaux
2311 Pear Dessert Plate
2312-13 Square Tremblay Plaque
2314-15 Round Tremblay Pierced
2316 Tremblay Tile
2317 Dining Round Salmon
2318 Salmon for Dining Room Coloured as Trout Salmon, Spotted Extra
2319 Hunt Beer Set
2321 Column
2322 Tremblay Green Centre
2323 Ball Figure
2324 Goat's Head Covered Vase
2325 Flower Pot & Column
2326 Hooped & Lagged Jug
2327 Figural Candle Holders
2328 Dog's Head Vase
2329 Ovid Vase
2330 Vase, Shape 93
2331-2 Chapman & Hall Vase
2333 Clodian Tile
2334 Tremblay Snake Handle Cigar Tray

2335-6 Tremblay Pierced Dessert Plate, Landscapes
2337 Caterer Jug
2338 Round Leafage Bread Tray
2339 Key Plate
2340 Stanley Dessert Plate
2341 Hanging Mask Matchholder
2342 Egyptian Jardinière
2343 Tremblay Butterfly Dessert Plate
2344 Swan Covered Vase
2345 Clodian Jardinière
2346 Turquoise Basket & Stand
2347 Flower Pot
2348 Bracket
2349 Deck Flower Holder
2350 Hooped & Lagged Jug
2351-3 Rosette Flemish Toilet Ware
2354 Hooped & Lagged Jug
2355 Rosette Jug
2356 Caterer Jug
2357-8 Hop Jug
2359 Hunt Jug
2360 Elizabethan Candelabra
2361-2 Matt Bread Tray
2363 Round Tremblay Plaques
2364 Ovid vase, No. 8
2365 Centennial Jug
2366 Rustic Fern Stand
2367 Leafage Broth Set
2368 Hanging Bracket
2369 Ellis's Vase
2370 Disraeli Pot
2371 Hop Jug
2372 Octagon Strawberry Tray
2373 Raleigh Biscuit Box
2374 Primrose Cheese Bell & Stand
2375 Leafage Bread Tray
2376 Narcissus Vase
2377 Fern Pot & Stand
2378 Deck Flower Pot & Stand
2379 Brewster Jug
2380 Harp Vase
2381 Elizabethan Teapot
2382 Cylindrical Vase – Trophies
2383 Deck Flower Holder
2384 Basket Cake Box
2385 Basket Jug
2386 Cleopatra Déjeuner Set
2387 Bramble Pot
2388 Centennial Jug
2389 Primrose Jug
2390 Bramble Jug
2391 Primrose Pot

2392 Sunflower Vase
2393 Leafage Bonbonnière,
No. 2
2394 Versailles Basket
2395 Limoges Candlestick
2396 Mayo Flower Basket
2397 Ivy Spill
2398 Tremblay Snake
Handled Cigar Tray
2399 Beehive Honey
2400 Rosette Small Spill
2401 Trophies Watering Can
2402 Individual Oyster Tray
2403 Goode's Vine Stand
2404 Garden Seat
2405 Sutherland Centre
2406 Boucher Single Centre
2407 Orchard Kettle
2408 Ivy Pattern Tile
2409 Butterfly Tremblay
Centre
2410 Pierced Tremblay
Dessert Plate, Landscapes
2411 Ivy Jug
2412 Crown Jug
2413 Rope Jug
2414 Brewster Jug
2415 Satyr Dessert
2416 Gothic Plates
2417 Crane Jardinière
2418 Double Mask
Watchholder
2419 Tremblay Cigar Tray
2420 Round Tremblay Plaque
2421 Flute Dish
2422 Leafage Tray
2423 Key Dessert Ware
2424–5 Tile, Embossed Centre
2426 Crane Tile
2427 Satyr Dessert Plate
2428 Lorne Plate
2429 Indian Tray
2430 Sunflower Vase
2431 Y Centre Stand
2432 Tea Taster, No. 8
2433 Regout Butter, No. 8
2434 Hopped & Lagged
Butter
2435 Hooped & Lagged Cruet
Set
2436 Cylindrical Vase,
Trophies
2437 Hunt Jug
2438–40 Trentham Vase
2441–2 Dragon Lamp
2443 Tremblay Dessert Plate,
Fruits
2444 Tremblay Snake
Handled Cigar Tray
2445 Tile

2446 Tile, Birds
2447 Laurel Pot
2448 Rosette Butter
2449 Satyr Dessert Plate
2450 Octagon Tremblay
Dessert Plate
2451 Matt Bread Tray
2452 Toast & Egg Rack
2453 Small Trophies Vase
2454 Tremblay Pen Tray
2455 Rosette Cruet Set
2456 Boucher Dessert Plate
2457 Tankard, Printed
Japonica
2458 Cable Jug, Printed
Japonica
2459 Leo Pot
2460–1 Rope Tobacco Jar
2462 Boucher Plain Dessert
Plate
2463 Bud Vase, No. 8
2464 Centre Vase
2465 Ruben Garden Seat
2466 Early English Tile
2467 Tremblay Tile
2468 Matt Tile
2469–71 Deck Tile
2472 Key Dessert Plate
2473 Pear Dessert Plate
2474 Snake Handled Card
Tray or Bread Tray
2475 Satyr Bread Tray
2476 Strawberry Cigar Tray
2477 Tremblay Cigar Tray
2478 Hanging Bracket
2479 Dolphin Bonbonnière
2480 Cupid Bracket
2481 Garden Pedestal
2482 Vase, 950
2483 Hooped & Lagged Jug
2484–6 Swan & Rush Toilet
2487 Bramble Jug
2488 Boucher Centre
2489 Boucher Dessert, Printed
Stork Pattern
2490 Salmon Dish
2491 Elephant Punch Bowl
2492 Sutherland Centre,
Pierced
2493 Rustic Vine Stand
2494 Sea God Sceaux
2495 Mayo Flower Basket
2496 Trophy Tobacco Jar
2497 Roman Vase
2498 Italian Vase & Column
2499 Chinese Tub & Stand
2500–1 Salisbury Vase
2502 Portle Vase
2503 Cylindrical Vase
2504–8 Dresser Spills

2509–11 Cylindrical Vase
2512 Dresser Spills
2513 Chinese Ring Handled
Jardinière
2514 Vase, Shape 950
2515 Vase, 27
2516 Chapman & Hall Vase
2517 Mikado Vase
2518 Vase, 27
2519 Orange Marmalade
2520 Pomade or Puff Box or
Small Tobacco Jar
2521 Snake Handled Jug
2522 Dolphin Cigar Tray
2523 Basket Sardine Box with
Shell on Lid
2524 Oyster Tray
2525 Beehive Honey Pot
2526 Oyster Tray
2527 Potpourri 381
2528 Rosette Vase
2529 Key Dessert, Early
English Printed
2530 Pekin Kettle
2531 Vase 941
2532 Twigg Tremblay Tall
Comport
2533 Romping Horse Vase,
298 Shape
2534 Globe Vase, 940
2535 Cylindrical Spill
2536 Dresser Spill
2537–8 Vase 1009
2539 Fluted Pot
2540 Strawberry Tray with
Parrot
2541 Strawberry Tray without
Parrot
2542 Parrot Jardinière
2543 Vase
2544 Ewer Vase, Cupid
Handle
2546–7 Pineapple Bread Tray
2548–9 Satyr Bread Tray
2550 Vine Sceaux
2551 Phoebus Strawberry Tray
2552 Bramble Jug
2553–4 Ship Dessert Plate
2555 Cornflower Individual
Butter
2556–9 Reed Horn
2560–2 Rosette Horn
2563 Bramble Jug
2564 Doric Jug
2565 Rosette Jug
2566 Pear Dessert
2567 Grape Dessert
2568 Large column
2569 Sickle Bread Tray
2570–1 Stanley Bread Tray

2572 Grape Bread Tray
2573 American Oyster Tray
2574 Delhi Vase
2575 Thistle Spill
2576 Stag Pen Holder
2577 Churn Butter
2578 Wicker Cheese Stand
2579 Dove Pen Holder
2580 Fly Match Box
2581 Fern Shape Pen Tray
2582 Boat Sardine Box
2583 Orchard Teapot
2584 Parrot Salt
2585 Double Salt
2586 Hooped & Lagged Cruet
    Set
2587 Pillar Candlestick
2588 Brewster Tobacco Jar
2589 Horus
2590 Bachelor Set
2591 Rosette Vase
2592 Triangle Vase, No. 27
2593 Japanese Vase
2594 Watteau Can
2595-6 Tremblay Snake
    Handled Tray
2597 Sunflower Individual
    Butter
2598 Salisbury Jug
2599 Fluted Pillar Candlestick
2600 Snake Handle Tazza
2601 Reed Horn
2602-3 Rosette Horn
2604 Hunt Mug

*Silver Decorated Series (Nos.
    2605-25)*

2605 Silver Salmon Dish
2606 Fern Pot
2607 Primrose Pot
2608 Deck Pot
2609 Bramble Pot
2610 Vine Biscuit Box
2611 Primrose Cheese Bell
2612 Vine Sceaux
2613 Raleigh Water Bottle
2614 Narcissus Vase
2615 Primrose Jug
2616 Orchard Teapot
2617 Satyr Bread Tray
2618 Satyr Plate
2619 Pear Dessert Plate
2620 Lotus Candlestick
2621 Indian Cake Tray
2622 Sunflower Individual
    Butter
2623 Bird Nest Salt
2624 Ivy Jug
2625 Dante Vase
2626 Vineyard Basket

2627 Pommier Basket
2628 Dresser Spill
2629 Buffalo Ware
2630 Tremblay Limoges
    Dessert Ware
2631 Puck Sardine Box
2633 Salad, Tall Foot
2634 Strawberry Set
2635-6 Pickle
2637 Puck Tea Ware
2638 Brewster Jug

*Argenta Ware (Nos.
    2639-86)*

2639 Rosette Butter
2640 Stanley Butter
2641 Rosette Kettle
2642 Hooped & Lagged Jug
2643 Hunt Jug
2644 Bacchanalian Jug
2645 Orchard Kettle
2646 Sardinia Box
2647 Strawberry Set
2648 Salad, Low or Tall
2649 Butterfly Tremblay
2650 Satyr Dessert
2651 Vine & Strawberry
    Dessert Plate
2652 Trefoil Strawberry Tray
2653 Rosette Beer Set
2654 Hop Beer Set
2655 Stanley Dessert
2656 Passion Flower Pot
2657 Punch & Judy Cruet Set
2658-9 Individual Butter
2660 Individual Card
2661 Umbrella Stand
2662 Ice Pail
2663 Individual Butter
2664 Spade Individual Butter
2665 Individual Butter
2666 Meadow Butter
2667 Sunflower Vase
2668 Stag Tile
2669 Matt Bread Tray
2671 Grape Bread Tray
2672 Churn Butter
2673 Meadow Butter
2674 Matt Sardine Box
2675 Crown Jug
2676 Mixed Pickle
2677 Burton Jug
2678 Trophy Tobacco Jar
2679 Hooped & Lagged
    Butter
2680 Mrs. Pollock's Centre
2681 Partridge Pie
2682 Fern Stand
2683 Elizabethan Teapot
2684 Octagon Strawberry Tray

2685 Elizabethan Candalabra
2686 Elizabethan Candlestick
2687 Parrot Jardinière
2688 Meadow Butter
2689 Hooped & Lagged
    Butter
2690 Cosy Set
2691 Dante Vase
2692-4 Punch Brandy & Soda
    Set
2695 Punch Grog Set
2696 Shamrock Jug
2697 Salisbury Jug
2698 Corn Cheese Bell &
    Stand, Argenta
2699 Churn Butter
2700 Tremblay Butter
2701 Round Leafage Bread
    Tray, Argenta
2702 Sunflower Comport,
    Argenta
2703 Peacock Tray
2704 Boat Sardine Box

*Argenta Ware (Nos.
    2705-27)*

2705 J M Strawberry Tray,
2706 Dove
2707 Bamboo Kettle
2708 Strawberry Set
2709-10 Horseshoe Individual
    Butter
2711-12 Hop Jug
2713 Primrose Jug
2714 Salmon Dish
2715-17 Sardine
2718 Churn Butter
2719 Meadow Butter
2720 Salad, Tall Foot
2721 Caterer Jug
2722 Passion Flower Pot
2723 Wheat & Poppy Pot
2724 Deck Flower Holder
2725 Elizabethan Flower
    Holder
2726 Tremblay Dessert Plate
2727 Leo Pot
2728 Peacock Pickle
2729 Horseshoe Individual
    Butter
2730 Punch Teapot
2731-2 Oak Teapot
2733-4 Teaware 152
2735 Wheatsheaf Teapot
2736 Wheatsheaf Teapot,
    Argenta
2737 Peacock Strawberry Tray,
    Argenta
2738 Lookar? Tray, Argenta
2739 Parrot Salt

2740 Cupid Bracket, Argenta
2741 Raleigh Tobacco Jar, Argenta
2742 Flowering Reed Jug, Argenta
2743 Matt Bread Tray, Argenta
2744 Vine & Strawberry Bread Tray, Argenta
2745 Barley Jug, Argenta
2746-7 Fan Garden Pot
2748-9 Peacock Individual Butter
2750 Ice Pail, Argenta
2750[sic] Cosy Set
2731[sic] Bacchanalian Sceaux
2752 Fan Strawberry Set
2753 Peacock Pickle
2754 Oyster Tray, Argenta
2755 Fan Strawberry Set
2756 Fan Strawberry Set, Argenta
2757 Fan Cheese Bell, Argenta
2758-9 Palms Cheese Bell
2760 Strawberry Set
2761 Fan Jug
2762 Fan Jug, Argenta
2763-4 Prince of Wales Jug
2765-7 Lobster Pot
2768 Stag Pen Holder
2769 Individual Strawberry Set
2770 Fan Garden Pot, Argenta
2771 Umbrella Stand
2772 Fan Jug
2773 Primrose Tile
2774 Strawberry Tile
2775-6 Rustic Umbrella Stand
2777 Large Column
2778 Embossed Plantagenet Toilet
2779 Rosette Toilet
2780 Seaweed Oyster Tray
2781 Passion Flower Tile
2782 Dolphin Cigar Tray
2788 Fan Punch Bowl
2789 Fan Dessert Ware
2790 Horseshoe Individual Butter
2791-2 Fan Dessert Ware
2793 Fan Salad, Argenta
2794 Monkey Salad, Argenta
2795 Monkey Cake Tray, Argenta
2796 Monkey Bread Tray

*Argenta Ware (Nos. 2797-2807)*

2797 Rhebus Tray
2798 Vase 1218
2799 Florentine Vase

2800 Cleopatra Tea Ware
2801 Oak Garden Seat
2802 Bamboo Jardinière
2803 Masked Handle Vase
2804 Snake Handled Bread Tray
2806[sic] Fern Pen Tray
2806 Bird Nest Bracket
2807 Strawberry Soup
2808 Fan Biscuit Jar
2809-10 Bramble Tea Ware
2811 Parrot Jardinière, Argenta
2812 Mayo Flower Basket, Argenta
2813 Tortoise Sardine Box with Rabbit Lid
2814 Ocean Oyster Tray, Argenta
2815 Fish Aquarium Plate, Argenta
2816 Fan Salad for Mounting, Argenta
2817-19 Fan Salad for Mounting
2820 Gipsy Strawberry Set
2821 Gipsy Strawberry Set, Argenta
2822 Sultan Garden Seat, Argenta
2823 Sutherland Centre or Flower Basket, Argenta
2824 Raleigh Flower Pot, Argenta
2825 Goode's Vine Stand
2826 Raleigh Sardine Box, Argenta
2827 Hanging Flower Basket, Argenta
2829 Alexandra Centre, Argenta
2830 Bow Handled Card Tray, Argenta
2831 Ocean Ice Pail
2832 Ocean Sardine, Argenta
2833 Ocean Butter, Argenta
2834 Ocean Sardine
2835 Ocean Butter
2836 Athletic Jug, Argenta
2837-8 Ocean Oyster Tray
2839 Mixed Pickle, Card Shape, Argenta
2840-1 Mixed Pickle, Card Shape
2842 Ocean Butter
2843 Basket with Wreath, Argenta
2844 French Basket & Stand
2845 Flower Pot
2846 Leafage Teapot, Argenta
2847-8 Oval Basket Plate

2849 Eggshape Salt, Argenta
2850 Bow & Basket, Argenta
2851 Leafage Pickle, Argenta
2852 Leafage Pickle
2853 Fluted Basket, 1050 Shape, Argenta
2854 Fluted Basket, 1050 Shape
2855 Oyster Barrel, Argenta
2856 Fan Jug, Argenta
2857 Fan Garden Pot, Argenta
2858 Fan Garden Seat
2859 Monkey Salad, Rustic Foot, Argenta
2860 Monkey Salad, Rustic Foot
2861 Orange Marmalade, Argenta
2862-3 Orange Marmalade
2864 Buttercup Butter, Argenta
2865 Buttercup Butter
2866-7 Smoking Cap Spittoon
2868 Ocean Cruet Set
2869 Ocean Candlestick
2870 New Matt Cheese Bell
2871 Fan Cruet Set
2872 Garden Strawberry Tray
2873 Fan Cruet Set, Argenta
2874 New Cheese Bell
2875 Ocean Candlestick, Argenta
2876 Ocean Cruet Set, Argenta
2877 Sunflower Butter
2878 Daisy Butter
2879 Swan Umbrella Stand
2880-2 Elizabethan Tea Ware
2883 Dessert No. 7, Argenta
2884 Dessert Acanthus, Argenta
2885 Dessert No. 8, Argenta
2886 Sunflower Butter, Argenta
2887-8 Elizabethan Teapot
2889 Bacchanalian Jug
2890 Strawberry Jug, Argenta
2891-2 Strawberry Jug
2893 Monkey Teapot, Argenta
2894 Gipsy Strawberry Tray, Argenta
2895-6 Gipsy Strawberry Tray
2897 Sickle Bread Tray, Argenta
2898 Sunflower Comport/ Centre, Argenta
2899 Gipsy Strawberry Tray
2900 Bonnett Bracket
2901 Bonnett Flower Pot
2902 Bonnett Bracket
2903 Bramble Tea Ware

2904 Greenaway Flower Pot
2905 Matt Cheese Bell,
  Argenta
2906 Ocean Bread Tray,
  Argenta
2907 Greenaway Flower Pot
2908 Ocean Bread Tray
2910 Monkey Ware
2911–12 Palm Bread Tray
2913 Fruit Dessert, 6 different
  fruits
2914 Fruit Dessert, Argenta
2915 Bouquet Salad
2916 Lobster Salad
2917 Swan Ewer
2918 Shell Toilet
2919 Fan Punch Bowl
2920 Passion Flower Tile
2921 Passion Flower Tile,
  Argenta
2922 Rubens Garden Seat,
  Argenta
2923 Fan Cheese Bell
2924 Fan Cheese Bell, Argenta
2925 Fan Cheese Bell
2926–7 Courney Copper
  Bracket
2928 Lobster Salad
2929–30 Fan Jardinière
2931 Vine Punch Bowl
2932 Fan Punch Bowl
2933 Strawberry Jug
2934 Shell Fish Dish
2935 Plain Fan Dessert
  (Renamed Chicago)
2936 Ocean Jug
2937 Fan Tea Ware, Argenta
2938 Courney Copper Bracket
2939 Apple Blossom Flower
  Pot
2940 Gipsy Strawberry Set
2941 Ocean Ice Pail
2942 Ocean Ice Pail, Argenta
2943–5 Ocean Pickle
2946 Ocean Plate
2946[sic] Ocean Dish
2947–8 Shell Oyster Tray
2949 Ocean Dish
2949[sic] Ocean Plate
2950 Ocean Pickle
2951 Vine Punch Bowl
2952–3 Ocean Shell Jug
2954 Spoon Warmer
2955 Ocean Pickle
2956 Fan Salad
2957 Fan Dessert Ware
2958 Fan Salad
2959 Fan Comport
2960 Fan Jug
2961 Fan Teaware

2962 Fan Teapot & Ware
2963 Ocean Tea Ware
2964 Strawberry Set
2965 Ocean Sandwich Tray
2966 Bouquet Plate
2967–9 Strawberry Jug
2970–1 Fan Tea Ware
2972–3 Athletic Jug
2974–5 Monkey Teapot
2976 Household Strawberry
  Set
2977 Fan Dessert Ware
2978–9 Ocean Pickle
2980 Border Dessert Ware
2981 Meadow Butter
2982 Individual Strawberry Set
2983 Punch Cruet Set
2984 Elizabethan Teapot
2985 Ocean Jug
2986 Fan Punch Bowl
2987 Fan Jug
2988–90 Shell Dessert Ware
2991–3 Sunflower Individual
  Butter
2994–5 Apple Blossom Flower
  Pot
2996–7 Franklin Strawberry
  Set
2998 Leau? Strawberry Set
2999 Leau? Bread Tray
3000 Leau? Strawberry Set
3001–2 Spoon Warmer
3003 Fan Flower Pot
3004 Fan Toilet Ware
3005 Bramble Jug
3006 Hop Jug
3007 Bramble Jug
3008 Hop Jug
3009–10 Shell Cruet Set
3011 Shell Butter
3012–14 Ocean Shell Salad
3015 Bramble Jug
3016 Garden Strawberry Set
3017 Ocean Sardine
3018–9 Ocean Butter
3020 Fruit Dessert Plate
3021 Ocean Fish Dish & Plate
3022 Chicago Dessert
3023 Garden Strawberry Set
3024 Dolphin Oyster Tray
3025 Shell Ice Pail
3026 Shell Oyster Tray
3027 Fan Punch Bowl
3028 Apple Blossom Flower
  Pot
3029 Kate Greenaway Flower
  Pot
3030 Vine Strawberry Set
3031 Fan Teapot
3032–5 Fan Tea Ware

3036–8 Kate Greenaway
  Flower Basket
3039 Wicker Dessert Ware
3040–2 Fan Umbrella Stand
3043 Leeds Dessert
3044–5 Seaweed Bread Tray
3046 Fan Dessert Ware
3047 Fruit Punch Bowl
3048 Fruit Strawberry Set
3049 Fruit Bread Tray
3050 Fruit Ice Tray & Plate
3051 Fruit Jug
3052 Cornfield Bread Tray
3053 Shell Fish Dish
3054 Shell Dessert Plate
3055 Fruit Pickles
3056 Fruit Punch Bowl
3057 Fruit Strawberry Set
3058 Fruit Bread Tray
3059 Fruit Ice Tray
3060 Fruit Jug
3061 Cornfield Bread Tray
3062 Shell Fish Dish
3063 Shell Dessert
3064 Fruit Pickles
3065 Fan Dessert Ware
3066 Fan Salad
3067 Fan Punch Bowl
3068 Fan Cheese Bell
3069 Fan Jug
3070 Fan Bread Tray
3074 Kate Greenaway
  Umbrella Stand
3075 Fan Dessert Ware
3076 Fan Salad
3077 Fan Bread Tray
3078 Fan Punch Bowl
3079 Fan Jug & Beer Set
3080 Fan Cheese Bell
3081 Ocean Sandwich Tray
3082–4 Tassle Umbrella Stand
3085 Fruit Umbrella Stand
3086–8 Lincoln Salad
3089 Shell Sardine, Boat Lid
3090–2 Lincoln Dessert Ware
3093–5 Lincoln Pickles
3096–8 Lincoln Jug
3099–3101 Tropic Dessert
3102–3 Shell Sardine, Boat Lid
3104 Fruit Umbrella Stand
3105 Fruit Sardine
3106–8 Fruit Butter
3109 Fruit Sardine
3110 Fruit Butter
3111–13 Fruit Spittoon
3114 Fruit Sardine
3115–17 Fruit Cruet Set
3118 Fruit Dessert
3119 Fruit Strawberry Basket
3120 Fruit Jug

3121 Fruit Punch Bowl
3122 Cornfield Bread Tray
3123 Fruit Bread Tray
3124 Fruit Strawberry Set
3125 Fruit Pickles
3126 Fruit Dessert Ware
3127 Fruit Punch Bowl
3128 Fruit Bread Tray
3129 Cornfield Bread Tray
3130 Fruit Pickles
3131 Fruit Jug
3132–3 Lincoln Umbrella
    Stand
3134–5 Sunflower Umbrella
    Stand
3136–8 Shell Oyster Tray
3139–43 Ocean Tea Ware
3144 Seaweed Teapot
3145–8 Seaweed Jug
3149 Shell Dessert Ware
3150 Sunflower Dessert
3151 Shell Fish Plate
3152–4 Sunflower Dessert
3155–6 Fruit Individual Butter
3157–8 Tropic Individual
    Butter
3159 Vine Strawberry Set
3160 Sunflower Umbrella
    Stand
3161 Lincoln Umbrella Stand
3162 Shell Dessert Ware
3163 French Cruet Set
3164 Berlin Match Holder
3165 Garden Pot with
    Primrose
3166 Garden Pot with Fern
3167–8 Garden Pot with
    Apple Blossom
3169–70 Lincoln Bread Tray
3171 Ocean Tea Ware
3172 Matt & Shell Fish Dish
3173–4 Lincoln Garden Seat
3175 Seaweed Jug
3176 Granville Butter
3177 Boston Butter
3178–81 Lincoln Cheese Bell
    & Stand
3182 Lincoln Flower Pot
3183 Carner? Centre
3184 Sutherland Centre
3185 Versailles Basket
3186 St. Cloude Basket
3187–8 Sunflower Jug
3189 Naiad Centre
3190 Seaweed Jug
3191 Seaweed Tea Ware
3192 Granville Butter
3193 Lincoln Tea Ware
3194–5 Lincoln Comport
3196 Lincoln Butter

3197 Sunflower Jug
3198 Seaweed Butter
3199 Sunflower Jug
3200–1 Lincoln Flower Pot
3202 St. Louis Strawberry Tray
3204–5 St. Louis Dessert Ware
3206–7 St. Louis Bread Tray
3208–10 St. Louis Oyster Tray
3211–14 St. Louis Jug
3215–16 St. Louis Molasses Jug
3217 St. Louis Plate
3218 Sportsman Pie
3219–21 Early English Dessert
    Ware
3222–3 Bird Plates
3224 Early English Dessert
    Ware
3225 St. Louis Plate
3226 St. Louis Oyster Tray
3227 St. Louis Jug
3228 St. Louis Molasses Jug
3229 Chicago Butter
3230 Partridge Pie
3231 Ocean Sardine
3232 Fan Jug
3233 Fan Tea Ware
3234 Ocean Teapot
3235–7 Gaiety Match Holder
3238 Chicago Butter
3239 Chicago Butter
3240–1 St. Louis Ice Tray
3242–3 St. Louis Salad
3244–5 St. Louis Fish Dish
3246–7 St. Louis Pickle
3248 Early English Pickle
3249–51 Alaska Salad
3252-3 Lincoln Flower Pot
3254 Early English Flower Pot
3255–6 Early English Pickle
3257 Early English Flower Pot
3258 Early English Umbrella
    Stand
3259 St. Louis Jug
3260–2 Lincoln Garden Seat
3263–4 Early English
    Umbrella Stand
3265–6 St. Louis Punch Bowl
3267–8 St. Louis Sardine
3269–70 St. Louis Butter
3271–2 Chrysanthemum
    Dessert Ware
3273 Chrysanthemum Jug
3274–7 Sunflower Tea Ware
3278–9 Chrysanthemum Jug
3280–1 Chrysanthemum
    Butter & Stand
3282 St. Louis Tea Ware
3283 St. Louis Jug
3284–5 Early English Milk Set
3286–7 Early English Sardine

3288 St. Louis Butter
3289 Lincoln Umbrella Stand
3290 Chrysanthemum Cheese
    Bell & Stand
3291 Chrysanthemum Oyster
    Tray
3292 Chrysanthemum Bread
    Tray
3293 Chrysanthemum Tea
    Ware & Butter
3294 Early English Flower Pot
3295 Apple Blossom Flower
    Pot
3296 Bramble Flower Pot
3297 Lincoln Flower Pot
3298 Fan Flower Pot
3299 Chrysanthemum
    Comport
3300 St. Louis Oyster Tray
3301 Chrysanthemum Jug
3303 St. Louis Strawberry Tray
3304 Chrysanthemum Oyster
    Tray
3305 St. Louis Sardine
3306 St. Louis Tea Ware
3307 St. Louis Jug
3308 Lincoln Jug
3309 Alaska Salad
3310 Ocean Jug
3311 St. Louis Fish Dish
3312 Trefoil Strawberry Dish
3313 St. Louis Salad
3314 Garland Strawberry Tray
3315 St. Louis Sandwich
3316 Chrysanthemum Jug
3317–18 St. Louis Oyster Tray
3319 Chrysanthemum Butter
    & Tea Ware
3320–1 St. Louis Oyster Tray
3322 Chrysanthemum Butter
    & Tea Ware
3323 Chrysanthemum Butter
3324–5 Chrysanthemum
    Oyster Tray
3326 Chrysanthemum Milk
    Set
3327 St. Louis Milk Set
3328 St. Louis Jug
3329 Chrysanthemum Jug
3330 Primrose Cheese Bell
3331 Fan Flower Pot
3332 Bramble Flower Pot
3333 Matt Cheese Bell
3334 Lincoln Cheese Bell
3335 Primrose Cheese Bell
3336 Chrysanthemum Cheese
    Bell
3337 Chrysanthemum Cheese
    Bell, Tall
3338 Sunflower Jug

3339 Fan Jug
3340 Chrysanthemum Bread
Tray
3341 Early English Flower Pot
3342 Chrysanthemum Jug
3343 St. Louis Jug
3344 Bramble Jug
3345 St. Louis Jug
3346 Chrysanthemum Dessert
Ware
3347 St. Louis Dessert Ware
3348 Fan Cheese Bell

**K Series (Nos. 3349-4189)**

3349 New Coral Jug
3350 New Grosvenor Jug
3351-2 New Coral Jug
3353-6 Grosvenor Flower Pot
3357 St. Louis Flower Pot
3358 St. Louis Sardine
3359 St. Louis Butter
3360 St. Louis Jug
3361 St. Louis Dessert Ware
3362-3 Daisy Flower Pot
3364-5 Grosvenor Flower Pot
3366 Salmon Dish
3367-71 Owl & Bat Lamp
3372-4 Plaque, King Lear &
His Companion
3375 Teapot
3376 Fan Toilet
3377 Matt Cheese Bell, New
Round Knob
3378-80 Grosvenor Salad
3381 Shell Salad
3382-5 Coral Salad
3386 Grosvenor Jug
3387 Grosvenor Sardine
3388 Grosvenor Tea Ware
3389 Grosvenor Oyster Tray
3390 Grosvenor Tobacco Jar
3391 Grosvenor Jug
3392 Grosvenor Tea Ware
3393 Grosvenor Tobacco Jar
3394 Grosvenor Sardine
3395 Grosvenor Oyster Tray
3396 Grosvenor Jug
3397 Grosvenor Tea Ware
3398 Grosvenor Oyster Tray
3399 Grosvenor Tobacco Jar
3400 Grosvenor Sardine
3401-3 Grosvenor Pickle
3404-6 Grosvenor Punch
Bowl
3407-9 Grosvenor Dinner
Ware
3410-12 Grosvenor Dessert
Ware
3413 Grosvenor Dinner Ware

3414 Grosvenor Dessert Ware
3415 Grosvenor Tea Ware
3416 Fan Flower Pot
3417 Lincoln Flower Pot
3418 Palm Cheese Bell
3419 Grosvenor Sardine
3420 Grosvenor Jug
3421-4 Daisy Flower Pot
3425-6 Lincoln Cheese Bell
3427 Cornfield Bread Tray
3428-9 Grosvenor Dinner
Ware
3430-3 Grosvenor Dessert
Ware
3432 [sic] Ocean Tea Ware
3433-4 [sic] St. Louis Tea
Ware
3435 St. Louis Ice Tray
3436 St. Louis Jug
3437 Sunflower Bread Tray
3438 Grosvenor Jug
3439 Grosvenor Tea Ware
3440 Grosvenor Salad
3441 Grosvenor Dessert
3442 Grosvenor Tea Ware
3443 Grosvenor Salad
3444 Grosvenor Sardine
3445-6 Chrysanthemum
Cheese Bell
3447-9 Luther Flower Pot
3450-1 Luther Jug
3452-8 Luther Cheese Bell
3459-61 Grosvenor Cheese
Bell
3462-4 Warncliff Jug
3465 Luther Salad
3466 Grosvenor Cheese Bell
3467 Caterer Jug
3468 Daisy Luther Pot & Lion
Head Column
'Gone to Phillips, London Nov
12 1890'
3469-70 Luther Flower Pot
'One done magnolia shape
for Maple & Co. June 10,
1891'
3471-3 Cucumber Salad
3474-5 Melon Salad
3476 Luther Flower Pot
3477 Column
3478 Grosvenor Flower Pot
3479 Grosvenor Jug
3480 Luther Flower Pot
3481 Tomato Salad
3482 Cucumber Square Salad/
Asparagus Dish
3483 Swan Vase
3484-6 Luther Dessert Ware
3487 Luther Sardine
3488 Luther Sardine Butter

3489 As 3488
3490 Lincoln Umbrella Stand
3491 St. Louis Flower Pot
3492 Luther Flower Pot
3493 Chrysanthemum Bread
Tray
3494 Chrysanthemum Tea
Ware
3495 Primrose Cheese Bell
3496 Sunflower Umbrella
Stand
3497 St. Louis Flower Pot
3498 Chrysanthemum Cheese
Bell
3499 Fan Tea Ware
3500 Lincoln Umbrella Stand
3501 Luther Flower Pot
3502 Bramble Flower Pot
3503 Primrose Cheese Bell
3504 Chrysanthemum Bread
Tray & Tea Ware
3505-8 Luther Bread Tray
3509 Fan Jug
3510 Bramble Jug
3511 St. Louis Jug
3512 Ocean Jug
3513 Coral Jug
3514-15 New Salad
3516 Jug
3517 Mug
3518-19 New Jardinière
3520-4 Flower Pot
3525 As 3519
3526 Chrysanthemum Cheese
Bell
3527 Chrysanthemum Dessert
Ware
3528 Chrysanthemum Jug
3529 Luther Ware
3530 Luther Sardine
3531-3 Magnolia Salad
3534-5 Luther Flower Pot
3536-9 Owl Lamp
3540-1 Magnolia Flower Pot
3542-8 Plain Lamp
3549-50 Plain Column
3551-3 Oak Garden Seat
3554 Sunflower Umbrella
Stand
3555 Lincoln Umbrella Stand
3556-8 Lincoln Garden Seat
3559 Grosvenor Flower Pot
3560 Chrysanthemum Ware
Cheese Bell
3561 Ocean Tea Ware &
Salad, Jugs
3562 Salmon Dish & Plates
3563 Ocean Fish Dish
3564 Fish Dish & Plates
3565 Fern Stand

3566 Strawberry
3567 Fan Toilet Ware & Salad & Jug
3568 Primrose Cheese Bell
3569 Sartago Salad
3570 AB Flower Pot
3571 Daisy Flower Pot
3572 St. Louis Jug & Bread Tray
3573 Hunt Tobacco Jar & Jug
3574 Fruit Garden Strawberry Set & Other Ware
3575 Oak Tea Ware
3576 Seaweed Jug
3577 Caterer Jug
3578 Dolphin Oyster Tray
3579 Early English Sardine & Bread Tray
3580 Grape Bread Tray
3581 New Butter
3582–4 Wicker Work Hanging Basket
3585–7 Leafage Hanging Basket
3588 Octagon Jug Stand, Rustic Pattern
3589 Bramble Flower Pot
3590 Grosvenor Bread Tray
3591 Grosvenor Plate
3592 New Fruit Butter
3593–8 Cruet Set
3599 Luther Daisy Flower Pot
3600 Luther Cheese Bell
3601–2 Warncliffe Jug
3603 Tunbridge Flower Pot
3604 Warncliffe Jug
3605 Tunbridge Jug
3606 [Illegible]
3607–8 Hunt Jug
3609–10 Grosvenor Jug
3611 Magnolia Flower Pot
3612 Fruit Umbrella Stand
3613 Fan Garden Seat
3614 Luther Flower Pot
3615 Daisy Flower Pot
3616 Tunbridge Flower Pot
3617 Daisy Flower Pot
3618 Magnolia Flower Pot
3619 Tunbridge Flower Pot
3620–1 Fluted Flower Pot
3622 Tunbridge Flower Pot
3623 Luther Flower Pot & Pedestal
3624 Oak Garden Seat
3625 Fruit Umbrella Stand
3626 Luther Pedestal & Ware
3627 Grosvenor Flower Pot & Ware
3628 Grosvenor Flower Pot
3629 Lion Head Column

3630 Daisy Flower Pot
3631 Lincoln Garden Seat & Other Ware
3632 Oak Garden Seat
3633–4 Toilet Ware
3635 Daisy Flower Pot
3636 Sunflower Umbrella Stand
3637–8 Tunbridge Flower Pot
3639–40 Luther Ware
3641–3 Vase
3644–5 Round Vase
3646 Lion Head Column
3647 Vase as 3644
3648 Luther Daisy Pot
3649 Luther Pedestal & Ware
3650 Chrysanthemum Ware
3651 Ocean Ware
3652 Fruit Ware
3653 Magnolia Flower Pot
3654 Grosvenor Ware
3655 Sunflower Jug
3656 Tunbridge Flower Pot
3657 St. Louis Ware
3658 Matt & Shells Ware
3659 Hunt Jug
3660 Trefoil Strawberry Set
3661 Early English Sardine
3662–3 Matt Bread Tray
3664 Buttercup Butter
3665 New Berry Butter
3666 Luther Pedestal
3667 Magnolia Flower Pot
3668 Fruit Ware
3669 St. Louis Ware
3670 Salmon Dish & Plates
3671 Matt & Shell Ware
3672 Fan Ware
3673 Ocean Ware
3674 Chrysanthemum Ware
3675 Tunbridge Ware
3676 Oak Tea Ware
3677 Strawberry Strawberry Set
3678 Illegible
3679 Primrose Cheese Bell
3680 New Berry Butter
3681 Early English Sardine
3682 Orange Base
3683 Salad Plate
3684 Bramble Jug
3685 Luther Daisy Flower Pot
3686 Luther & Magnolia Ware
3687–9 Owl Salad
3690–1 Griffin Salad
3692 St. Louis Ware
3693–3709 Vase
3710–11 Magnolia Flower Pot
3712 Tunbridge Flower Pot
3713–15 Griffin Flower Pot

3716 Griffin Pedestal
3717 Luther Pedestal
3718 St. Louis Jug
3719 St. Louis Salad
3720 Ocean Sardine
3721 Fan Jug
3722 Lincoln Salad
3723 Matt Bread Tray
3724 Tunbridge Flower Pot
3725 Griffin Flower Pot & Pedestal
3726 Matt Sardine
3727 Tunbridge Flower Pot
3728 Griffin Flower Pot
3729 Grosvenor Ware
3730–2 Game Pies
3733 Luther Pedestal
3734 Lincoln Dessert Ware
3735–6 (Stained Glass) Window Pattern Toilet Ware
3737 Window Pattern Lamp
3738 Window Pattern Jug
3739 Window Pattern Biscuit Box & Salad
3740 Window Pattern Jug
3741 Glass (Window) Pattern Flower Pot
3742 Window Pattern Pedestal
3743 Magnolia Salad & Flower Pot
3744–6 Squirrel Salad
3747 Magnolia Salad
3748 Magnolia Flower Pot
3749 Luther Pedestal
3750 Fruit Matt Strawberry Tray
3751 Franklin Strawberry Tray
3752 Strawberry Strawberry Tray
3753–5 Fluted Shell Salad
3755 [sic] Sunflower Jug
3756–7 Grosvenor Jug
3758 Tunbridge Jug
3759 St. Louis Flower Pot
3760–64 Leopard Flower Pot
3765 Flemish Jug
3766–71 Magnolia Flower Pot & Pedestal
3772 St. Louis Jug
3773 Tunbridge Jug
3774 Luther Jug
3775 Tunbridge Jug
3776 Luther Flower Pot
3777 Luther Jug
3778–80 Magnolia Flower Pot
3781 Luther Flower Pot & Pedestal
3782–3 Luther Cheese Bell
3784 Luther Jug
3785 Leopard Flower Pot

3786 Fan Jug
3787 St. Louis Jug
3788 Leopard Flower Pot
3789 Flower Basket
3790 Luther Jug
3791 Sardine
3792 Butter
3793 Flower Pot
3794 Cheese Bell
3795 Grosvenor Flower Pot
3796 Griffin Flower Pot & Pedestal
3797 Daisy Flower Pot
3798 Grosvenor Bread Tray
3799 Early English Sardine
3800 Luther Jug
3801 Luther Daisy Flower Pot
3802 Magnolia Pot
3803 New Umbrella Stand
3804 Umbrella Stand
3805 Chrysanthemum Cheese Bell
3806 Shaded Toilet Ware, Star Shape
3807 Shaded Toilet Ware, Stafford Shape
3808–9 Shaded Toilet Ware, Chester Shape
3810 Shaded Toilet Ware, Star Shape
3811 Shaded Toilet Ware, 587 Shape
3812 [Illegible] Dessert Plates to Match Mintons
3813 Chelsea Shape Toilet Jug
3814–15 Stafford Shape Toilet Jug
3816–20 Wicker Dessert Ware
3824 Gisse ? Edge Dessert
3825 Magnolia Flower Pot
3826 Luther Flower Pot
3827 Fluted Flower Pot
3828 Luther Flower Pot
3829 Fluted Flower Pot
3830–1 Chelsea Toilet Jug
3832 Chelsea Shaded Toilet Ware
3833 Fluted Flower Pot
3834–6 Star Shape Toilet Ware
3837–50 Italian Pattern Flower Pots & Pedestals
3851 Hexagon Umbrella Stand
3852 Sunflower Umbrella Stand
3853 Garden Seat
3854 Garden Seat, Different Pattern
3855 Basketwork Umbrella Stand
3856–7 Daisy Luther Flower Pot
3858 Italian Flower Pot & Pedestal
3859 Griffin Flower Pot & Pedestal
3860 Italian Flower Pot & Pedestal
3861–2 Luther Flower Pot & Pedestal
3863 Magnolia Flower Pot & Pedestal
3864 Lion Head Column
3865 Griffin Pedestal
3866 Magnolia Flower Pot
3867 Chary Cheese Bell
3868–9 Star Shape Toilet Ware
3870–4 Tunbridge Flower Pot
3875 Italian Flower Pot
3876 Oak Garden Seat
3877–9 Italian Flower Pot & Pedestal
3880 Maneshead Jug
3881 Chelsea Toilet Jug
3882–3 Ruben Garden Seat
3884 Quinsy Umbrella Stand
3885 Griffin Pots & Pedestal
3886 Stafford Shape Toilet Ware
3887 Cheap? Cheese Bell
3888–91 Italian Flower Pot & Pedestal
3892 Quinsy Umbrella Stand
3893 Octagon Umbrella Stand
3895–3902 Italian Flower Pot & Pedestal
3903 Italian Flower Pot & Pedestal; Quinsy Umbrella Stand
3904–5 Quinsy Umbrella Stand
3906–7 Italian Flower Pot & Pedestal
3907–8[sic] Magnolia Salad
3909 Griffin Flower Pot & Pedestal
3910 Lincoln Garden Seat
3911 Sunflower Umbrella Stand
3912–14 Tunbridge Flower Pot
3915 Tunbridge Jug
3916 Game Pie
3917 Sunflower Jug
3918 Luther Cheese Bell
3919 Quinsy Umbrella Stand
3920 Tunbridge Jug & Flower Pot
3922 Early English Sardine
3923 Quinsy Umbrella Stand
3924 Griffin Flower Pot
3925 Quinsy Umbrella Stand
3926 Tunbridge Jugs & Flower Pot
3927 Sunflower Jug
3928 Magnolia Flower Pot
3929 Tunbridge Flower Pot & Jugs
3930–1 Game Pie
3932–3 Italian Pot & Pedestal
3934–5 Luther Cheese Bell
3936 Quinsy Umbrella Stand
3937 Lincoln Garden Seat
3938–9 Fruit Umbrella Stand
3940–2 Ruben Garden Seat
3943 Italian Flower Pot & Pedestal
3944 Griffin Flower Pot & Pedestal
3945–7 Cushion Garden Seat
3948–9 Italian Flower Pot & Pedestal
3950–4 Quinsy Umbrella Stand
3955–7 Griffin Flower Pot
3958 Quinsy Umbrella Stand
3959–60 Griffin Flower Pot & Pedestal
3961–5 Lowell Flower Pot & Pedestal
3966 Magnolia Flower Pot
3967 Lowell Flower Pot & Pedestal
3968 Luther Tea Ware
3969 Ocean Cremes or Mustards
3970–1 Fan Cremes or Mustards
3972–6 Lowell Flower Pot & Pedestal
3977–8 Paper Basket Work Garden Seat
3979 Magnolia Flower Pot
3980 Magnolia Salad
3981–2 Grosvenor Salad
3983–4 New Salad
3985–6 New Lamp
3987 Fan Biscuit Box
3988 Elephant Biscuit Box
3989 Procession Biscuit Box
3990 Basket Umbrella Stand
3991 Basket Garden Seat
3992 Basket Umbrella Stand
3993 Basket Garden Seat
3994–6 Paper Basket Garden Seat
3997 Paper Basket Umbrella Stand
3998–9 Ruben Garden Seat
4000 Lowell Pedestal
4001 Lowell Flower Pot &

Pedestal
4002 Lowell Flower Pot
4003 Lowell Flower Pot &
   Pedestal
4004 Quinsy Umbrella Stand
4005 Ruben Garden Seat
4006–9 Italian Salad
4010–11 Lowell Salad
4012 Ocean Salad
4013 Stephanotis Salad
4014 Sturkheim ? Salad
4015 Griffin Salad
4016 Elephant Biscuit Box
4017 Fan Biscuit Box
4018 Ocean Salad
4019 Magnolia Salad
4020 Lowell Salad
4021–3 [Illegible]
4024–6 Magnolia Salad
4027 Griffin Pedestal
4028 Griffin Pot
4029 Lowell Pedestal
4030 Lowell Pot
4031 Lion's Head pedestal
4032 Magnolia Pot
4033 Lowell Pedestal
4034 Lowell Pot
4035–6 Stag Salad
4037 Heraldic Salad
4038 Ruben Garden Seat
4039 Basket Umbrella Stand
4040–1 Stag Salad
4042 Procession Biscuit Box
4043–4 Lowell Salad
4045 Heraldic Salad
4046 Wicker Umbrella Stand
4047 Wicker Paper Basket
4048 Wicker Umbrella Stand
4049–50 Wicker Paper Basket
4051 Wicker Umbrella Stand
4052 Italian Flower Pot

4053 Lowell Flower Pot
4054 Lowell Pedestal
4055–7 Hunt Jug
4058–64 Italian Flower Pot
4065 Lowell Flower Pot
4066 Lowell Pedestal
4067–8 Lowell Flower Pot
4069 Oak Garden Seat
4070 Lincoln Umbrella Stand
4071 Italian Pedestal
4072–3 Magnolia Flower Pot
4074 Lowell Flower Pot
4075 Magnolia Flower Pot
4076 Tunbridge Jug
4077–8 Heraldic Salad
4079 Lowell Flower Pot
4080–3 Victoria Flower Pot
4084 Lowell Salad
4085 Procession Biscuit Box
4086 Fan Biscuit Box
4087 Lowell Salad
4088 Heraldic Salad
4089–90 Lincoln Salad
4091 Grosvenor Salad
4092 Magnolia Salad
4093 Lowell Salad
4094 Heraldic Salad
4095 Grosvenor Salad
4096 Elephant Biscuit Box
4097 Luther Jug
4098–9 Shar Salad
4104–5 Lowell Salad
4106–6a Shar Salad
4107 Shar Biscuit Box
4108 Shar Salad
4109 Procession Biscuit Box
4110–17 Teapots, Shape 152
4118 Magnolia Flower Pot
4119 Italian Pedestal
4120 Magnolia Flower Pot
4121 Italian Pedestal & Flower

Pot
4122 Parapet Teapot
4123 Hunt Jug
4124–5 Shar Salad
4126–7 Lowell Salad
4128–9 Heraldic Salad
4130 Daisy Luther Flower Pot
4131 Bramble Flower Pot
4132 Teapot, Shape 152
4133–4 Silver Shape Jugs
4135–42 Italian Flower Pot
4143–6 New Fluted Flower
   Pot
4147–50 Altered Italian Flower
   Pot
4151 Magnolia Tile
4152 Spiral Tile
4153 Italian Pot & Pedestal
4154–5 Lowell Shape
4156 Heraldic Shape
4157 Tomato Salad
4158–64 Victoria Flower Pot
4165–70 Screw Top Tankard
4176–82 Loving Cup, Screw
   Top, 3 Handled
4183–6 Screw Top Whiskey
   Bottle
4187 Loving Cup
4188 Quinsy Umbrella Stand
4189 Fruit Umbrella Stand

**Q Series - Tiles**

421·5 Classical
426·8 Cupids & Fish
429 Boy Fishing
430–1 Midsummer's Night
   Dream
436 Cupids & Fish
437–8 Children Series
439–41 Cupids & Fish
442–4 Children Series

## GEORGE JONES MAJOLICA PATTERN NUMBERS

This list was compiled from shape books in the Wedgwood Archives. These are not complete, and are of a late date (see Chapter Four). In most cases different colour variations, usually in the ground, were given letter prefixes. The pattern numbers are usually found painted in a reserve on the bottom of a piece. Sizes are given where available.

1450 Twigs Garden Seat
   (17¾in. × 11 ½ in.)
1458 'Palissy Vase', dk. bl. gr.
   (15 in. × 8½ in.)
1459 'Palissy Vase', turq. gr.
1473 'Potting Pot & Stand',
   Acorn
1481 Rustic Jardinière, rope
   trim (8 in.)

1750 'Rustic Stilton Cheese
   Stand', full, half & no. 3
   sizes
1754 'Morning Glory Wooden'
   Tub Flowerpot & Stand (8
   or 9 in.)
1758 'Partridge Game Pie
   Dish', (8, 9 or 10 in.)
1800 'Lotus Jug', brown gr.

1802A 'Eastern Plants Jug',
   turq. gr.
1804 Leaf Dessert Set:
   'Centrepiece, low comport,
   elevated comport & dessert
   plates'
1806 'Foliage Jug', pink gr.
1809 'Chestnut Jug', turq. gr.
1809 ½ 'Potting Pot & Stand',

cow lid
1831 'Sardine Box & Stand',
  turq. gr.
1841 'Flowerpot & Stand',
  turq. gr. (6½ in. × 8½ in.)
1841A 'Flowerpot & Stand',
  pink gr.
1841½ 'Flowerpot & Stand',
  dk. bl. gr.
1842 'Dog Trough', pink gr.
1845 'Rustic Butter Tub &
  Stand'
1846 'Barrel Jug'
1848 'Shell Sardine' (5 in. ×
  6½ in.)
1849 'Spittoon', turq. gr.
1877 Eagle Wall Bracket (9½
  in. × 8½ in.)
1885 'Snowdrop Flowerpot'
  in. pink gr. (6, 7, 8 or 9 in.)
1885B 'Snowdrop Flowerpot',
  dk. bl. gr.
1886 'Snowdrop Flowerpot',
  turq. gr.
1887 Lily of the Valley
  Jardinière & Stand, turq. gr.,
  3 sizes
1889 Tile, White Flowers, dk.
  bl. gr.
1891 Tile, dk. bl. gr.
1893 Tile, dk. bl. gr.
2200 'Goat Stilton Cheese',
  pink, half size
2201 'Goat Stilton Cheese',
  pink, full size
2209 Tile, pink gr.
2212 Lily of the Valley
  Jardinière & Stand, pink
2214 'Flowerpot & Stand',
  pink
2218 'Rustic Toast Rack'
2220 'Double Butter or Honey
  Tub'
2225 'Dove Jardinière' (7½ in.
  × 11 in.)
2227 'Fleur de Lis Flowerpot
  & Stand', turq. gr. (8 in.)
2230 Wild Rose Stilton Cheese
  Stand, 3 sizes
2244 Cherub & Dolphin
  Centre (15½ in. h. × 13½ in.
  w.)
2245 Waterlilies Dessert Set:
  'Centre piece, low comport
  elevated comport, &
  dessert plates'
2247 Draped Woman Centre
  (12 in.)
2253 'Michael Angelo Vase
  Stand'

2253A Mermaid Wall Bracket
2259 l/s (14¾ in. h.)
2262 'Fox Game Pie Dish',
  turq. gr. (9 in. × 10 in.)
2263 'Fox Game Pie Dish',
  pink gr.
2274 Cherub Centres
2275 Cherub & Waterlily Vase
  (8¾ in.)
2280 'Fox Game Pie Dish',
  rockingham gr.
2281 Ribboned Garden Seat,
  turq, gr.
2282 Faun & Shell Centre (9
  in.)
2288 'Twin Bacchanalian tub'
  (12½ in. l. × 10 in. h. × 7½
  in. w.)
2295 Lily of the Valley
  Jardinière, mazarine bl.
2297 'Swan Flowervase', turq.
  gr. (8 in. × 10 in.)
2297A 'Swan Flowervase', dk.
  bl. gr.
2507B Garden Seat, dk. bl. gr.
  (17¾ in. × 11½ in.)
2509 Iris Jug (Alton pattern?),
  dk. bl. gr.
2510 Snow Drop Jardinière,
  pink gr.
2510½ Snow Drop Jardinière,
  dk. bl. gr.
2511 Draped Woman Centre
  (11¾ in. × 5¾ in.)
2514 Swag Jardinière dk. bl.
  gr. (9 or 11 in.)
2536 'Small Dove Tray'
2540 'Triamphora Vase', dk.
  bl. gr., rams' heads (15½ in.
  × 7 in.)
2541 'Cupid Standing in Shell'
  (7½ in. × 6 in.)
2542 Pineapple Teapot (sizes
  18, 24, 30, 36)
2548 Iris & Waterlily
  Jardinière, turq. gr., l/s
  or s/s
2551 'Square Foliage', dk. bl.
  gr.
2551A 'Square Foliage', turq.
  gr.
2551B 'Square Foliage', pink
  gr.
2553A Globe Vase, w/ivy,
  beetles & frogs, turq. gr.
  (6½ in. × 5 in.)
2555 Bramble Jardinière (l/s
  12 in.)
2557 Two Cherubs Centre
  (14½ in. × 11 in.)

2562 Rustic Cherub Centre (9
  in. × 7 in.)
2563 'Cucumber Tray'
2564 'Carlton Luncheon Tray'
2566 'Larger Dove Tray' (10½
  in. l.)
2577 'Boy Candelabra' (15½
  in. × 9¼ in.)
2584 Leaf Dessert set: 'Low
  comport, elevated comport
  & dessert plates', turq. gr.
2586 'Goat Stilton Cheese
  Stand', turq. gr., half or full
  size.
Also 2586A & 2586B, probably
  dk. bl. gr. & pink gr.
2587 'Robin Biscuit Box',
  white gr. (8 in. × 7 in.)
2587A 'Robin Biscuit Box',
  turq. gr.
2587B 'Robin Biscuit Box', dk.
  bl. gr.
2587C 'Robin Biscuit Box',
  lavender gr.
2588A 'Triple Holly Tray', turq.
  gr. (14 in.)
2588B 'Triple Holly Tray', dk.
  bl. gr.
2590 'Triamphora Vase'
2593 Cupid Leaf Dish (11½
  in.)
2702 'Marmalade Jar'
2704 'Sphinx Candlestick' (8
  in.)
2714 'Oval Sphinx Jardinière'
  (6 in. × 8¾ in.)
2715 'Cupid Candlestick'
2735 Nautilus Spoon Warmer,
  turq. gr., l/s
2741A Primula Jardinière, dk.
  bl. gr., s/s (6½ in. dia. × 6½
  in. h.);l/s 8 in. dia. × 8½ in.
  h.)
2743 Wooden Box Jardinière
  s/s (7⅞ in. h. × 7 in. w.); l/s
  (9 in. h. × 8½ in. w.)
2763 'Salmon Dish' l/s (23
  in.); s/s (19 in.)
2764 'Mackerel Dish' (15 in.)
2776 'Holly Mask Jug', dk. bl.
  gr., (sizes 6, 12, 24, 30)
2776C 'Holly Mask Jug', turq.
  gr.
2777 'Mottled Jug. Rope
  Handle' (sizes 6, 12, 24, 30)
2781 'Europe-Park Centre':
  stag & doe beside tree
  trunk pedestal (10¼ in. × 10
  ¾ in.)
2782 'W. Chinon Camel'

Centrepiece (9¼ in. × 8¾ in..)

2784 'Neptune Jardinière', turq. gr. (23 in. × 10 in. × 9½ in.)

2789 Draped Cherub Pedestal Centre, 'not pierced' (13¾ in. × 8¾ in.)

2790 Draped Cherub Pedestal Centre, 'pierced'

2792 'Basket Jug', dk. bl. gr. (sizes 6, 12, 24, 30)

2795 'Pineapple Kettle' (sizes 18, 24, 30)

2796 'Ornamental Tray' Birds on Nests, turq. gr.

2796B 'Ornamental Tray', dk. bl. gr.

2797 Cornucopias Centre (16 in. h.)

2797C Cornucopias Centre, with white baskets

3205 'Dog Comport' turq. gr. (8½ in. × 11 in.)

3206 'Asia' Centrepiece, turq. gr. (10¼ in. × 10¾ in.)

3207 'Africa' Centrepiece, w/ lion, turq. gr. (10¼ in. × 10¾ in.)

3216 Tripod Basket Dish w/ ladles (7½ in. × 9½ in.)

3221 'America' Centrepiece, turq. gr. (10½ in. × 10¾ in.)

3224 'Amphorea Jardinière', dk. bl. gr. (16½ in. × 16¼ in.)

3225B Bamboo & Wicker Dessert Set: 'Low comport, elevated comport & dessert plates'

3227 'Giraffe Centre', (14½ in. × 14 in.)

3228 'Hunting Claret or Beer Jug', w/or w/out cover, l/s, s/s

3230 'Elephant Vase' (11¾ in. × 6½ in.)

3256 'Bamboo Jug' (sizes 6, 12, 24, 30)

3259 Hummingbird Jardinière, turq. gr. (17½ in. × 11½ in.)

3259B Hummingbird Jardinière, dk. bl. gr.

3262 'Neptune Shell' Centre (15 in. h., shell 10½ in. broad)

3262A 'Neptune Shell' Centre, 'white shell tinted'

3263 'Rose Basket', dk. bl. gr., pink lining, 3 sizes (7 in. × 9 in.)

3263A 'Rose Basket', turq. gr.

3263B 'Rose Basket', white gr.

3263C 'Rose Basket', white w/ bamboo tinted handle

3264 'Hunter's Scroll Game Pie Dish, Sportsman Lid', (round 7 in. or 9 in.)

3265 'Bird Marmalade & Stand', turq. gr.

3268 'Hunter's Scroll Game Pie Dish w/Fawn Handle' (Round 7 in. or 9 in.)

3268A 'Hunter's Scroll Game Pie Dish w/Fawn Handle', turq. gr.

3269 Ivy Urn, dk. bl. gr., robin on lid (12 in. × 7 in.)

3269A Ivy Urn, turq. gr.

3270 'Lily Candlestick w/Bird'

3271 'Oval Wicker Basket', turq. gr. (10 in. × 6 in.)

3271A 'Oval Wicker Basket', different colour gr.

3272 'Round Basket', turq. gr. (9½ in.)

3273 'Flower Basket', hanging, turq. gr. (11 in. × 8 in.)

3278 'Oval Egg Stand', w/six egg cups

3279 'Beehive Stilton Cheese Stand'

3240 'Apple Blossom' Stilton Cheese Stand, Turquoise gr., full size (also in dk. bl. gr.), covered cheese plate also avail.

3241 'Apple Blossom' Stilton Cheese Stand, half size

3280 'Smoking Set: Spill, Cigar Box, Dog Ash, Fox Ash, Lucifer Box, Tobacco Box'

3290 'Oval Stephanotis Jardinière' (7 in. × 15½ in.), dk. bl. gr.

3290A 'Oval Stephanotis Jardinière', turq. gr.

3291 'Fern Fish Dish', white drainer

3292 Basket Jug

3295 'Small Pine Jardinière', dk. bl. gr.

3295A 'Small Pine Jardinière', probably turq. gr.

3296 'Oblong Pine Jardinière' (16¾ in. × 16 in. × 4½ in.)

3296A 'Oblong Pine Jardinière', probably turq. gr.

3297 'Hunters Scroll Jardinière' dk. bl. gr. (6¼ in. × 17¼ in.)

3297A 'Hunters Scroll Jardinière', turq. gr.

3298 'Parroquet Jardinière', dk. bl. gr.

3298A 'Parroquet Jardinière', turq. gr.

3299 'Apple Blossom' Cheese Dish, turq. gr.

3300 Strawberry Set w/3 spoons, turq. gr.

3302 'Stephanotis Small Round Flowerpot', dk. bl. gr. (7 in. × 7¾ in.)

3302A 'Stephanotis Small Round Flowerpot', turq. gr.

3303 'Apple Blossom' Jug, turq. gr., (sizes 6, 12, 24, 30, 36)

3304 'Apple Blossom Tea & Coffee Tray: Tray, teapot, coffee pot, cream, sugar box, cup & saucer'

3305 'Apple Blossom Butter & Stand', turq. gr.

3306 'Apple Blossom Honey' turq. gr. A(also in dk. bl.)

3307 'Apple Blossom Jug Stand'

3312 Waterlily Pad Dessert Set: 'Centrepiece, low comport, elevated comport & dessert plates'

3316 'Apple Blossom Mug'

3320 'Mermaid Shell' Centre (15 in. × 10½ in.)

3321 Strawberry Tray, mottled centre

3321A Strawberry Tray, pink centre

3321B Strawberry Tray, dk. bl. gr., pink centre

3323 Tile, White Flowers, dk. bl. gr.

3323A Tile to match 3323

3326 Bird & Dragonfly Flowerpot, turq. gr. (10 or 14 in.), stand also avail.

3327A Shell Dessert Set: 'Low comport, elevated comport, dessert plates'

3330 'Small Rose Basket' as 3263, but smaller, turq. gr.

3330A 'Small Rose Basket', white gr.

3330B 'Small Rose Basket', dk. bl. gr.

3330C 'Small Rose Basket', pink gr.

3331 'Tortoise Spittoon'
3332 'Tortoise Matchbox'
3333 'Tortoise Ashtray'
3335 Dark bl. gr. Pedestal (3 ft. h. & 11 in. broad at top)
3341 'Tower Stilton'
3346 Foliage Jug
3347 'Small Round Flowerpot to match' No. 3297
3349 'Double Bullfinch Tray'
3349A 'Double Bullfinch Tray', dk. bl. gr.
3350 'Wagtail Tray'
3352 White Cornucopia Vase, side support
3357 'Open Towers' Jardinière, turq. lining
3363 Pink Flowers Dessert Set: 'Low comport, elevated comport, oval comport, dessert plates', turq. gr.
3369 Bird on Leaf Dish w/ Cattails (12 in. × 10½ in.)
3371 'Hare Game Pie Dish', Hen & Chicks (11 in.)
3372 Tile, White Flowers, dk. bl. gr.
3377 'Bird Carlton Set'
3380 'Indian Garden Seat', turq. gr., (17¾ × 14 in.)
3381 Pine Vase, side support
3382 'Pine Flower Stand' (10½ in. h.)
3384 'Wren Holder', Menu Holder, s/s or l/s (5½ in.)
3386 'Pitcher Plant Flower Stand' (9½ in. × 9 in.)
3388 Pine Vase, tripod base
3390 Trefoil Dish, leaves & flowers on pink gr., with butterly on rim
3390B Trefoil Dish, dk. bl. gr.
3391 Jardinière, bent branch legs, white flowers, moths, dk. bl. gr. (7½ in., 8½ in. or 9½ in.)
3394 Stephanotis Tile, turq. gr.
3397 'Wren Holder', l/s (5½ in. h.)
3401 'Oyster Plate', turq. gr., pink shell centre
3403 Low Comport, green centre, turq. rim, pink flowers (11½ in. h.)
3403B Low Comport, dk. bl. gr.
3404B Draped Cherub 'Figure Comport', dk. bl. gr. (13 in. h.)
3405 'Apple Blossom' Cabaret

Set, turq. gr.
3407 Stork Soup Tureen, no cover, w/lining
3408 Cyclamen Vase (8 in. h.)
3409 'Stork Jug', w/or w/out metal cover, turq. gr.
3410 Dresser Set w/'Low Powder, Lucifer Box, Flat Candlestick, Ring Tray, Pin Tray, Match Stand, Comb Tray, Tall Candlestick, Tall Pomade', each item separately priced. All w/ modelled flowers & butterflies.
3412 Cattail & Bird Stilton Cheese Stand, dk. bl. gr.
3413 Stork Soup Tureen, dk. bl. gr., no lining, w/cover
3414 Stork Soup Tureen, fitted as tea caddy
3416B Game Pie Dish, l/s 10 in.; s/s 8 in.
3429 'Spring Flower'
3436 'Butterfly Spill'
3437 'Butterfly Spill, no fly'
3439 Flowered Jug (sizes 6, 12, 24, 30)
3440 Bird Nest Jug w/Bird Handle (sizes 12, 24, 30, 36)
3441 'Sardine Stand' (Pelican top)
3443 Leaf Dish, white gr.
3443A Leaf Dish, crimson gr.
3443B Leaf Dish, black gr.
3444 Begonia Leaf Dish, red rim
3445 Caladium Leaf Dish (10 in. × 12 in.)
3446 'Leaf Comport'
3449 Wild Rose Jardinière (8 in. × 10 in.)
3450 Monkey Handled Teapot, dk. bl. gr., cream jug also avail.
3456 Rustic Vase w/pink flower
3457 Rustic Jug (sizes 6, 12, 24, 30)
3458 Monkey Handled Jug, dk. bl. gr.
3464 Stork Tile, dk. bl. gr.
3465 Monkey Tea Set w/tray, teapot, two cups & saucers, sugarbox, & milk jug. 'Sugarbox with two monkeys' cost extra.
3466 Baskets Centre (10½ in. h.)

3467 Wild Rose Jug (sizes 6, 12, 24, 30)
3468B 'Punch' Punch Bowl, turq. gr.
3469D Garden Seat, dk. bl. gr. (19 in. h.)
3470 'Crocus Vase'
3476 Butterfly & Wheat Sheaf Bread Tray, rectangular
3477 Butterfly & Wheat Sheaf Bread Tray, round
3483 'Trinket & Flower Holder', cattails design
3484 'Lotus' (possibly a Stilton dish, not illustrated)
3490 'Terrier Ashtray', dk. bl. gr., turq. lining
3491 'Cat Ashtray', dk. bl. gr., turq. lining
3498 Double Dolphin & Cupids Sweetmeats Dish (10¾ in. h. × 13½ in. l.)
3507 Hummingbird Hanging Basket, turq. gr. (11½ in.)
3516 Hops Beer Set: Jug (size 24 or 30), 2 mugs & tray
3517 Fish Game Pie Dish
3518 Lobster Game Pie Dish
3520B Gondolier
3523 Basket Egg Holder, turq. gr., w/eggcups
3524 Basket Egg Holder, w/ out fittings
3525 Low Rustic Bowl, oak leaves, turq. lining
3526 Low Footed Waterlilies Bowl, turq. gr., pink lining
3528 Wild Rose Tile
3529 Butterfly Tile, turq. gr.
3530 Seagull Tile
3531 Seagull Tile
3533 Basket
3534 Basket, turq. gr.
3542 Children Pedestal Centres (9 in. h. × 6 in. w.)
3544 Seagull Tile
3545 Leaf Basket
3546B Strawberry Fish w/ large ladle, cream jug, sucrier & spoon, dk. bl. gr.
3547 'Sardine Box, Basket in Boat'
3550 'Jay Tray', turq. gr.
3551B 'Dog Biscuit Tray', dk. bl. gr.
3557 Barrel Caviar Set w/two dishes, salt shaker and toast rack
3558 Jay Flower Basket, pink lining

3559B Butterflies Bowl, dk. bl. gr.

3562B Drum Cabaret Set w/l/s or s/s tray, dk. bl. gr., turq. lining

3567 Swallow & Calla Lily Jardinière, turq, gr., l/s (17½ in.); s/s (12 in.)

3568 Swan Jardinière, turq. gr., l/s (17½ in.); s/s (14 in.)

3569 Game Pie Dish

3571 Swans & Cattails Tile

3571A Tile to match 3571

3572 Tile to match 3571

3573A Wild Rose Stilton Cheese Keeper, full size

3574 Double Sauce Boat, dk. bl. gr., two ladles priced separately

3575 Log Planter, turq. lining

3576 Basket Jug, dk. bl. gr. (sizes 12, 24, 30)

3579 Bulb Footed Jardinière, (10½ in. h. × 8½ in. w.)

3580B 'Crocus Vase', dk. bl. gr. (7 in.)

3581B 'Snowdrop Vase', (5½ in.)

3582B 'Primula Vase', dk. bl. gr. (8 in.)

3583B 'Cyclamen Vase', dk. bl. gr. (8 in.)

3586 Bulb Jardinière, dk. bl. gr. (14¾ in. h.)

3592B Candleholder, dk. bl. gr.

3594B Daisy Jardinière, dk. bl.

gr. (10 in. h. × 10 in. w.)

3598 'Lady Pedestal Fountain' (h. of figure 18 in., w. of trough 13 in.)

4000s Bone China

5202B Calla Lily Jardinière, dk. bl. gr. (3 ft. 9 in.)

5204 Daisy Stilton Cheese Keeper, dk. bl. gr., full or half sizes

5206 Daisy Butter Dish, dk. bl. gr.

5207 Hanging Basket to match 3598

5208 Cupids Urn, dk. bl. gr. (17½ in.)

5209 'Egyptians Vases' (12 in. h.)

5210 Calla Lily Flowerpot

5212 Bird & Dragonfly Flowerpot, no birds (10 in.)

5213 Wild Rose Jardinière, w/out raised birds

5215 Calla Lily Jug

5216 Strawberry Butter Dish

5217 Waterlilly Butter Dish

5219 Primula Rustic Jardinière, pink lining (9 in., 11 in. or 13 in.)

5220 Calla Lily Garden Seat, dk. bl. gr. (18 in. × 12 in.)

5232 Basket Dish w/ladles, pink ribbon on handle, turq. lining.

5233 Basket w/Bees, turq. lining, pink ribbon on handle

5235 Brown Basket, turq. lining

5237 Large Basket Weave & Chinamen Urn

5238 'Apple Blossom' Cakeplate, turq. gr.

5246 Sea & Sky Jug, turq. & dk. bl. gr., (sizes 6, 12, 24, 30)

5250B Low Jardinière, dk. bl. gr., turq. lining, (14½ in. × 5½ in.)

5252B Bacchanalian Jug, dk. bl. gr. (sizes 6, 12, 24, 30)

5254 Kneeling Woman Wall Bracket (11¾ in. × 5¼ in.)

5255 Boar's Head Game Pie Dish (10 in.)

5258 Stag Wall Bracket (9 in. × 7 in.)

5259B Jardinière, dk. bl. gr., turq. lining, l/s (11 in.); s/s (9 in.)

5260 Rustic Primula Umbrella Stand (20 in. × 11 in.)

5261 Rustic Primula Garden Seat (20 in. × 11 in.)

5262 Goldfinch Jardinière, dk. bl. gr. (16¾ in. × 15¼ in.), 3 sizes

5266 'Waterlily Dish'

5276 Strawberry Luncheon Tray

6000s 'Ivory' Wares

7000s Bone China

## W. T. COPELAND MAJOLICA SHAPES

This list has been compiled using the Majolica Fixing Books 1869–79, books of sepia photographs of Copeland shapes (some of which have handwritten notes indicating that they were made in majolica) and one of the China Ornament Books, which includes a few early majolica designs, whose Ornament Numbers are indicated below. I am indebted to Robert Copeland who assisted me in the compilation of this list. All records consulted are in the archives of the Spode Museum in Stoke-on-Trent.

Acanthus Bracket

Albion Garden Pot

Albion Garden Seat

Albion Lily Pan

Albion Lily Pan, New Plinth

Alhambra Garden Seat

Alhambra Garden Pot

Alhambra Vase, 12 & 18 in.

Angel Front Vase & Stand

Aquatic Vase

Arabesque Bottle, No. 8

Arabesque Cigar Tray

Arabian Basket & Stand

Arabian Garden Seat

Arctic Jug

Argyle Candelabra

Ashantee Hall Stool

Bamboo Spill

Bamboo Teapots, 18, 24, 30

Barley Beaker

Barley Jugs, 6, 9, 12, 18, 24, 30

Basket Work Basket & Stand, Square

Basket Work Honey & Stand

Basket Work Vase, Pierced Top, Round

Basket Wall Flower Holder

Baskets, to hang on frame

Bath Baskets

Bath Baskets, Double

Beaded Butter & Stand

Bear [figure]

Bears One and Two Handled
  Mugs
Beauchamp Covered Vase, 2
  sizes
Beauvais Bowl
Beavais Cream Jug
Beauvais Japan Pot
Beauvais Jugs
Beauvais Teapot
Beehive Honey Pot
Beehive Match Pot
Belgian Lion
Bird Centre
Bird Comports, Tall & Low
Bird Nest Basket
Bird Nest Egg Basket
Bird Roll Tray
Bloodhound
Bon Bon Stand, Octagon Foot
Bone Picker [dog]
Bow Flower Holder
Boy with Sutherland Basket
Bread Plates, 10 & 12 in.
Brighton Spoon Tray
Brind Garden Pot
Brind Garden Seat
Brind Match Pot
Bryant Match Box
Bullrush Honey Pot
Bullrush Matchpot
Bullrush Pickle
Bullrush Spill
Bullrush & Frog Flower
  Holder
Bullrush & Swan Flower
  Holder
Butter, Covered Oval or
  Round
Butterfly Flower Holder
Byzantine Embossed Garden
  Pot
Byzantine Vase

Cactus Vase, no. 14
Cairo Basket & Stand
Cairo Garden Seat
Caltha Cheese Stand
Canboy Violet Pots
Castle Match Pots
Cauliflower Teapots (18, 24,
  30, 36)
Cavalier Pets Group
Cellini Covered Vase
Centennial Jug (Washington
  Medallion)
Cigar Ash Pan
Convulvus Beaker
Convulvus Basket
Convulvus Two Handled
  Beaker, 18, 30

Corinthian Bracket
Corinthian Pillar
Corinthian Tobacco Jar
Cornucopia, to fit frame
Cornucopia Flower Holder,
  No. 9
Crab Dish, No. 10
Cradle Cigar Tray
Crescent Oyster Tray
Cupid Basket
Cupid at Sea
Cupid Candelabrum
Cupid Cornucopia
Cupid, Seated & Single Basket
Cupid, Seated & Bulrush
  Basket
Cupid & Shell Bracket, Large
Cupid & Shell Centre
Cushion Garden Seat

Daisy & Buttercup Lily Pan
Deerhound
Delhi Candlesticks
Devonshire Butters
Diana Centre
Dog, Hens & Chickens
Dolphin Flower Holder
Dolphin Salt Cellar, No. 29
Dolphin & Boy Centre
Dolphin & Shell Tazza
Donkey & Paniers
Donkey Garden Pots
Dove Basket
Dutch Season Figure

Eagle Jug
Eclipse Basket
Element Jugs, 4 sizes, No. 5
Element Pedestal, Large
Elements, Set
Elephant
Elgin Pillar & Seat
Elgin Two Handled Vase
Etruscan Embossed Vase
Extinguisher

Falstaff in Basket
Faun Centre
Fern Tray, Oval
Fern Centre
Fern Comport & 4 in. Pedestal
Fern Low Foot Comport
Fern Dessert Plate, No. 12
Fern Dessert Plate, Autumnal
  Tints, No. 18
Fig Leaf Garden Pot & Stand
Fisher Boy Centre
Flemish Extinguisher & Stand
Floral Centre
Floral Comport, Tall or Low
Florence Basket

Flower Trough, Straight or
  Curved
Four Dutch Seasons Set with
  Floral Comport
Four Seasons Figures
French Fiddler
French Shepherd &
  Shepherdess
French Shepherd
  Candelabrum
French Shepherd &
  Shepherdess Candlesticks
Frog Cream
Frog Flower Holder, Triple
Frog Violet Holder
Frogs & Bulrushes Flower
  Holder
Fruit Dish, Triple

Game Pie Dish, Large
Georgian Butter & Stand
Georgian Vase
Gothic Basket & Stand
Grecian Basket
Grecian Fluted Pedestal
Grecian Vase
Grecian Violet Pot
Griffin Handled Vase
Griffin Head Vase

Hen Coop
Hyacinth Spill
Hooded Garden Pot
Hyacinth Match Pot
Hyam Wall Creeper, Small

Iris Garden Pot
Italian Garden Pots, 3, 4, 5
Italian Vase
Ivy Bracket
Ivy Covered Vase

Japanese Claret Jug
Japanese Vase
Jugs, 12, 18, 24
Jugs, Stone Body, 12, 18, 24,
  30

Lambeth Jug
Lapogena Flower Holder
Laurel Pillar, Large (3 parts)
Lazy Cooper
Leaf Dish
Leafage Orange Pan
Leafage Round Orchid Pan
Leafage Vases, 8 & 11 in.
Leafage Wall Creeper
Leamington Basket & Stand
Leda & the Swan Ewer
Lily Pan, Embossed
Lion on Pedestal
Lions' Head Garden Seat

Lotus Butter & Stand
Lotus Candlestick
Lotus Covered Butter & Stand
Lotus Cream
Lotus Jugs
Lotus Piano Candlestick
Lotus Taper
Lotus Vases & Stands
Lotus Violets
Lotus Wall Creeper
Lotus & Swan Flower Stand

Madeira Basket, Large or Small
Madras Garden Pot & Stand,
  Large
Maiolica Ewer, No. 15
Mandarin Cream
Meander Vase
Milan Lamp
Milan Shape Bottle
Monkey
Monkey on Tortoise, 'Sloth &
  Mischief'
Mooresque Flower Holder, 6
  in.
Mooresque Urn, No. 22
Musical Instruments Jewel
  Casket, No. 11

Naiad Centre
Nasturtium Saucer
Neptune Cup
Neptune Spoon Tray
Nile Jugs, 12, 18, 24, 20

Oak Garden Pot & Stand
Oak Jugs, 9, 12, 18, 24, 30
Oak Rose Basket & Stand
Orchid Wall Flower Holder,
  Pan or Creeper, No. 26
Oriental Garden Pot, 1, 2, 3, 4,
  5, 6
Oval Extinguisher & Stand
Owl, Large
Oyster Plate, Round

Pansy Garden Pot & Stand, 3,
  4, 5, 6, 7
Pansy Individual Butter or
  Pickle
Pansy Lily Pan, 18¼ in. h.
Paris Tripod Spill
Partridge Game Pie Dish
Pelicans Pillar
Pembroke Beaker
'The Pets', Group
Pillar Vase & Base
Pine Jugs (9, 12, 18, 24, 30,
  36)
Pitcher Plant Flower Holder
Plover Egg Stand
Plover Flower Stand

Pompeian Etruscan Embossed
  Vases
Poppy Taper
Primrose Flower Holder, No.
  25
Primrose Garden Pot & Stand,
  Sizes 3, 4, 5, 6
Protât Comport
Protât Covered Vase
Protât Cupid Bracket

Raphaelesque Bottle, No. 24
Raphaelesque Claret Jug, No.
  20–3?Reed Jardinière
Reed Pedestal
Reed Sparrow Nest
Renaissance Garden Pot, 3
  sizes
Renaissance Jardinière, New
  Oval or Round
Renaissance Jugs, 12, 18, 24,
  30
Renaissance Vase, Two
  Handled, 3 sizes, No. 16
Ribbed Stilton Cheese Pan &
  Cover
Ribbon & Bamboo Handled
  Basket, Oval 8¾ in.
Roll Tray, No Birds
Roman Piper & Companion
Roman Vase, Large
Rose Baskets & Stands
Round Jardinières, 2 sizes
Rustic Butter & Stand
Rustic Centre
Rustic Honey Pot & Stand
Rutland Cheese Stand &
  Cover
Rutland Garden Pot & Stand,
  3, 4, 5, 6
Rutland Garden Seat

Salmon Covered Pot
Sanda [?] Vase
Sardine Box
Satyr Head Covered Vase, No.
  7
Satyr Head Jug
Scroll Covered Vase, No. 13
Scroll Two Handled Vase, 2
  sizes
Season Pedestal, New
Seasons Pillar
Sentinel Dog, Borzoi
Serpent Pedestal Covered Vase
Setter Dog
Shell Basket, 3 sizes
Shell Basket with Handle
Shell Bracket, 3 sizes
Shell Celery Dish, Triple
Shell Dish, Oblong

Shell Embossed Vase,
  Unhandled
Shell Miniatures
Sleigh Sardine Box
Sitting Gardener
Spaniel Letter Weight
Spittoon, Plain
Spoon Tray, Large
Square Plinth
Squirrel Hat Stand
Stafford Basket, Double
  Covered
Stag Hound Reclining
Stag Hound Standing
Stork Centre
Strawberry Basket
Strawberry Basket, Handled
Stump Garden Seat
Swan Flower Holder
Swan Tazza
Sweet Pea Match Pot
Sweet Pea Spill
Swiss Honey Pot & Stand

Tabby Cat Milk
Terriers, Group
Trays
Trays, Stone Body
Triamphora & Stand, Large
Triple Cornucopia Flower
  Holder
Triton with [Conch] Shell
  Centre, Large, No. 27
Triton with Scallop Shells
  Comport, Large, No. 28
Tulip Leaves
Tulip Jug, 6, 9, 12, 18, 24, 30,
  36
Tumblers, Stone Body
Two Handled Vase with
  Heads

Vienna Card Tray
Vine Jugs
Vine Wall Creeper, Small
Vintage Claret Jug, No. 21
Vintage Garden Pots & Stands,
  3 sizes
Violet Embossed Lily, 6 in.
Violet Pot
Violet Seller

Warwick Vase, No. 17, small
'Waste Not Want Not' Bread
  Plate
Watch Stand
Wheel Barrow
Whitby Oyster Tray
Wicker Edge Card Tray
Wild Boar, 'after Planch at
  Derby'

Woodcock Lid Game Pie Dish,
No. 30

Yokahama Vase

**Copeland Majolica Tiles**

Aquatic

Buttercup & Four Leaf
Butterfly Tile, No. 2
Daisy & Buttercup
Elements
Fleur de Lys, No. 3
Flower Centre Tile, Nos. 31–6
Four Elements Tiles

Gothic Tile, No. 5
Gothic Tile, No. 6
Italian Embossed Slab
Italian Embossed Tile
Leaves Tile, No. 4
Oriental Embossed Tile
Embossed Tile as sent to Paris

## GRIFFEN, SMITH & CO. ETRUSCAN PATTERNS (1884 Catalogue)

INDIVIDUAL BUTTER
A1 Lilly Leaf Conventional
A2 Leaf on Plate
A3 Begonia Leaf
A4 Geranium Leaf (new);
  Geranium Leaf (old)
A5 Smilax
A6 Pansy
A7–1 Wicker
A7–2 Wicker and Begonia
A8 Shell

LEAVES, B1–B12

TRAYS
C1 Oak Card
C2 Oak Fruit
C3 Begonia and Wicker
C4 Tray Ash
C5 Tray Pin
C6 Berry Tray
C7 Geranium Cake
C8 Napkin Cake
C9 Tea Pot Stand
C10 Spice Tray
C11 Ind. Berry Tray
C12 Oak Bread
C13 Grape
C14 Shell Cake

PLATES, FRUITS &c.
D2 Leaf on Plate, 6 or 7 in.
D3 Begonia, 7 in.
D4 Fruit, 5 or 6 in.
D5 Maple Plate, 7 in.
D6 Fruit
D7 Fruit, 3½ or 4 in.
D11–1 Fruit
D12–1 Fruit
D13 Plate, 6 in.
D14 Fruit
D15 Bamboo Plate, 6 in.
D16 Cauliflower Plate, 6 or 7
  in.
D17 Sun Flower Fruit
D18 Strawberry Plate, 7 in.
D19 Grape Fruit
D21 Shell Plate, 5, 6, or 7 in.
D22 Fruit

D23 Fruit
M4 Rose Plate, 4 in.

JUGS
E1 Straight, 24s, 30s, 36s
E2 Rustic, 6s, 12s, 24s, 30s, 36s
E4 Conventional, 12s, 24s, 30s,
  36s, 42s, 48s, 54s
E3 Rose, 12s, 24s, 30s, 36s,
  42s, 48s, 54s; Ind Col'd;
  Ind. Green
E5 Corn, Ind. Green; Ind.
  Col'd
E6 Baseball
E7 Fern, 12s, 24s, 30s, 36s
E12 Corn, 30s, 36s
E16 Thorn, 6s, 12s, 24s, 30s,
  36s, 42s
E20 Sun Flower, 6s, 12s, 24s,
  30s, 36s, 42s
E26 Shell, 62, 12s, 24s, 30s,
  36s, 42s
E27 Coral, 42s, 48s, 52s

COVERED JUGS
E22 Bamboo Molasses Jug
E23 Sun Flower Molasses Jug
E30 Coral Molasses Jug
E27 Coral, 42s, 482, 54s
E3 Ind.

TEAPOTS, SUGARS AND
  CREAMS
E8 Bamboo Cream
E9 Bamboo Sugar
E10 Bamboo Tea Pot
E13 Cauliflower Tea Pot
E14 Cauliflower Sugar
E15 Cauliflower Cream
E17 Bird Cream
E18 Bird Sugar
E19 Bird Tea Pot
E24 Shell Tea Pot, large or
  small
E25 Shell Sugar, large or small
E26 Shell Cream, large or
  small
E31 Corn Teapot, 24s, 30s

SPOONERS
E11 Bamboo
E21 1 Bird
E21 8 Shell

CUSPADORES
F1 Lilly
F2 Pine Apple
F8 Sun Flower
F9 Shell

FLOWER POTS, F5–F7

BASKETS
G1 Begonia
G2 Wicker

SAUCE DISHES, H1–H3, Daisy

SOAPS, 14

COMPORTS, SALADS, &c.
J1 Maple Comport
J2 Maple Centre
J3 Daisy Salad
J4 Cake Stand
J5 Grape Comport
J6 Card Comport
J7 Lilly Salad
J8 Shell Salad
J9 Cauliflower Comp., 6 or 7
  in.
J10 Shell Comport
J11 Shell Centre
J12 Shell Centre

INDIVIDUAL SALTS, K1

COVERED BUTTERS
K2 Cow
N2 Butterfly
N3 Bamboo
N7 Shell

MUGS, VASES, &c.
L5 Lilly Mug
L6 Celery
L7 Small Vase
L8 Small Vase
L10 Hanging Soap
L11 Hanging Soap
L13 Oak Mug

L14 Oak Vase
L15 Salt & Pepper
L16 Oak Brush Vase
03 Mug

BOWLS
M1 Lilly, low
M2 Lilly, high
M3 Rose, high
M4 Rose, low

M8 Bamboo
M9 Cauliflower
M10 Cigar Box
M12 Shell

NAPPIES
M5 Shell, 6, 7, or 8 in.
M6 Shell, 8 in.

SARDINES, N1 & N4

COVERED CHEESES
N5 Lilly
N6

TEAS AND COFFEES
01 Bamboo
02 Cauliflower
04 Shell Tea
05 Shell Coffee
06 Shell Coffee (Moustache)

# ANNOTATED BIBLIOGRAPHY

## BOOKS & PAMPHLETS

Atterbury, Paul, ed., *The History of Porcelain* (William Morrow & Co., New York, 1982).

Barber, Edwin Atlee, *The Pottery & Porcelain of the United States & Marks of the American Potters* (Feingold & Lewis, New York, 1976). A reprint of the above works, which were previously published in 1893 and 1904, respectively. Remains the single most important source of information about the pottery industry in the United States during the nineteenth century.

Barnard, J., *Victorian Ceramic Tiles*, 2nd edn (Studio Vista, London, 1979).

Barrett, Richard Carter, *Bennington Pottery & Porcelain* (Crown Publishers Inc., New York, 1958).

—— *A Color Guide to Bennington Pottery* (Forward's Color Productions, Inc., Manchester, Vt., 1966).

Batkin, Maureen, *Wedgwood Ceramics, 1846–1959* (Richard Dennis, London, 1982). The only authoritative book covering this period thoroughly; very useful illustrations. A must for collectors of Wedgwood majolica.

Battie, David and Turner, Michael, *The Price Guide to 19th and 20th Century British Pottery* (Antique Collectors' Club, Woodbridge, 1987).

Bemrose, Geoffrey, *19th Century English Pottery and Porcelain* (Faber & Faber, London, n.d.).

Bernard, Roger and Renard, Jean-Claude, *Gien Faience* (Société Nouvelle des Faienceries de Gien et Les Editions Sous le Vent, Gien, 1985 et Paris 1981).

Binns, R. W., *Worcester China: A Record of the Work of Forty-Five Years 1852–1897* (Bernard Quaritch, London, 1897).

Blacker, J. F., *The ABC of Collecting Old Continental Pottery* (Stanley Paul & Co., London, 1913).

—— *Nineteenth Century Ceramic Art* (Stanley Paul & Co., London, 1911).

—— *The ABC of English Nineteenth Century Pottery and Porcelain* (Stanley Paul & Co., London, 1922). An update of *Nineteenth Century Ceramic Art*.

—— *Collecting Old English Pottery* (Coles Publishing Co., Ltd., Toronto, 1980).

Branin, M. Lelyn, *The Early Potters and Potteries of Maine* (Wesleyan University Press, Middletown, Conn., 1978).

Briggs, Asa, *Victorian Things* (B. T. Batsford, London, 1988). A fascinating account of the things of the age. Creates a useful framework for understanding Victorian ceramics.

Buffet-Challie, Laurence, *Art Nouveau Style* (Academy Editions, London, 1982).

Bunt, Cyril G. E., *British Potters and Pottery Today* (F. Lewis Publishers Ltd., Leigh-on-Sea, 1956). Appendices list potters in 1710–1715, 1787, 1802 and 1954.

Burton, Angela, *Maws Tile Company, 1850–1900* (Dissertation, Dept. of Ceramic Sculpture, North Staffordshire Polytechnic, June 1981).

Buten, Harry M., *Wedgwood ABC But Not Middle E* (Buten Museum of Wedgwood, Merion, Pa., 1964).

—— *Wedgwood Rarities* (Buten Museum of Wedgwood, Merion, Pa., 1969).

Cameron, Elizabeth, *Encyclopedia of Pottery & Porcelain: The 19th & 20th Centuries* (Faber & Faber, London, 1986). This is an invaluable reference which includes many of the majolica manufacturers worldwide. Each entry includes a very useful bibliography.

Chaffers, William, *Marks & Monograms on European and Oriental Pottery & Porcelain*, 15th edn (William Reeves, London, 1974).

Charles, Bernard, *Pottery and Porcelain: A Glossary of Terms* (Hippocrene Books, New York, 1983). Absolutely indispensable to anyone interested in ceramics. The alphabetical entries are supplemented by a very useful 'Classified List of Entries'.

Charleston, Robert J., ed., *World Ceramics* (Paul Hamlyn, London, 1968).

Clement, Arthur Wilfred, *Our Pioneer Potters* (Privately Printed, New York, 1947). Good on English potters in the United States.

Collard, Elizabeth, *Nineteenth Century Pottery and Porcelain in Canada* (McGill University Press, Montreal, 1967).

Cox, Warren E., *The Book of Pottery and Porcelain*. revised edn (Crown Publishers, Inc., New York, 1970).

Coysh, A. W., *British Art Pottery* (David & Charles, London, 1976).

Cruikshank, Graeme, *Scottish Pottery: A Brief History* (Shire Publications, Aylesbury, Bucks, 1987).

Curtil, Henri, *Marques et signatures de la faience française* (Editions Charles Massin, Paris, n.d.).

Cushion, J. P., *Handbook of Pottery and Porcelain Marks*, 4th edn (Faber & Faber, 1980). Includes 'Index of Names and Dates of Manufacturers, Retailers, Wholesalers and others who registered designs from 1842 to 1883'.

Danckert, Ludwig, *Directory of European Porcelain: Marks, Makers and Factories*, 4th edn (N.A.G. Press Ltd., London, 1981).

Day, Lewis F., *Everyday Art* (London, 1882).

Denker, Ellen & Bert, *The Warner Collector's Guide to North American Pottery and Porcelain* (The Main Street Press, New York, 1982).

Domanovsky, Gyorgy, *Hungarian Pottery* (Corvina, Budapest, 1968).

Dresser, Christopher, *Principles of Decorative Design* (London, 1873).

Dudson, Audrey M., *Dudson: A Family of Potters since 1800* (Dudson Publications, Hanley, 1985).

Durant, Stuart, *Ornament* (Macdonald & Co., London, 1986).

Eastlake, Charles, *Hints on Household Taste* (London, 1868).

Edinburgh Libraries & Museums Committee, *The East of Scotland Potteries* (Edinburgh, 1969). Most of the information appears to have been taken from Fleming.

Ernould Gandouet, Marielle, *La Céramique en France au XIXème siècle* (Grund, Paris, 1969). A must for those interested in French majolica.

Evans, Paul, *Art Pottery of the United States: An Encyclopedia of Producers & their Marks*, 2nd edn (Feingold & Lewis, New York, 1987). Excellent reference, includes some of the larger American majolica manufacturers and an addenda on tiles. Extensive and invaluable footnotes.

Fleming, J. A., *Scottish Pottery* (Jackson & Co., Glasgow, 1923. Reprinted by E. P. Publishing Ltd, East Ardsley, Yorkshire, 1973). Still the single best source of information on this subject. Many other works rely heavily on his writing.

Furnival, William J., *Leadless Decorative Tiles, Faience and Mosaic* (Stone, 1904).

—— *Researches on Leadless Glazes* (Stone, 1898).

Garrett, Rhoda and Agnes, *Suggestions for House Decoration in Painting, Woodwork and Furniture* (Macmillan, London, 1876).

Gates, William Jr and Dana E. Ormerod, *The East Liverpool, Ohio Pottery District* (*Journal of the Society for Historical Archaeology*, Vol. 16, Nos. 1-2, 1982).

Gillard, Michele-Cécile, *Faience de Gien: Formes et Décors* (Charles Massin Editeur, 1987).

Gloag, John, *Victorian Taste*, 2nd edn (David & Charles, Newton Abbot, 1972).

Godden, Geoffrey A., *An Illustrated Encyclopaedia of British Pottery and Porcelain* (Herbert Jenkins, London, 1964).

—— *Antique China and Glass under £5* (Baker, London, 1966).

—— *British Pottery, an Illustrated Guide* (Barrie & Jenkins, London, 1974).

—— *Encyclopaedia of British Pottery and Porcelain Marks* (Barrie & Jenkins, London, 1964).

—— *Encyclopaedia of British Porcelain Manufacturers* (Barrie & Jenkins, London, 1988).

—— *Jewitt's 'Ceramic Art of Great Britain 1800-1900'* (Barrie & Jenkins, London, 1972). Invaluable resource, but it's still worth consulting the earlier editions for their illustrations. This edition is updated and corrected, and includes some new illustrations. Most importantly the index includes all firm names.

—— *Minton Pottery and Porcelain of the First Period, 1793-1850* (Herbert Jenkins, London, 1968). The only work which covers this period thoroughly.

—— *Ridgway Porcelains*, 2nd edn (Antique Collectors' Club, Woodbridge, 1985).

—— *Victorian Porcelain* (Herbert Jenkins, London, 1961).

Grant, Maurice Harold, *A Dictionary of British Sculptors from the XIIIth century to the XXth century* (Rockliff, London, 1953).

Haggar, Reginald G., *The Concise Encyclopedia of Continental Pottery & Porcelain* (André Deutsch, London, 1960). A handy, general reference.

—— *English Art Pottery, 1865-1915* (London Art Dealers' Club, London, 1975).

Henrywood, R. K., *Relief-Moulded Jugs, 1820-1900* (Antique Collectors' Club, Woodbridge, 1984). Does not include majolica glazed jugs, but is a good source on some of the firms who made them.

Herbert, Tony, *The Jackfield Decorative Tile*

*Industry* (Ironbridge Gorge Museum Trust, Telford, 1978).

Hess, Alan, *Some British Industries: Their Expansion and Achievements, 1936 56* (Information in Industry, London, 1957). Includes an article on Thomas Poole.

Hillier, Bevis, *Pottery and Porcelain, 1700-1914: England, Europe and North America* (Weidenfeld & Nicolson, London, 1968).

Hopper, Robin, *The Ceramic Spectrum: A Simplified Approach to Glaze & Color Development* (Chilton Book Co., Radnor, Pa., 1984).

Howe, Bea, *Antiques from the Victorian Home* (B. T. Batsford, London, 1973).

Hughes, G. Bernard, *English & Scottish Earthenware, 1660-1860* (Abbey Fine Arts, London, n.d.). Useful, but it does rely very heavily on both Jewitt and Fleming.

—— *Victorian Pottery and Porcelain* (Spring Books, London, 1959).

Hughes, Kathy, *A Collector's Guide to Nineteenth Century Jugs* (Routledge & Kegan Paul, London, 1985). This work on relief-moulded jugs includes those with majolica glazes.

James, Arthur E., *The Potters & Potteries of Chester County, Pennsylvania*, 2nd edn (Schiffer Publishing Ltd., Exton, Pa., 1978). This edition is updated and expanded. A very good chapter on Phoenixville; reproduces the Etruscan 1884 Catalogue in full.

Jervis, W. P., *The Encyclopedia of Ceramics* (Blanchard, New York, 1902). The format and classification of some entries is a little erratic, and he did rely heavily on both Barber and Jewitt, but there is some very informative original research.

—— *A Book of Pottery Marks* (Wright, Tyndale & van Roden, Philadelphia, Pa., 1897).

Jewitt, Llewellyn, *The Ceramic Art of Great Britain*, 2 vols (Virtue & Co., London, 1878; 2nd edn, 1883). This is the only source of information about many firms. The 1883 edition is preferable.

Jones, Owen, *The Grammar of Ornament* (Studio Editions, London, 1986). A reprint of the 1856 edition.

Ketchum, William C., Jr, *Early Potters and Potteries of New York State, 1650-1900*, 2nd edn (Syracuse University Press, Syracuse, New York, 1987). Completely revised and updated, this edition includes valuable information about the New York majolica makers.

—— *Pottery & Porcelain* (Alfred A. Knopf, New York, 1983). One of the Knopf Collectors' Guides to American Antiques, it is well formated and includes useful features, such as a detailed list of American pottery and porcelain manufacturers.

Klamkin, Marian, *The Collector's Book of Wedgwood* (David & Charles, Newton Abbott, 1971).

Kovel, Ralph and Terry, *The Kovels' Collectors' Guide to American Art Pottery* (Crown Publishers Inc., New York, 1974). Contains valuable bibliography after each article.

Kybalová, Jana, *Ceramic Marks of the World* (Hamlyn, London, 1981). Particularly useful for Eastern European marks.

Lami, Stanislaus, *Dictionnaire des sculpteurs de l'école française aux dix-neuvième siècle* (Librairie Ancienne Honore Champion, Paris, 1914).

Lehner, Lois, *Ohio Pottery & Glass, Marks & Manufacturers* (Wallace-Homestead Book Co., Des Moines, 1978). Very useful.

—— *Lehner's Encyclopedia of U.S. Marks on Pottery, Porcelain & Clay* (Collector Books, Paducah, Ky., 1988). Absolutely indispensable to anyone interested in American Ceramics, with over 1,900 firms and 8,000 marks. There are articles about every firm with individual bibliographies.

Lesur et Tardy, Adrien, *Les poteries et les faiences françaises*, 6 vols, (Tardy, Paris, 1957-60). Invaluable reference including 20th century firms and their marks. The first 3 volumes are alphabetical entries by place names and the 4th volume is a supplement and index to these. The final volumes contain black and white plates.

Lewis, Griselda, *A Collector's History of English Pottery*, 3rd edn (Antique Collectors' Club, Woodbridge, 1985).

Lidstone, James Torrington, *The Thirteenth Londoniad* (1866). An amusing collection of awful poems about different potteries, among them several majolica makers.

Liveing, Edward, *The Story of Royal Cauldon* (Dissertation, University of Keele, c.1975).

Lloyd Thomas, D. and E., *Victorian Art Pottery* (Guildart, London, 1974).

Lockett, Terence A., *Collecting Victorian Tiles* (Antique Collectors' Club, Woodbridge, 1982).

Mackay, James, *The Dictionary of Western Sculptors in Bronze* (Antique Collectors' Club, Woodbridge, 1977).

Malgras, Gilbert-Jean, ed, *Faiences de Strasbourg* (Nouveau Tardy, Paris, 1985).

Marks, Mariann K., *Majolica Pottery: An Identification and Value Guide* (Collector Books, Paducah, Ky., 1983). Beautiful full colour illustrations with captions, no text.

—— *Second Series Majolica Pottery: An Identification and Value Guide* (Collector Books, Paducah, Ky., 1986).

May, Harvey, *The Beswick Collectors' Handbook* (Kevin Francis Publishing, London, 1986).

McCabe, James D., *The Illustrated History of the Centennial Exhibition* (Reprint of 1876 edn, National Publishing Company, Philadelphia, 1975).

McVeigh, Patrick, *Scottish East Coast Potteries, 1750–1840* (John Donald Publishers, Edinburgh, 1979). Too early to discuss majolica, but gives backgrounds of several potteries which later did manufacture it.

Meigh, Alfred, *Meigh's Lists* (Forsbrook, Staffordshire, n.d.). Compiled from 18th/19th-century directories and records, this lists all known Staffordshire potters and potteries.

Messenger, Michael, *Pottery & Tiles of the Severn Valley: A Catalogue of the C. H. Temple Collection* (Remploy, London, 1979).

Miller, Judith and Martin, *Miller's Antiques Price Guide*, Vols I–X (Miller's Publications, London, 1979–88).

Neuwirth, Waltraud, *Markenlexikon für Kunstgewerbe: Keramik* (Selbstverlag Dr. Waltraud Neuwirth, Wien, 1978).

—— *Markenlexikon für Kunstgewerbe: Wiener Porzellan* (Selbstverlag Dr. Waltraud Neuwirth, Wien, 1978).

Palme, Per, *Svensk Keramik* (Forum, Stockholm, 1947).

Pappas, Joan and A. Harold Kendall, *Hampshire Pottery manufactured by J. S. Taft & Company, Keene New Hampshire* (Forward's Color Productions, Manchester, Vt., 1971).

Paton, James, *Jugs: A Collectors' Guide* (Souvenir Press, London, 1976).

Pelka, Otto, *Keramik der Neuzeit* (Klinkhardt & Biermann, Leipzig, 1924). Useful.

Penkala, Maria, *European Pottery* (Charles E. Tuttle, Rutland, Vt., 1960).

Physick, John, *The Gamble Room* (Victoria & Albert Museum, London, 1977).

Purviance, Evan and Louise, *Zanesville Art Pottery in Color* (Wallace-Homestead Book Co., Des Moines, 1978).

Ramsay, John, *American Potters & Pottery* (Hale, Cushman & Flint, Clinton, Mass., 1939). Known to be unreliable.

Rebert, Charles, *American Majolica, 1850–1900* (Wallace-Homestead Book Co., Des Moines, 1981). Some good illustrations.

Reilly, Robin and Savage, George, *The Dictionary of Wedgwood* (Antique Collectors' Club, Woodbridge, 1980).

Rhead, G. Wooliscroft and Frederick Alfred, *Staffordshire Pots & Potters* (EP Publishing, 1977). This is a reprint of the 1906 edition.

Rickerson, Wildey C., *Majolica Collecting for Fun & Profit* (Pequot Press, Chester, Conn., 1972).

Riley, Noel, *Tile Art: A History of Decorative Ceramic Tiles* (Chartwell Books, Secaucus, NJ, 1987).

Robinson, Sir John Charles, *Catalogue of the Soulages Collection* (1856).

Roentgen, Robert E., *Marks on German, Bohemian & Austrian Porcelain, 1710–present* (Schiffer Publishing Co., Exton, Pa., 1981).

Rumsby, John, ed., *Tiles and Architectural Ceramics: Bibliography*, 2nd edn ed. by Edwin Chapman (Tiles & Architectural Ceramics Society, 1988). A very thorough bibliography which helpfully notes the whereabouts of some of the rarer references.

Saint-Clair, Anne, *Le dictionnaire des antiquités et de la brocante* (Nouvelles Editions Marabout, Verviers, Belgique, 1979).

Sandon, Henry, *Royal Worcester Porcelain: From 1862 to the Present Day* (Barrie & Jenkins, London, 1973).

Schwartz, Marvin D., *Collector's Guide to Antique American Ceramics* (Doubleday & Co., New York, 1969).

Shinn, Charles and Dorrie, *The Illustrated Guide to Victorian Parian China* (Barrie & Jenkins, London, 1971).

Smith, G. M., *Belleek Porcelain & Pottery: A Handbook for the Collector* (Toucan Press, Guernsey, 1979).

Spargo, John, *Early American Pottery and China* (The Century Co., New York, 1926). Very useful, contains a chronological list of potters and a marks section.

Statham, Claire, *Making Ceramic Tableware* (Cheddleton Flint Mill Industrial Heritage Trust, Hanley, 1976).

Tilmans, E., *Faience de France* (Editions de Deux-Mondes, Paris, 1953).

Van Lemmen, Hans, *Victorian Tiles* (Shire Publications Ltd., Aylesbury, 1986).

Wakefield, Hugh, *Victorian Pottery* (Herbert Jenkins, London, 1962).

Walker, Francis A., ed., *International Exhibition 1876, Reports & Awards Group II* (J. B. Lipincott & Co., Philadelphia, Pa., 1877).

Waring, J. B., *Masterpieces of Industrial Art*, 3 vols (1863).

Watkins, Lura Woodside, *Early New England Potteries and their Wares* (Cambridge University Press, 1950).

Weiss, Gustav, *Ullstein Porzellanbuch* (M. Wien, Ullstein, 1964). Useful marks section.

Whiter, Leonard, *Spode* (Barrie & Jenkins, London, 1970, reprinted with new colour plates, 1989).

Young, Jennie J., *The Ceramic Art: A Compendium of the History and Manufacture of Pottery and Porcelain* (Sapper, Low, Master, Searle and Rivington, London, 1879).

## ARTICLES
'At the Source', *Pottery & Glass*, May 1949, pp. 31–4. Article about S. Fielding & Co.

'At the Source', *Pottery & Glass*, January 1947, pp. 25–8. The story of Thomas Poole Ltd.

Atterbury, Paul, 'Minton Majolica: The Revival of Sixteenth and Seventeenth-Century Italian Earthenwares', *Connoisseur* 192, August 1976, pp. 304–8.

Barber, Edwin Atlee, 'Recent Advances in the Pottery Industry', *Popular Science Monthly* Vol. XL, No. 3, January 1892.

—— 'The Rise of the Pottery Industry', *Popular Science Monthly* Vol. XL, No. 2, December 1891. Both of the above articles are very useful, especially good on tiles.

Bergesen, Victoria, 'English Majolica of the Nineteenth Century', *The Ceramics Index*, Vol. 1, No. 10, October 1987, pp. 4–8.

Branin, M. Lelyn, 'The Providence and Bay View Potteries in South Amboy, New Jersey', *Spinning Wheel*, June 1975, pp. 13–17.

Brown, Nell, 'I, Too, Collect Majolica', *Hobbies*, March 1939, pp. 72–3.

Brown, Philip and Dorothy, 'Poisonous Tiles', *Glazed Expressions*, No. 16, Spring/Summer 1988, pp. 2, 11.

Buxton, Virginia Hillway, 'The Other Roseville', *Spinning Wheel*, April 1975, pp. 28–30. Discusses Roseville's commercial wares.

'Ceramics at Philadelphia', *The American Architect & Building News* Vol. I, Nos. 31–37, 39–43, 29 July 1876–14 October 1876.

Clarke, J. F. Gates, 'Rebekeh at the Well Teapots', *Spinning Wheel*, July/August, September, November, December 1978. This four-part series discusses the Edwin Bennett factory and a number of other producers of rockingham glazed ware.

Colls, R. H., 'The House of Booths & Colcloughs', *Pottery & Glass*, August 1951, pp. 73–5.

Cooke, Nigel T., 'The Forgotten Spittoon', *Antique Collecting* Vol. 23, No. 6, November 1988, pp. 51–4.

'Crest of the Wave: A Visit to Grafton China', *Pottery & Glass*, December 1956, pp. 400–1.

'The Devon Phoenix: Problems and Progress of Rebuilding', *Pottery & Glass*, August 1952, pp. 62–3.

Elliot, J. W., 'Relief Ornamentations on Staffordshire Earthenware and Stoneware', *Connoisseur* 194, January 1977, pp. 31–6.

Ellis, Anita, 'Late Victorian Revivals', *The Antique Collector*, November 1985, pp. 84–9.

Fay, A. 'Villeroy & Boch: art et industrie céramique', *La Revue du Louvre et des Musées de France* 35, No. 4, 1985.

Fitzpatrick, Nancy R., 'The Chesapeake Pottery Company', *Maryland Historical Magazine*, March 1957, pp. 65–71.

Fitzpatrick, Paul J., 'Chesapeake Pottery', *Antiques Journal*, December 1978.

Francis, Victoria, 'Victorian Majolica', *Antique Collector*, January 1977, pp. 73–7.

Gillard, M. C., 'La Faience de Gien', *L'Estampille*, September and December 1985.

Godden, Geoffrey, 'Victorian Ceramic Artists', *Apollo*, January–June 1959.

Greene, John, 'W. B. Simpson & Sons – 150 Years Old, Alive and Well in Clapham Common', *Glazed Expressions*, Spring 1983, p. 4.

'Grimwades at Norfolk Street', *Pottery Gazette & Glass Trades' Review*, September 1964, pp. 988–9.

Hampson, Rodney and Eileen, 'Brownfields, Victorian Potters', *Northern Ceramics Society Journal* 4, 1980–1, pp. 177–218.

Harrison, Desmond. 'Brownfield of Barlaston Hall', *Six Towns Magazine*, September 1972, pp. 32–3.

Haslam, Malcolm. 'Bernard Palissy', *Connoisseur* 190, September 1975, pp. 12–17.

Hayot, Monelle, 'La Faience de Gien', *L'Oeil* 293, December 1979, pp. 44–9.

Henrywood, Richard K., 'Relief-Moulded Jugs – Some Recent Discoveries', *Antique Collecting* 23, No. 4, pp. 55–60.

'High-quality Tableware & Popular Novelties: Versatile Range of Products by Fieldings', *British Bulletin of Commerce*, November 1954, p. 30.

'Histories of Famous Firms, City of Stoke-on-Trent', *British Bulletin of Commerce Survey*, 3 parts (November and December 1954; January 1955).

Holland, Eugenia Calvert, 'Edwin Bennett and the Products of his Baltimore Pottery', *Maryland Historical Society*, Summer 1973.

Hoover, Mary W., 'Reminiscences in Collecting Majolica', *Hobbies*, March 1939, pp. 69–70.

'Horace Poole', *Pottery & Glass*, April 1954, p. 111.

Keno, Leigh, 'Odell & Booth Brothers', *Art & Antiques*, March/April 1980.

Kevill-Davies, Sally, 'A Sardine Box', *Antique Collecting*, December, 1985, pp. 58–9.

'Maw & Co's. Encaustic & Other Tiles', *The Building News*, February 15, 1867, pp. 131 ff.

Mell, George, 'Candle Extinguishers', *Antique Collector*, November 1976, pp. 60–1.

Morse, Barbara White, 'High Art Majolica Tiles of the U.S. Encaustic Tile Works', *Spinning Wheel*, March/April 1982, pp. 40–5.

Morse, Florence L., 'Hampshire Pottery', unpublished ms.

Muter, Grant, 'Minton Secessionist Ware', *Connoisseur* 204, August 1980, pp. 256–63.

Nilson, Lisbet, 'Down From the Attic', *Connoisseur*, February 1984, pp. 68–73.

Pennypacker, Frances W., 'Majolica and its Makers', unpublished ms, November 1942.

'Progress by Stoke Fancies Potter', *Pottery Gazette & Glass Trades' Review*, April 1962, pp. 510–11. An article about Shorter & Son.

Ramsay, John, 'American Majolica', *Hobbies*, May 1945, pp. 45–8.

Rayle, Rubye, 'A Dessert Service Started It', *Hobbies*, March 1939, p. 77.

'Romance of a Family Firm [S. Fielding]', *Pottery & Glass*, August 1956, pp. 252–5.

W. B. Simpson & Sons, Ltd., 'W. B. Simpson & Sons, 1883–1925', *Glazed Expressions*, Spring 1983, p. 5.

*Staffordshire Daily Sentinel*, 14 July 1873. An obituary of William Brownfield.

Stradling, J. G., 'American Ceramics and the Philadelphia Centennial', *Antiques* 110, July 1976, pp. 146–58.

—— 'East Liverpool, Ohio: an American Pottery Town', *Antiques*, June 1982.

Thompson, Christopher, 'Ostentation and Vainglory: Minton Peacock in Australia', *The Australian Antique Collector*.

Van Houten, Edna M., 'Majolica Links the Past and Present', *Hobbies*, March 1939, pp. 74–6.

van Lemmen, Hans, 'Pugin's Ceramic Stove for the 1851 Great Exhibition', *Glazed Expressions* 7/8, Summer/Autumn 1984, pp. 1–2.

Wadsworth, Philip S., 'Fouque … Arnoux, A Family of Potters in France and England', *Apollo*, February and March 1956.

'Wannopee Pottery', *The New Milford Historical Society Newsletter*, n.d.

Weidner, Ruth Irwin, 'The Majolica Wares of Griffen, Smith & Co.', *Spinning Wheel*, January/February and March/April 1980.

Williams, Lena, 'Majolica, Like Gold is Where You Find It', *Hobbies*, March 1939, pp. 70–1.

Woldbye, Vibeke. 'Shells & the Decorative Arts', *Apollo* 120, September 1984, pp. 156–61.

'The World of Royal Doulton', *Tableware International*, February 1978, pp. 2–23. A brief history and synopsis of current wares of each of Royal Doulton's subsidiaries.

Wraight, Carolyn, 'Zanesville, Ohio 1', *Glazed Expressions* 11, Winter 1985, pp. 4–5.

Wright, Margaret Bertha, 'Deck Faience', *Crockery and Glass Journal*, 13 October 1881, reprinted from *Art Amateur*.

Young, Jennie J., 'Pottery, Old and New', *The Contemporary Review*, February 1884.

## EXHIBITION CATALOGUES

Aslin, E. and Atterbury, P. *Minton 1789–1910*, Victoria & Albert Museum, London, 1976.

Barber, Edwin Atlee, *Catalogue of American Potteries & Porcelains*, Pennsylvania Museum & School of Industrial Art, Philadelphia, 1893.

Cecil, Victoria, *Minton Majolica*, Jeremy Cooper Ltd, 1982.

Dell'Ava, Suzanne, *Céramique art nouveau: France 1900*, Musée d'art et d'histoire, Genève, 1980.

Dell'Ava, Suzanne and Fabienne Sturm, *Fruits et légumes: faience et porcelaine*, Musée d'art et d'histoire, Genève, 1978.

*Early Arts of New Jersey: The Potter's Art c. 1680–1900*, New Jersey State Museum, Trenton, 1956.

Fine Arts Society, *The Aesthetic Movement and the Cult of Japan*, 1972

Hurst, A., *A Catalog of the Boynton Collection of Yorkshire Pottery*, Yorkshire Philosophical Society, 1922.

Keene, K. H., *American Art Pottery, 1875–1930*, Delaware Art Museum, Wilmington, 1978.

McCrum, S., *The Belleek Pottery*, Ulster Museum, Botanic Gardens, Belfast, 1973.

Minton, *London Exhibition of 1862: Catalogue of the Principal Works*, London, 1862.

*Porcelain & Pottery of New Jersey, 1688–1900*, Newark Museum, Newark, 1947.

*Pottery & Porcelain of New Jersey prior to 1876*, New Jersey Museum, Newark, 1915.

Stoke-on-Trent City Museum & Art Gallery, *Minton Tiles, 1835–1935*, 1984.

Swann, Michael, *The Catalogue of 'Focus on Tiles': The Private Collection of Michael Swann*, Derby City Museum, The Strand, 14 June–23 August 1986.

*Victorian Tiles*, Wolverhampton Art Gallery, 1978.

*Villeroy & Boch, 1748–1930*, Rijksmuseum, Amsterdam, 1977–8.

*Wenger's Collection of Pottery*, Etruria, Stoke-on-Trent, 1914.

## PERIODICALS

The researcher will find it useful to examine all available copies of the following periodicals.

*American Potter* (Trenton, 1888–1903).

*American Pottery & Glassware Reporter* (Pittsburgh, 1879–82).

*American Pottery Gazette* (New York, 1905–10).

*Art Journal Illustrated Catalogues*, 4 vols (1851–79).

*The Art Union*, 10 vols (1839–48).

*The Artist and Journal of Home Culture*, 1880–94.

*The Ceramic Gazette & Journal of Decorative & Home Adornment* (Teddington, 1881).

*China & Pottery World* (New York, 1893–7).

*China, Glass & Pottery Review* (New York, 1897–1908).

*The Clayworker* (Indianapolis, 1884–1933). Although this is a trade publication primarily for brickmakers, Barber wrote for them regularly about various ceramics.

*Crockery & Glass Journal* (New York, 1874–1905).

*Glazed Expressions* (Tiles & Architectural Ceramics Society, 1981–).

*Northern Ceramic Society Journal.*

*Northern Ceramic Society Newsletter.*

*The Potter: A Journal for the Manufacturer &c.* (1893).

*The Potter* (London, 1902).

*Potteries Advertiser* (Hanley, 1897–1912).

*The Pottery Gazette.*

*The Pottery Gazette Diary* (London).

*The Pottery Gazette & Glass Trades Journal* subsequently *Glass Trade Review* (London 1878–9).

*The Pottery Gazette Yearbook* subsequently *The Pottery Gazette Reference Book; The Pottery Gazette Buyer's Reference Book,* 1881– ).

*Pottery & Glass* (New York, 1908–15).

*The Pottery & Glass Record* subsequently *Pottery & Glass* (London 1918– ).

*Pottery & Glass Salesman* (New York, 1910–42).

*The Pottery & Glass Trades' Journal* (London 1878–9).

*The Pottery & Glass Trades' Review* (London, 1877–9).

*The Pottery & Glass Trades' Weekly* (London, 1904).

*Pottery, Glass & Brassware Salesman* (O'Gorman Publishing Co., New York, 1913–19).

*Pottery & Glassware Reporter* (Pittsburgh, 1879–1926).

*Scottish Pottery Historical Review.*

*Scottish Pottery Society's Archivist's Newsletter*

*Spinning Wheel* (Mount Vernon, 1945–83).

Wedgwood Club, *Old Wedgwood,* 13 vols (Boston, 1935–48).

Wedgwood International Seminar, *American Wedgwoodian* (1962– ).

## DIRECTORIES

*Business Directory of London* (J. S. C. Morris, London, 1864).

*Directory of Glass Factories & Potteries of the United States & Canada* (Commoner & Glassworker, Pittsburgh, 1902 & 1903).

*Keates's Gazetteer & Directory of the Staffordshire Potteries, Newcastle & District* (J. Keates, Hanley, 1875–6).

*Kelly's Post Office Directory* (London, 1887).

*Mercantile Directory of London* (1891).

*Merchants & Manufacturers Pocket Directory of London* (Ashbee & Co., London, 1868).

*Potteries Directory* (1907).

*The Staffordshire Potters' Directory for 1868* (Unwin Brothers, London, 1868).

*West London Directory* (Allen, London, 1869).

## OTHER RESOURCES

Boote, T. & R., *Catalogue.*

*Carter & Co's. Tiles,* J. Fleming & Co., Leicester, n.d.

Craven Dunnill & Co., Ltd, Price Lists, 1885, 1888; Catalogues, 1879, 1892, 1905, n.d.

Gibbons, Hinton & Co., Ltd., *Tiles,* n.d.

Griffen, Smith & Co., *Catalogue of Majolica* (Phoenixville, Pa., 1884). Reprinted Brooke Weidner, 1960.

Jones, George & Sons, *Catalogue,* Stoke-on-Trent, 1924.

Local Newspaper Cuttings, Vol. 4, Hanley Library, July 1899.

*Malkin Tiles Catalogue E,* n.d.

Mansfield Brothers, Catalogue, J. Fleming & Co., Leicester, n.d.

Maw & Co. Catalogues, c.1862, 1888, 1890, 1893, 1907.

Phillips, New York Sale Catalogues, September 26, 1985; July 2, 1986; October 25, 1986; July 10, 1987; December 5, 1987.

Wedgwood, Josiah, & Sons, *Catalogue of Bodies & Glazes & Shapes Current for 1940–1950,* 1947.

—— Tile Catalogue, n.d.

Wedgwood Club, Minutes, Boston, 1957–63.

*Wedgwood 1880 Illustrated Catalogue of Shapes,* Wedgwood Society, London, 1971.

# INDEX